Healing the Heart of a Woman

Laura Gagnon

Dedication

This book is dedicated to every hurting woman. May you be encouraged and awakened to the truth that sets you free.

Acknowledgements

Thank you, Holy Spirit for Your inspiration and guidance in this labor of love.

To my husband Norm, for being a constant source of wisdom and encouragement.

To my family, may this book become a foundation of truth and understanding that you continue to build upon throughout your lifetime.

And to my mother, Beverly Mansfield; thank you for loving me during the hard times and teaching me the important lesson of perseverance.

A special note of thanks to Tina Preston for encouraging me to write this book.

Introduction

This book is for every woman. Every color. Every race. From every walk of life. Those in bondage, those that are free. From the homeless, the downtrodden and those that feel forgotten; to the influential, successful business woman of today. Doctors, lawyers, homemakers, school teachers and everything in between. The addict. The advocate. The gay and gender confused. The abused, the defiant, the rebel and reformer. We are different, but deep down, we are all sisters. We are on various pages in life, in understanding, in complex relational dynamics between God, ourselves and others. I have met many women and as I've listened to them share about their lives there seems to be a common denominator among all of us. We struggle to believe in ourselves and we struggle to stop listening to those old familiar voices that try to tell us we are just not "good enough." How similar we are in the fact that we wrestle with those voices in our head that want to tell us we are unworthy. This book reveals why people listen to the voices that magnify their weaknesses and insecurities, and offers a path to inner healing. As women, we often share similar elements of our stories that speak of pain, disappointment and damaged self-image. I pray that you will allow me to help you through your journey to discover the real you. If we can learn to lay down the judgments of ourselves and others, together we can help each other heal.

Perhaps you are wondering why you should read this book or what makes this book any different than the multitude of other books written by other brilliant and amazing authors. First of all, something led you to pick up *this* book. I do not believe in coincidences. In the kingdom of God, there is meaning to everything that occurs. I believe there is a message inside these pages that is intended for you. There is something for everyone. The second reason is God has given me life experience to be able to identify with things that women find in common. Perhaps you will discover similarities in some of our journeys, and as you do, realize that inside these pages are answers for your healing, freedom and victory. Partly biographical, I write of my own personal experiences to offer hope, encouragement and prayers written specifically for inner healing, transformation, deliverance and breakthrough. We will also take a closer look at some of the real women in the Bible with scandalous reputations, because they were women Jesus loved and adored just like you and me. Jesus does not care who He offends and He makes no apologies. He is 100% committed to our healing and restoration.

Though this book is written with the female reader in mind, I encourage men to read it in hopes that they will understand the women in their life a little better, as well as their spiritual role as a husband and father. Many of the issues discussed in this book are common to all of us. The issues of unresolved pain and confusion regarding our true identity affect people much deeper than they may realize. Those issues have left individuals and families broken. God wants to heal the hope for your family and future. He wants to restore each person's true identity and I'll show you why it is found through a relationship with Jesus Christ. His desire is to set people free from their pain, misconceptions about themselves and God, and heal hearts and lives.

Every person has a need to feel understood. God understands your pain and longs to set you free! I, too, am intimately acquainted with pain. I know your suffering. I know the heartache of feeling rejected and unwanted. I know the fear of living with secrets that destroy a person from the inside out. I understand the pain and regret from personal choices that left me devastated from embarrassment and filled with self-loathing. I know what it's like to have such shame you can hardly face yourself, much less confess it to another human being. I know the embarrassment, feelings of inferiority and anger from things such as poverty, dysfunctional family dynamics, absent parents and physical, sexual and emotional abuse. I've been the drunk and the drug addict. I've been the person who couldn't keep a job, and the mom who risked having her kid taken away because I hated myself too much to want to live responsibly. I've been the adulterous woman looking for love in all the wrong places and creating a mess out of my life. I know the sting of rejection and self-hatred from not feeling loved. I know what it feels like to lose your home, your life, stability and have to dig yourself out of a pit so deep it feels like you'll never get out. I know what it feels like to lose everything and have to start over – sometimes from my own mistakes, and other times because I simply said yes to God. I've been there when everyone you hoped you could trust walks away and you wonder why life is so painful. I know the agony of feeling abandoned and question whether God exists. I know what it's like to blame God for all my pain, and say, "I hate You!" one minute, and a moment later whimper a cry that says, "How can I trust You?" when all my dreams were shattered and lying in pieces. Worst of all, I know the shame of it all when the devil tells your story in such a way so that what others see is the worst possible picture of who you are and you feel you will never escape the shame. In the midst of whatever mess you may be in the middle of, or the pain, the shame, the regret and the myriad of emotions you may have experienced; I'm here to tell you the truth. What you've endured is not your destiny, and what you've done is not who you are. May you discover the magnificent beauty of the real you!

Table of Contents

CHAPTER ONE

Why We Do the Things We Do

"I can't believe I'm going through this again!" she cried, as tears spilled down her face. "I'm so stupid! What is wrong with me?" she asked, "I'm not a bad person, really I'm not." She looked up at me with beautiful, big green eyes. "I don't treat people bad; at least I don't think so. I work hard. I'm a professional woman, you know. I have a good job. That should count for something, shouldn't it?" She looked at me as though she was desperately searching for signs of confirmation that she was a good person. I nodded. "Of course it counts," I said, consoling her. "Why do I always get rejected? What is wrong with me?" I took a breath, patted her hand and waited. I knew there was more. A *lot* more. A flood of emotion swept over her like waves crashing on a rocky shoreline. Tearfully, she went down the list of reasons she felt were adequate to justify her desire for love, marriage and family. "Why do I keep ending up with a broken heart?" she asked me. "Do you know how much time I've wasted on this relationship?" "Eight years!" she exclaimed. "Eight years of my life down the drain!" "And three years before that with someone else. I wanted to have a family," she sobbed, reaching for another tissue. "Look at me. I'm in my thirties. It's probably never going to happen now." I knew that look on her face. I'd been there too. All she could see was her dreams crushed and no hope for the future. "I'm sorry," she whispered. "I hate falling apart. I must look awful. I just don't understand why I'm not good enough." She put her head down and wept uncontrollably.

That scene may sound familiar. A lot of us know that story. It was my story, too. Looking for love in all the wrong places and never understanding why I ended up feeling rejected and broken hearted. Married and divorced by 22, I jumped right from one disastrous relationship to another without even thinking twice. The first one was mentally unstable, controlling and abusive. Our marriage was short lived but it was full of physical, emotional and even sexual abuse. Every part of the abuse was degradation in some form. It was intended to break my spirit so that my husband could make me compliant to the use of control. Fear controlled my life. Thankfully, I was strong willed, because it was that determination to survive that made me fight for freedom. A person can endure a lot of things but one thing we have to dig deep to find within ourselves is the will to live. That is something no one else can do for us. I finally stood up and began to fight and once I did, I never stopped. It finally came to an end when one night, for no apparent reason, my husband decided his steak was overdone, decided to throw a fit and smash up the entire house. He quickly became out of control. He got out a gun, loaded it and shoved it in my face. Only by that time, my emotions were so beyond broken that instead of feeling fear, I was just numb. I wanted to be free from all the torment. "Do it," I taunted. "You want to kill me? Stop threatening and just do it." I think I was a bit over the edge myself to taunt a fool with a gun, but I was tired of being held hostage in my marriage. He had resorted to sleeping in the car outside the house just to make sure I didn't go anywhere without him knowing. He disabled the car every time he wasn't going to be home. There were repeated outbursts, threats, and abuse in front of our 2 year old daughter. I couldn't take it anymore. My sanity was holding on by a thread. I was actually beginning to convince myself that the only way out was if he was dead. I started thinking of ways he could 'have an accident.' Thank God I never acted on those thoughts. I got out before I could do something crazy and even more regrettable. That night the police intervened just at the right time. They asked me if I wanted to leave and I said yes. Only I had nowhere to stay for more than just a night, so I returned the next day. A couple months later, a woman from work helped me and I took my daughter and got out for good. It was far from over; my estranged husband and his equally crazy girlfriend harassed and stalked me repeatedly over the next two years. Restraining orders meant nothing to him. He broke into my apartments, vandalized my vehicle and made life absolutely maddening. My life was turbulent and emotional for quite some time, but while I was fresh out of that relationship, I found someone else. I was starving for love. Desperate people do desperate things in order to feel loved, and I definitely felt insecure and alone. The problem was, I had never experienced real love and I had no prior role model upon which to base a healthy love relationship.

The second man seemed more stable, at 20 years my senior and an established career in real estate. I wanted to feel secure and he wanted sex and convenience. He introduced me to cocaine and we drank a lot, but it seemed so... grown up, I guess you would say. We played house for a number of years and though it took longer to get violent, it did. It was equally toxic and abusive. It was a codependent relationship which so degraded the way I felt that I found myself extremely depressed and devoid of any real desire to live. I repeatedly overdosed on alcohol. This man was quick to tell me that I was worthless and a failure, and though it hurt terribly, I couldn't disagree with him. Nothing could shut out the voices in my head that told me I was nobody. I was convinced my child was better off without me. Those negative thoughts were leading me right off a cliff and I didn't know how to stop it. I was convinced that I needed that man to survive because I didn't believe in myself any longer, and so I clung to him long after common sense told me to let go. I didn't feel stable enough to provide for myself and my daughter, and I kept trying to hold on to the only means of support to which I had become accustomed. I desperately wanted someone to take care of me, but I was so needy in the relationship I couldn't help but add to the destruction. I wasted a lot of years trying to satisfy the inner desire for love and fulfillment. I spent almost 10 years of my life with the wrong person and came out of it bitter, broken, penniless and without a shred of self-esteem left.

It didn't stop me from trying to find love, though. I was so desperate for affirmation and love that I settled for compromise and a hope that maybe something would fill the gaping hole in my heart. The next time around, I made an even worse choice. I chose a drug addict and a guy that told me "I needed to be broken," because I wasn't submissive enough. I thought I was actually pretty compliant. I rescued him from rehab, brought him into my home, and I hadn't even known him more than a week or two. He was an unemployed, womanizing druggie, still married and a deadbeat dad to three kids he wasn't permitted to see. He knew all the right things to say because he was a user in every sense of the word. I sure knew how to pick 'em. I repeatedly chose the same type of emotionally distant, abusive person that was unwilling and unable to love me. I wasn't just being irresponsible; I was acting irrational and senseless. I was driven by fear and a need to be affirmed and loved, yet I thought so little of myself that I continued to accept any form of counterfeit love available.

Without any concept of my own value, I found new ways of sinking even lower in my pit of misery. This man (much like my first husband) thought I needed to learn a lesson, and his way of 'breaking me' was to choke me from within about an inch of my life. It still took me another couple of weeks and a few more fearful episodes to finally kick him out. I spent all my rent money trying to support another individual in his addiction, and I left myself with even more emotional scars, if that was possible. The really shameful part is the fact that I had just renewed my commitment to Christ and gotten water baptized for a second time only a few weeks earlier. The enemy came in like a flood to pull me right back into the lifestyle I was trying to leave behind. I was living a tortured life and I did not know why. I couldn't see where there was one cataclysmic wrong turn in life that put me on the highway to hell. Maybe I'd always been on the wrong road in life and never understood that. I knew I was lost, I just didn't know how to find the right exit and get going in the right direction. I couldn't seem to find the answer to where everything went terribly sideways and left me a preposterous mess. Life just kept bottoming out.

It is amazing to me how many lovely women get caught up in the same sort of insanity. One definition of insanity is doing the same thing over and over expecting different results. Far too many women get caught up in the thrill of the chase and the idea of conquering the unavailable man. They are addicted to the emotional roller coaster that leaves them with the same disappointing ending time after time. The devil knows that dance. *Come on, Sis.* If Katy Perry's song *"Hot n' Cold"* seems to be your theme song then it's time to get off the dance floor and make some changes. No more dancing with the devil! He knows what buttons to push and just how to pull you into the game. Each time a relationship ends in rejection your heart becomes a little more jaded and bitter. When a relationship ends a little twinge rises up inside of you and you tell yourself, *"Next time around, I will be smarter…I will play the game a little better…"* And you try very hard to believe in yourself, but every time the feelings of inferiority, insecurity and rejection increase, so you have even greater expectations from the next person in order to satisfy the needs of your battle scarred heart. Life isn't a game and hearts are not toys to be played with. If a man isn't mature or emotionally healthy enough to know what he wants, then he isn't ready to treat you the way you deserve. Raise the bar on your expectations! In all fairness, this type of relationship problem works both ways. Women can be just as much at fault as men, but if you can see the snares in advance, the truth can set you free and help keep you from putting your foot in the trap. The problem with many people is they have a spirit of rejection attached to their life that sends messages to the spirit realm. Those 'messengers' act as magnets to pull the wrong people into another person's life because those they attract also have the wrong spirit attachments. This is how Satan keeps people feeling broken, inferior, and rejected. This is how he reinforces his lies and a faulty belief system in his victims. Over and over he sets the stage to produce a certain outcome so that negative experiences serve to re-write a person's sense of identity. Their belief system conforms to negative emotional experiences rather than what God says in His word. In the mind of his victims, the power of deception becomes stronger than their real identity. Those negative emotions serve to defile hearts through deep disappointment and bitterness. A spirit of rejection works in association with insecurity and jealousy. All of these are fear based emotions. Insecurity needs constant reassurance. Jealousy will cause a person to feel frustrated that they are not being shown the love and attention they think they deserve. Jealousy complains and accuses others. It produces suspicion and mistrust towards others. These responses in turn can cause rejection to occur. When a person feels rejected, the next tendency to manifest is a feeling of competition in order to gain what is desired. Regardless of what relational dynamics are affected, competition arises out of a root of jealousy and that spirit will put people at odds with one another.

Jealousy is a relationship killer because it is not content unless there is a winner and a loser. Competitors compete to win. Jealousy is the result of covetousness and a lack of trust. It is a self-centered emotion because it wants to possess the object of its desire. Many times one or both participants in the relationship will also have a spirit of rejection working in their life. A spirit of rejection withdraws from relationships as a means of self-preservation. Those carrying a spirit of rejection tend to reject others while they still feel they have a measure of control. That is why relationships built around these dynamics fizzle out or leave a lot of emotionally charged responses. Victims are left wondering what they did wrong and they tend to want to try to stabilize an unhealthy relationship. When a person is on an emotional roller coaster, they often feel they can't quit the unhealthy relationship because of the underlying desire for love, intimacy and affirmation. In co-dependent relationships both parties must agree to change or stabilization is nearly impossible to achieve. Double-mindedness is at the heart of the issue. One or both participants have difficulty determining what they really want because they have opposing thoughts that constantly lead them in different directions. It often feels like a bi-polar relationship. You're not crazy, but it can make you feel like it if you can't bring yourself to get help and get healed.

Jealousy will cause people to lust after things that are unhealthy or unintended for them. When people lust after relationships or other things that are not God's desire for them, they may resort to the use of manipulation, guilt, condemnation or force in order to obtain and hold on to what their soul craves. This could be a love interest, status, power, position or something else; but, for the most part, where you find jealousy at work you will also find lust. Lust and envy fuel jealousy. James 3:16 in the New Living Translation says, **"For wherever there is jealousy and selfish ambition, there you will find disorder and evil of every kind."** Jealousy is a strongman spirit that has the potential to cause anger, rage, dissention, contention, strife and competition. It is the opposite of love.

Do you see how all these things tend to become entangled? It can be quite difficult to sort out. If a person wants to be healed then they must come to the realization that their own belief system is in need of an overhaul. If we don't do something different we will always get the same results. Our soul craves spiritual sustenance to make it whole. It craves whatever it doesn't have and will attempt to fill that void with whatever seems appealing. When a person's soul has a black hole that empty vacuum will become filled with darkness if they don't fill it with light. Darkness attracts the wrong spiritual forces and others that have darkness in them. What we are full of has the potential to either attract or repel others. Read the first chapter of the book of John. When people love the darkness of their own hearts more than they love the truth and the light of Christ, they will not come to the light. That is serious food for thought, isn't it? Understanding truth about ourselves can sometimes be one of the most difficult things to face, but we need to learn to see truth as our friend. The more truth we embrace, the more we can live in the light and be filled with light. *The light of Christ attracts a different type of person into our lives.* Every person gets to make the choice of what they want to attract into their life. If the power of evil influences is stronger than the holiness within them, that person is left without the spiritual strength to resist what is unhealthy for them. Our only defense against darkness is purity and truth. When we fill our soul with the food it craves we are then filled with light. Light *attracts* light. In John 8:12 Jesus said that He is the light of the world and those that follow Him will never walk in darkness, but have the light of life. When a person refocuses their passion on the One who is worthy of their affections He will

> "The more truth we embrace, the more we can live in the light and be filled with light."

6

not only fill us with light and truth, but He will send out red flags and warn us if we begin to get into dangerous waters. Fill your soul with light and give it the ability to be in health and prosper.

I was convinced all men were the same, until I met a man that didn't act like all the others. As it turns out that man had a great family life and excellent role models for parents. He always spoke very highly of his parents and family life, and it made all the difference. He also had a strong relationship with the Lord. He started telling me how a man should treat a woman and let me in on a few secrets about the way men think. One thing he said is that men know pretty quickly whether or not they want to be serious with a woman. Generally speaking, people have a good idea if someone else has qualities they value. My friend also told me to write a list of what I felt were important qualities in a man, and that I should pray for God to send me the man with those qualities. I thought, *"This man is different."* I started to raise the bar on my expectations. Sometimes others that have settled will try to convince you that you should too. Haven't you settled long enough? Isn't it time to stop cooperating with those familiar spirits that set you up for failure? You have to recognize the trap, break the pattern and get healed before you repeat the same cycle all over again. The reality is you cannot change a man with commitment fears and trust issues. You cannot force someone to change for you. They have to want to change for themselves. You cannot train a man how to be a man of integrity that treats women with respect, honor and dignity. Only a father or a mentor can do that. A man that is accountable to God has both. Everyone needs to be accountable to someone other than just themselves. If your desire is for a spouse, then you deserve someone with a quality set of values and someone that recognizes your worth. You know that list I mentioned a moment ago? Men have their lists, too. It might only be in their head, but trust me, they have a list of expectations and desirable qualities in the woman they want to settle down with. If you want to attract a person that is healthy emotionally then you need to become the right woman for the right man. You need healing from those unloving pursuits, for though it is different from alcohol, drugs or other addictions, it is still an addiction. The prayers in this book can help you break the relational patterns that leave you hurt and disappointed.

Why do we come unhinged and throw sensibility out the window in order to degrade ourselves? Why do we consent to less than acceptable behavior from people that we don't have to tolerate? One person's crazy might not be another person's crazy, but I think you know what I mean. People find themselves repeating illogical, unloving patterns in their lives, and each time it only adds to the brokenness of their already bruised and bleeding hearts. The truth is many women have allowed their self-image to conform to what they tell themselves, and what they have allowed others to imply about them. Our own thoughts about how we perceive ourselves have dictated a faulty self-image into the mirror of our souls and that is often what we reflect back to the rest of the world. Many of us have allowed painful, shameful or embarrassing experiences to define our perception of ourselves. We have accepted the negative opinions and inconsiderate remarks of rude and selfish individuals and allowed them to impact our self-esteem more than those that love us and think the best about us. We have sought the approval of those in the world that don't like us, respect us, or have our best interests at heart.

Many people struggle with identity issues and a lack of self-worth. When a person does not feel loved or *lovable*, they begin to reject themselves. Self-hatred and rejection issues often occur in childhood and remain with a person their entire life, unless they do something on purpose to deal with it. There can be many things and various life situations that leave a person dealing with emotional pain, anger, bitterness, regret, feelings of guilt, shame or remorse. All of these things, when left unhealed, can be internalized and turn into a variety of other physical, mental, emotional and spiritual issues.

Self-rejection, self-hatred, shame, insecurity, and identity issues are at the heart of many physical issues. Negative self-talk comes from a spirit of rejection, abandonment and lack of fatherly/parental love. When a person attacks themselves through self-hatred and rejection, the body eventually begins to come into agreement with what is going on spiritually and begins to attack itself. This is where a lot of autoimmune disease comes from. The immune system, which is supposed to defend the body against potential risks and foreign germs, begins to go to war against the body. When a person doesn't love themselves, the body comes into agreement with a spirit of infirmity and unloving spirits, which then begins to manifest the poison of a person's thoughts and words. The person has come into agreement with a spirit of death rather than life. When we reject what God says about us it causes agreement with unbelief rather than faith. The longer it continues the more fear, anxiety, illness and other spirits grow stronger, eventually weakening a person so much they often cannot recover. Repentance and breaking agreement with those negative words are the only way to turn the situation around so that the body can begin to heal. The keys to healing are this: seek forgiveness for yourself and your ancestors, for some problems are spiritually rooted in generational sin. Forgive those in authority and others that you have blamed for hurting, offending or disappointing you, and a willingness to invite God to heal the wounds of your heart.

I am not a doctor, but there is a great deal of evidence that ties physical issues such as depression, weight and eating disorders, diabetes, addictions, migraines, lupus, MS, many forms of stomach and digestive system disorders and other things to spiritually rooted issues. Self-rejection, self-hatred, bitterness and guilt cause the inner emotional conflict that separates a person from themselves and God. These things result in emotional and physical disorders as well as disease. There are certain diseases, characteristics and family traits that can be traced back through the family tree. If people do not deal with the things that happen in their families, those things will get passed down from one generation to the next. Broken relationships, inherited disease and generational curses will reproduce if someone doesn't intentionally do something to stop it. I have written more about that subject in the chapter dealing with generational curses. Separation from self, others and God causes fear, stress, feelings of rejection and other unloving thoughts. God created us and He knows what will release our healing. He is the source of truth and can help us discover our path to healing and wholeness. Every addiction is tied to a direct connection with a need to feel loved. Even the choice to enter into an alternative lifestyle is directly related to a need to feel loved and accepted. The need is filled with an illegitimate method of trying to achieve acceptance, love and validation. Many people turn to the alternative lifestyles as a result of a negative response to a negative emotion sustained through some life event. Fear of not being accepted or understood by the opposite sex, or fear that the opposite sex is not safe can turn a person to seek comfort in same sex relationships. Again, this is not the person's true identity; it is one that they have adopted for themselves based on the lies a person has told themselves, deception from the enemy and the attack of a person's self-image. Satan is the one that attacks people's sense of identity. First he breaks the spirit, then seduces people with a perverse spirit

> "The keys to healing are this: seek forgiveness for your sins and your ancestors, for some problems are spiritually rooted in generational sin. Forgive those in authority and others that you have blamed for hurting, offending or disappointing you; and invite God to heal the wounds of your heart."

to draw people into a homosexual lifestyle. What Satan cannot accomplish by breaking a person's spirit, he accomplishes through rebellion, lying, and seducing spirits; but people are not born homosexual. There is no medical evidence to support this. It is more likely that they have inherited tendencies towards certain sins from unbroken curses. Familiar spirits may have been with a person all their life in order to convince them that they are a certain way, but feeling and emotions are not evidence of truth. Do you know how I am sure that people are not born this way? Because in Romans 1:18-32 God condemns it in His word. He would never condemn homosexual behavior if it was genetically inherited and beyond a person's ability to change. God is not unjust. Alternative lifestyles directly contradict the truth of Genesis 1:16-28 that tells us we are made in His image and likeness. God is not double minded and He does not contradict His word. If the enemy can convince a person that they are not the person God created them to be they will live out of that faulty belief system. Now, if that touched a nerve and caused a sense of defensiveness to rise up within you, please know that it is not my intention to offend. I simply ask you to continue reading, pray the prayers at the end of each chapter, and see for yourself if God reveals His truth to you. Let your heart be open to receive understanding. If you've believed a lie about your identity wouldn't you rather find out the truth? I hope you will agree to keep seeking!

Rejection is the enemy's trap. Satan wants us to be afraid to trust again. He will whisper all sorts of thoughts in our ears to keep people disconnected. From the Latin, *diabaulus,* to the ecclesiastical Greek word *diabolos*, it means 'to slander, attack or accuse.' It also means 'to divide.' The Spanish word, *diablo*, refers to an evil spirit, the devil, or a diabolical person that separates and causes division. The devil is one who, spiritually speaking does everything in his power to separate us from God and others. He is the accuser, and will whisper suggestions to make us suspicious and unbelieving of others. He suggests the thoughts, and if we don't silence that voice, *we* become that voice of accusation to others. We become the tool that creates division in relationships. Once again, the spirit of fear is behind that voice of accusation. Fear breeds suspicion. Ultimately, people can end up sabotaging relationships because of what they allow to influence their thoughts and verbalize to others. It's so important to work through our own issues and make a choice to be healed. I know it's not easy to trust once a person has been hurt, but love is a choice just as much as fear or bitterness is a choice, and love will overcome all.

I'll tell you why people do the crazy things they do. It's because they don't know how to change the internal dynamics that drive them, and they don't take time to fix the broken places. They don't know who they are. When people don't feel worthy enough to be treated well they succumb to the acceptance of unloving thoughts. Convictions are compromised in the hope that they will be accepted, loved and validated. Far too many people don't understand the enemy of their souls and Satan takes advantage of our ignorance. Our ears are so accustomed to hearing the voice that tells us God does not care about us that we listen to accusations against ourselves, too. The enemy whispers his lies to accuse anyone and everyone making our pain someone else's fault, when he is the one that provoked others to act hurtful and inconsiderate towards us. He spins his lies in order to make us angry, defensive and rebellious. He speaks to people in the first person, as if the thoughts are coming from us. He doesn't want anyone to be able to figure out his game. *Because if you really understood his game*, you'd stop listening and start fighting back.

Every time the enemy introduces a counterfeit form of love, he does it with the intention to produce more broken relationships, anger, bitterness, and disillusionment. It may or may not be a love interest. It could just as easily be a parental role model or someone else we admire; but when these relationships fail for one reason or another, the person is left with a feeling of abandonment, hurt, and betrayal. As an act of self-preservation, many people make unholy vows to keep others at a distance. An unholy vow sounds like this: *"I will never let anyone hurt me like that again!"* Sometimes those vows are made against people in authority, a role model or a specific gender. Those secret vows, even though they may never be spoken aloud, will cause the person's heart to harden. The danger is a person can't just harden their heart against getting hurt. They harden their heart towards God, too, without realizing that is what they are doing. God works through human vessels. To the degree that we make ourselves vulnerable to others is the same degree to which we can achieve intimacy with God. Satan knows this, too. Who do you think put the thought there to make those vows in the first place? The person will begin to lose sensitivity to conviction of wrongdoing, the ability to give and receive love, and the gift of feeling compassion and empathy towards others. It is the same as constructing walls of concrete, one block at a time, never realizing that they are constructing prison houses for themselves in which they become the captive. These individuals are broken on the inside and hard on the outside. These deep disappointments leave people feeling rejected, insecure, broken and disconnected from themselves and God. It is so important to renounce those unholy vows!

Fear is at the root of all rejection. Everything the enemy does is to produce separation from ourselves, God and others. Whether a person realizes it or not, subconsciously those feelings of rejection and fear are often projected onto God. If a person anticipates rejection, they will withdraw and avoid communication. We all tend to know where we have sin in our life. We know our secret faults and it makes us feel unclean and unworthy of acceptance with God. Those feelings cause a person to become defensive and protective of things that leave them vulnerable to the enemy. The fear of rejection causes people to stay distant and separated from God, rather than realizing His great love and forgiveness towards them. Our God is full of mercy and will not reject anyone that comes to Him! He is one person that we never have to fear being transparent with, because He already knows everything about us. Many people struggle with feeling safe and secure in their relationship with God. Those that doubt His love and acceptance find themselves struggling with resistance that prevents their full surrender to the Lord. Instead of drawing close to Him, a person with trust issues will keep themselves at a distance. Separation causes people to begin to conform to a different belief system. The more we are separated from God, the more we elevate our own thoughts and ideas as a measuring rod for truth. The more a person is deceived by their own thoughts, the more they open themselves up to deception from the enemy, and he will always try to get people to reject who they are in Christ. It keeps them disconnected from the God that can heal them. May I offer you some good news? The closer you get to the Lord, the more you will find out your fears are unfounded!

The truth is our approval rating has nothing to do with us, but all about what Jesus has done through His shed blood, cross and resurrection. His love and acceptance are based on the truth that God is love and has made a way for us to bridge the gap of separation. If our approval or our righteousness can be attained through our own efforts, then it makes Christ's death in vain. Dear reader, if your thoughts condemn you, then I suggest that there is something amiss in your relationship with God. The Bible tells us God *is* love. **"Beloved, let us love one another, for love is of God; and everyone who loves is born of God and knows God. He who does not love does not know God, for God is love. In this the love of God was manifested toward us, that God has sent His only begotten Son into the world that we might live through Him. In this is love, not that we loved God, but that He loved us and sent His Son to be the propitiation for our sins. Beloved, if God so loved us, we also ought to love one another."** (1 John 4:7-11). The good news is, Holy Spirit is available to show us what the problem is, and He is able to lead us into the truth that makes us free. The blood of Jesus is powerful enough to cleanse our conscience of guilt, regret, shame, and many other unprofitable thoughts that lead to self-rejection, condemnation and other negative feelings. When you search the scriptures for yourself it becomes *your* truth, and nothing can take it from you.

Our heavenly Father loves us so much that He always has people ready and able to help us, and He often has people already in place that have answers for our lives. It is us that are sometimes not ready to hear those answers, and so we struggle unnecessarily, sinking deeper and deeper into despair because we are not yet teachable. There is a way out of every hopeless situation. Holy Spirit is like the Coast Guard ship that continuously circles those lost at sea, waiting for the right time to send in a diver or a rescue crew. Like an expert lifeguard, He knows when a person has worn themselves out in the struggle and is ready to receive help without fighting back. They have come to an important part of their understanding; they cannot save themselves. It is a crucial moment but one that He waits for, knowing that surrender is the only way to receive help. There is a way to overcome the enemy and get a fresh start in life, but we have to be willing to grab that lifeline of hope when God tosses us a life preserver. His hand is outstretched, waiting for us to respond. Today could be your day to grab His hand and be pulled out of deep waters. If you feel like you're drowning, call on Jesus Christ and He will send help. I guarantee it. He will pull you out of danger and put your feet back on solid ground.

CHAPTER TWO

Defining Moments

My earliest memory is one of my father. Of all the things I could remember, this particular thing became ingrained in my mind, and so along with this particular memory, it also became a defining moment in my life. Memories are powerful. Is it any wonder that the enemy of our souls will try to suppress the ones that make us smile? Is it any wonder that at times it can seem harder and harder to remember the memories that edify who we really are and remind us of the love and beauty of life, and the goodness in the world around us? Memories are powerful indeed. They possess the ability to imprint our minds with images that transfer into the way we see ourselves and shape our world view.

I looked at my daddy lying on the bed next to me. "Close your eyes, Teeny, and go to sleep. You're tired." He always called me Teeny. That was his nickname for me. I looked at him closer. As I stared into his eyes it was almost as if I could see beyond his tired, bloodshot eyes. Dad always made me feel awkward. I didn't like being close to him. Something didn't feel right. It was like no one was home on the inside. I felt sad for him in a way, because something about him seemed...*weak*. Frail, almost. He said things that didn't make sense sometimes. I didn't know what it was about him, but looking at him disturbed me and made me feel very uncomfortable. I rolled over and pretended to go to sleep.

That was my earliest memory from the age of three. Defining moments occur at various times in our life. Something happens that leaves a lasting impression on us, but how we choose to respond to that particular moment has the capacity to mold us and shape us into who we eventually become. The problem is that most often people choose a negative response to a negative emotional trigger, which begins to send messages to their psyche about many things. These "messages" begin to shape a person's view of themselves, others and God. Most people grow up not knowing who they are or that they are made in the image of God. Ignorance to this truth makes a person vulnerable. It allows other life situations and more negative "defining moments" to change a person from who God intended them to be, and transform them into something they are not. It's important to understand that the enemy cannot create a false identity without first changing our belief system. He does this by creating, over and over again, circumstances that will injure our emotions and self-image. When he does, he reinforces the lies that are aimed at convincing us that our feelings are truth. Our thoughts and feelings may tell us we are rejected, inferior, unattractive, incapable, incompetent, overweight, or any number of things. When we listen to the wrong voice long enough, it has the capacity to create a new belief system, and with it, create a new identity that is no longer in our Father's image.

Only the voice of our Father who created us can call us into our truest identity, destiny and purpose. As a nation of people, most of us have become like unmoored boats, tossed about at sea, aimlessly drifting further and further away from the plan and purpose God has for us. We have lost our compass. We have affixed invisible labels to ourselves that magnify how we feel about ourselves, without realizing that they act like a rudder on a ship. Those labels begin to direct our path in life.

I think the fact that my father was so terribly disconnected to himself and his family left me wondering about my own identity. If Dad didn't know who he was, then who was I? When people do not have a sense of knowing who they are they begin to define themselves by what happens to them in life experiences rather than looking for truth. Experiences and circumstances may be the facts, but they are not always truth. I was three years old when I had the sudden realization that something was definitely very "off" about my dad. Years later I would discover that it had a name, Paranoid Schizophrenia. Just the name of the condition speaks volumes. *Paranoid* Schizophrenia. Paranoia means full of fear. *Schizophrenia* is known as a dissociative identity disorder. The disorder is linked to chronic problems with behavior and emotion. Many forms of insanity and mental illness come from a deaf and dumb spirit. The spirit itself is not deaf and dumb, but can cause things such as mental illness, illogical speech, seizures and other things. The remedy is found in the gifts of the Holy Spirit to bring healing. I used to be on anti-anxiety pills, anti-depressants, tranquilizers and it wasn't doctors or prescription pills that healed me. It was a deliverance issue, and Jesus healed me. Over half of those that are thought to have this disorder also have issues with substance abuse, depression and anxiety issues. The whole nature of the disorder causes a person to become so emotionally unstable that they detach from reality and withdraw into themselves. They isolate themselves in their own personal prison within their own mind. For a while, I was on that path too. It really bothered me that Dad was mentally unstable. I had a lot of mixed emotions. For many years, I felt sorry for him. I pitied his existence and wondered why he wasn't more of a man. Even the alcoholic father of one of my friends seemed more preferable than my own father. I didn't know exactly what to think about my dad.

As I grew older and I had to deal with the difficulties of a person with mental illness, I grew to resent him. My mother had to fill the role of both parents, and as Dad became more and more of an emotional invalid, he also became one physically. Depression overwhelmed him. He could not hold a job and lay in bed all day, every day. By the time I was around 10 years of age, I would go to school, come home, and take care of my little brother and my dad while Mom worked. God bless her, she did the best that she could to try to hold it all together. One thing she taught me was perseverance. Whatever life throws at you, you simply can't give up. She never did, although I am sure she felt like it many times. My sister was quite a bit older than I and was able to dodge the house a bit more through school activities, friends and work, but emotionally she could not escape either. Family dynamics took their toll on everyone. I was angry about so many things and I was embarrassed that my dad wasn't like a normal dad. I hated the fact that he was a whiner and was self-absorbed to the point that the whole household revolved around him. He was emotionally weak, incapable of providing, parenting or offering any sort of relationship, yet even though he refused to get out of bed he managed to somehow rule the household. I wanted to be able to depend on my dad but I could not, and that made me fearful and depressed. He made me feel ashamed to identify with my family. I blamed him for our poverty, and the fact that as much as I wanted to, I could never blend in and feel like a normal part of my peers. The presence of constant fear made me a nervous child. I was sick a lot of the time and terribly insecure. I lived with the feeling that my world could come crashing down around my head at any moment, and that began to shape my self-image, personality and world outlook.

Fathers and mothers alike may be physically alive, but emotionally absent or unable to instill a sense of identity in their children. These things shape the person that child will eventually become. If a parent does not know who they are, they cannot tell you who you are. This lack of knowledge allows fear to dictate certain responses. These responses end up creating a new self-image in a person based on fears, feelings of inadequacy, inferiority, and fear that they will lose approval or acceptance from others. People unknowingly accept the lie of rejection that separates us from our real selves, God and others. This is the nature of *spiritual* schizophrenia.

The spirit of fear works to separate the individual from their heavenly Father by attaching negative labels to the person's psyche, and in the process, disconnects them from their true identity. Once a person accepts those labels as a reality, it becomes even harder to remove them. In that regard, there are a lot of people who are spiritually schizophrenic. They simply allow the wrong things to form in their belief system, and in the process, disconnect themselves from their Father. There are even many Christians that are not walking in their true identity.

There is a humorous quote that says, "I am acting like I'm ok. Please don't interrupt my performance!" I think sometimes we don't realize how we have grown accustomed to the play acting we do in an effort to portray ourselves in a certain light. We clothe ourselves with garments we have made for ourselves. Some people wear impressive designer labels of self-importance; some wear the tailored suits of a work-a-holic, while others array themselves with stately robes of self-righteousness. We dress ourselves up, adorn ourselves with glittery chains of bondage and entertain our little fantasies with the wistful hope that somehow we can change what we believe about ourselves on the inside by changing how we present ourselves to the rest of the world. Once again, we've listened to the whispers of that sly old serpent and taken his suggestions. What we have failed to realize is that we're still making fig leaves for ourselves. Every time we receive a lie into our belief system and receive it as truth, we put ourselves in chains.

Some wear the unbecoming prison garb of their bondages and shame, others put on the dowdy frocks of defeat and self-pity, while others still may don the putrid rags of the homeless drunk. What we choose to wear is often the manifestation of our belief system. Sometimes it is obvious and other times the lies that affect our identity manifest in very subtle ways. It's not always the lie that is most obvious that grabs our attention. It is the lie that sounds so reasonable to believe. There is the familiar voice that brings our focus back to our own shortcomings and makes us feel that we are unapproved in some way, or that we cannot please God. It puts the emphasis on our own performance rather than on what Jesus has already done for us. It is the lie of condemnation that brings us back under legalism; trying to earn what we feel we cannot achieve through grace. It is taking on the garments of the slave rather than wearing the robes of freedom. It is wearing a yoke of bondage that makes us slaves to the negative voices in our head. Regardless of the clothes we wear, no matter how good we think we may look or how poor; we must ask ourselves if we have allowed ourselves to become something that is not true to our real identity. Have we allowed ourselves to become something that we are not? Have we, in fact, traded in our robes of royalty and clothed ourselves in spiritual poverty? What we need to understand is that the garments of grace are the only ones that truly matter.

A poverty spirit is not just about financial poverty or social class. A spirit of poverty is a state of mind, but it also brings a curse. It is a lying spirit that tells a person they are unworthy. A poverty spirit will sound like it's your own thoughts telling you that you are not good enough, unable to change or become anything different. It gives unloving spirits a place to operate in a person's life, telling them that they are rejected, inferior and labels them with all kinds of negative thoughts. A spirit of poverty magnifies impossibilities and creates hopelessness and despair, which in turn attempts to make God small in the eyes of its victim. If a person believes God is too small or powerless to change their situation, or their mountains of impossibilities can only be removed by self-effort, their faith will wither and the person remains bound by unbelief. A poverty spirit will attempt to curtail anyone that tries to break free by declaring the voice of reason and once again remind the person of 'who they are or where they've come from.' It is an attempt to injure the faith and growth of those who desire real change and actively pursue their freedom. A spirit of poverty also causes a lack of discernment because the person that has this operating in their life has absorbed and believed a variety of lies. The more deception a person believes the harder it is for them to discern truth. These deceptions in the belief system cause rebellion and pride to be elevated in a person's life which is also a key to why they remain in spiritual poverty.

What a person believes about them and God has a direct relationship to other behaviors. They can become fearful of lack and allow fear to cultivate other negative thoughts and behaviors. A spirit of poverty does affect finances, but it is much more than that. Negative thought patterns and unconfessed sin allows a spirit of poverty to reproduce the effect of a curse into a person or family until it is dealt with correctly. Fear and unbelief resist the growth of faith. This is why a person (or family) will often display not just financial hardship or an inability to prosper, but spiritual poverty in their thought life as well. When we reject truth and accept the lies and thoughts that tell us we are not who God says we are we align ourselves with thoughts that cannot please Him. Only faith pleases God. Answers to prayer come as a result of faith, not fear, unbelief or worry. Rejection of truth causes us to be out of alignment with God. I remember a time when I had been struggling with feelings of inferiority and felt I could just not please God. I had been a Christian long enough to know the truth, but I had allowed disappointment and discouragement to begin to tell me that nothing I did counted for any good. It was like mental score-keeping. The voices in my head told me everything I had done to do well and live right were not enough to please God. What I did not seem to realize for a very long time is that by accepting those voices as my reality, I was at the same time rejecting grace. I was allowing those voices to clothe me in unbecoming garments of doubt, self-pity, condemnation and despair. I was trading in my robes of royalty and didn't even see that was what I was doing. My reasoning was bringing me back under condemnation and legalism, and that brought a whole lot of other emotions along with it. Though I fought it in my head and with scripture, I just could not seem to get rid of the emotional torment. I knew I was in a wrestling match with the enemy but I didn't seem to know how to end it. To make matters worse, I kept having dreams that I knew were speaking about identity.

In one dream, I saw a large snake coming after me and I felt a dark presence all around me. I kept fighting it and telling it to go, and then I heard the enemy answer as if he was talking to someone else. The voice whispered, *"But I don't have to go, because she isn't really submitted."* I was shocked, but that was an eye opener for me. I started to see the reality of how the spirit realm saw it. We simply cannot have our sin and our freedom, too. We have to give up some things. All unbelief is sin, according to scripture, because it is a direct rejection of God himself. God resists the proud, and I had unknowingly elevated my emotions above His word. God was trying to tell me through my dreams that I could not fulfill my destiny with the clothes I had made for myself. They weren't becoming to His bride, and they were not an accurate representation of His love and the work of grace in my life. His grace comes to those who are willing to admit they have believed lies and humble themselves by asking God to forgive them. His grace comes to those who are willing to ask Holy Spirit to come teach them the truth. We must be teachable if we want to understand and get free. When I did these things, I had another dream where a large snake was coming after me and it had come up behind my head. Instead of being fearful, I grabbed it just as it was about to strike, reached for a meat cleaver and cut off its head. When I awoke, I knew the meaning of the dream. Submission is what cuts the enemy's head off and removes his ability to whisper his lies and accusations in our ear. If we are to get free and walk in our true identity, it takes more than understanding. It takes a commitment to change. It takes a commitment to renounce those lying, demonic spirits that made room for the enemy to come in and steal from us. It takes a commitment to live for Christ and believe the truth of God's word. If we want to be secure and self-confident individuals, then we must discover our real identity as it is found in Christ. We must settle the issue once and for all.

CHAPTER THREE

Settling the Identity Issue

If we are going to settle our identity issues we must first make sure we ask the right questions. What foundation are we using to determine truth? One cannot secure an anchor into shifting sand. It has to be anchored in something steadfast, immovable and proven. The world and a philosophy of humanism would try to tell us that everything is subjective. At the whim of man, we can decide what it true or not true. Humanism rejects religious convictions and denies any moral value that proves to be superior to that of humanity. It centers around humans, their values, capacities and worth. Humanity is at the center of determining man's purpose, destiny and how we fit into society. The foundations of our nation have eroded because humanism has replaced the convictions for morality and relationship with God. When a people or a nation does not know foundational principles of which they came from, to whom they belong, or in whose image they are created; it causes them to be vulnerable to deception. **"My people perish for lack of knowledge..."** (Hosea 4:6)

The demand for self-rule has caused us to elect leaders that promise to give us what we say we want: *free choice to live without conscience and con-viction*. If we really understand who we are, we would not be led astray by those voices that promise us freedom while bringing us quietly into bondage. Humanism displays no regard for our creator, and places self on the throne of judgment and righteousness. It displays an independent spirit that believes self is capable of living apart from God and making our own decisions of what is moral and immoral. Yet, even the philosophy of humanism, especially in medicine, has at its core belief a deep concern for human welfare, and the values and dignity of the care of those in need. As a nation of people and throughout the world many people continue to depart from a humanistic philosophy in favor of godlessness. If that were not true, we would not see such a war against humanity. There is a battle in the fight for choice to prevail against anything that poses a perceived threat against the demand to live as we please. What we see in the world around us is that many people do not wish to be inconvenienced with the imperfect, the genetically flawed or unwanted children. We do not wish to be burdened with the elderly, the sick and disabled; and so, we have made room for a culture so desensitized by death that we actually promote ending human life as a viable approach to solving the perceived problems of society. We have adopted 'choice' and euthanasia as a means of eliminating those who stand in the way of our proud and arrogant moral corruption. Fear and selfishness promote an agenda to bring us under condemnation and judgment, and remove us even further from the conviction of our conscience. Thus, we have made humanity the highest authority and fooled ourselves into thinking we can live without conscience or accountability to God. For many, 'self' has become the god of America because a nation of people has made a god after their own image. What we need to understand is this is a spirit of rebellion. It is the same spirit of pride and arrogance that was cast out of heaven thousands of years ago, the same spirit that took a third of heaven's angels with him as they were eternally condemned for their disobedience and rebellion. It was Lucifer, that fallen angel, that was cast out of heaven because he said in his heart, **"I will ascend into heaven...I will exalt my throne above the stars of God,...I will also sit on the mount of the congregation on the sides of the north...I will ascend above the heights of the clouds...I will be like the Most High."** (Reference to Isaiah 14:13,14).

Since that time, the enemy of our souls has waged war against mankind in an effort to retaliate against the Holy One who has condemned him to eternal damnation in the lake of fire. Satan does this with every attempt he makes, trying to become the father of those that will choose his ways. It's only fair to advise you, dear reader, that you are simply a pawn to him. *A piece of the game, if you will.* Your soul is his prize. Unfortunately, whether you want to be in the game or not, you are. Your soul is the part of you that makes up your intellect, your mind and emotions. It is often referred to as a completely separate part, the spiritual part, of a human being. It is the part of a person's moral and emotional nature that makes up their personality and identity. Your body is flesh and will one day die, but your spirit is eternal. The only question that really matters is where you will dwell when your flesh dies. Your spirit wants an answer to this, too. That is why your spirit searches for truth. Satan, the deceiver, has to play the game even though the outcome is already fixed. He tries to convince people that he is more powerful than God, but his power is not equal to God. He will always be inferior because he cannot be more powerful than the One that created him. God gave mankind the right to be called sons and daughters of the Most High, not to the angels. John 1:12 tells us **that "To those who did receive Him, He gave the right to become children of God..."** Satan's hope is in the power of his lie. His ability to score against mankind depends on our ignorance of scripture, spiritual laws, and understanding of who God created us to be. The clock is ticking, and his intention is to take as many souls as possible with him into the lake of fire. If a person really understands all that is available to them in Christ, there is no way they would agree to be deceived! Like any predator, Satan takes advantage of people when they are hurt, offended, disappointed and most vulnerable. He makes prey out of his victims by introducing a lie that will bring them into captivity and re-create them in his image.

So many people are searching for truth, enlightenment, and fulfillment. Their quest for knowledge and understanding has filled them with many confusing thoughts and ideas. The New Age path of "enlightenment" often appeals to those that are searching because it includes a smorgasbord of ideas, beliefs and allows an individual to pick and choose from a variety of philosophies that include good works, paths to enlightenment, and spiritual development. New Age concepts of religion also seem to appeal to those that have had their creative expression squelched by parents or other people of influence, especially those that had a fundamental belief system that seemed restrictive in some manner.

New Age beliefs support many paths to seeking spiritual "light" or enlightenment, which basically encourages curiosity seekers to find whatever works for them; whether it be meditation, trances, tarot cards, mediums, astrology, spirit guides, or other forms of seeking spiritual revelation. It's the 'all roads lead to the same place' train of thought or the thinking that both darkness and light are equally good. It's not the searching that is wrong; it is going to the wrong source for information. Some people are so accustomed to listening to the wrong voice that they mistake the voice of the enemy as the voice of God. Scripture tells us that Satan is known as the father of lies, (John 8:44). No devil willingly volunteers the truth because 'their job' is to be like their father. They are under his authority and power. Neither can anyone expect truth from those that are under the influence of the deceiver. Satan is the authority over those that serve him; mediums, spirit guides, palm readers, tarot card readers, fortune tellers and anyone else that looks for information through occult practices invites a curse, death and destruction into their life. Satan, as the deceiver he is, uses portions of truth to sound believable and then purposely misleads people. James 3:15 tells us that the wisdom from the earthly realm is unspiritual and demonic. Any information obtained by occult practices is not holy, pure or from God's spirit. It is from the underworld and its demons. It simply does not make sense to seek advice or counsel from someone that is proven to be a liar! A devil's only motive is to lure a person's soul into darkness and eventually, eternal damnation.

New Age philosophies and Christianity are not compatible. New Age beliefs tend to view God as a source of energy or an alternative path to enlightenment rather than viewing God as a person. That is not what the Bible teaches. God refers to Himself as Father; He is a *person* with a mind, will, and emotions. This person has a voice. He communicates with mankind. The Bible says in Genesis 1:26-28 that mankind is made in His image. In the image and likeness of God we are made; meaning, we each have a mind, will and emotions. We have a body. We have a soul. We are not just a lump of 'energy' floating around in the universe. Does energy have a soul, a mind to make choices, feelings, and have opinions? No. The energy theory also cannot explain how we have emotions, because energy has none. Inside your body is the real you. Your body is just a house for your spirit. God doesn't need to use a natural type of house. We do. Someday, the house is going to fall off and the real you will live somewhere forever. The question is *where* will you spend eternity? There are only two options: heaven and hell. Energy, if that's all the entire universe is made of, wouldn't care one bit where you spent eternity, but your spirit does! Your spirit KNOWS it will live forever. Your spirit knows and searches for truth because it has to settle the question of where will it go when your flesh dies! This is at the quest for every person searching for truth. When a person is unsure, they are willing to search everywhere. They must come up with an answer that gives them peace with God.

Every aspect of God whether in the form of Father, Son or Holy Spirit is as a *person*. Read the Bible and you'll see this is true. God never represents Himself as someone He is not. He has emotions; He has feelings, character, integrity, standards and a value system. Energy does not. New Age beliefs tend to support ideas and philosophies that support independence from God. Self-fulfillment, self-seeking, and replacing "self" in exchange for God, supports the idea that truth and fulfillment are obtained outside of Jesus Christ and relationship with our Creator. Christianity promotes a humble Father/child relationship. One can never deny the person of Jesus Christ and expect to enter into God's holy heaven, for it is written, **"nor is there salvation in any other, for there is no other name under heaven given among men by which we must be saved,"** (Acts 4:12). The Bible tells us the wages of sin is death. We are eternally separated from God if our sins are not atoned for by the shed blood of Christ. This is the only way to the Father and into relationship with God. **"If you confess with your mouth the Lord Jesus and believe in your heart that God has raised Him from the dead, you will be saved. For with the heart one believes unto righteousness, and with the mouth confession is made unto salvation. For the scripture says, 'Whoever believes on Him will not be put to shame."** Romans 10:9-11.

In every other religion in the world, righteousness is self-made through good works, not imputed through a Holy God. In every other religion, there is a demand to earn acceptance or favor to that particular god or belief system through proving oneself in whatever acts or beliefs supported by that particular brand of religion. In no other religion has man or a so-called god given their life to redeem mankind from their sins. *They have no power or authority to do so.*

The truth is there is nothing we can do to be holy or good enough to enter into God's holy heaven outside of the blood of Jesus covering our sin. Our righteousness comes from Christ, not anything we can do to try to argue or defend how good we are. When we accept Christ as our Savior, not only does He forgive our sin and wipe the slate clean, He actually puts His righteousness in us. His Spirit lives within us so that we never again have to feel separated from God. Never again do we have to question or wonder who we belong to. Never again do we have to feel fatherless, rejected, and question whether God loves us. His acceptance is so complete that He decided long ago - before He ever went to the cross - that He would be the sacrifice for our sins instead of us having to pay the penalty of death and eternal separation. That is how great His love is for mankind. Ultimately, all searching for some form of god that we can relate to is trying to find a place of acceptance, a place that builds up our self-worth, and to obtain some sort of peace within ourselves, with others, and with God. Jesus Christ is the only one whose name Jehovah Shalom means "Prince of Peace." Jesus Christ did come in the form of a MAN, because it was a form humanity could relate to; yet Christ remained divine in order to redeem mankind from the penalty of our sin.

Many people question whether or not God exists. Intellect and an analytical mind can hinder a person from recognizing what others find through their faith. Some turn to science as a means of trying to prove their hypothesis. The big bang theory and evolution fail to explain how life is produced. Life is produced after like kind. Dogs produce dogs. Cats produce cats. Humans produce humans. DNA is reproduced from DNA. That is what science has proven. Frogs, toads, amphibians, monkeys or gorillas have never produced a human being. Life can only be produced from its origin. Science has their ways of testing data and proving a particular hypothesis, and some very analytical minds may have difficulty attempting to believe in a God they cannot see, touch, hear, smell or taste. God is unfathomable in light of the fact that He lives outside of time and beyond any measurable limits. Science may attempt to use a scientific approach in order to prove that anything that cannot be measured cannot exist. Yet, the attempt to prove God does not exist using scientific logic is a flawed concept. Science is incapable of proving what does *not* exist. Science operates on drawing certain conclusions based on data that has been collected and analyzed, but science can never prove with absolute certainty that God does not exist. If that were true, it would have to provide absolute proof in order to substantiate that claim. At best, science can only provide an unjustified opinion based on assumption.

Many of us would agree that intelligent design is found in nature and elsewhere in the universe. Do energy or dust particles have intelligent design inherent in them? No. As much as people may try to come up with their own logic and reasoning to disprove His existence, there is far too much tangible proof in the world and throughout the universe to deny His existence. There are eyewitness testimonies of people who claim to have had personal encounters with Jesus Christ and miracles that cannot be explained outside of a divine, supernatural intervention. Even science and archaeological discoveries have proven that certain things spoken of in the Bible existed, which helps substantiate various truths found in scripture. There are other methods of proving things that do not appear visible to the human eye. Take love, for example. Love cannot be measured by any scientific calculations, but I do not need anyone to convince me that the love my husband or children have for me, or my love for them is not real. Love is an emotion, but the tangible proof is in the actions that support the truth that love exists. So it is with God. God is also divine love. (See 1 John 4:8) **"In this the love of God has sent His only begotten Son into the world that we might live through Him. In this is love, not that we loved God, but that He loved us and sent His Son to be the propitiation for our sins."** This kind of love is based on a deliberate choice of the one who loves and is not conditional upon the behavior of the one which is loved. It is a love that actually suffers in selfless giving so that the one that is loved can receive the very best the other has to offer. Unconditional love thinks the best about others. It is patient, kind, and only has a desire to put the best interests of another person ahead of themselves. It goes far beyond the human capabilities of love, but this is truly how God loves us. Just because a person hasn't experienced it yet doesn't mean it doesn't exist. It simply means the relationship is not yet established in intimacy, where the individual senses a deeply meaningful connection with Christ. Ultimately, the discovery of whether or not God exists can only be arrived at through faith. Some would say, "I'll believe it when I see it!" That is what Thomas, one of Jesus' disciples said. (read John 20:25). Yet Jesus said, **"Blessed are those who have believed without seeing."** (John 20:29) God designed the reality of His kingdom to be revealed to those who are spiritually ready to receive it, and hidden from the scoffers, unbelieving and those that oppose Christ's message. Faith is what unlocks the ability to believe and receive. **"Now faith is the substance of things hoped for, the evidence of things not seen,"** (Heb. 11:1). Faith assures us of things we expect, and convinces us of the things we cannot see. Without faith, it is impossible to please God, but even if we deny Him, it does not mean that He ceases to exist.

This chapter is not intended to be an exhaustive list of apologetics, but I will say this: children do not grow up looking for reasons to disprove God's existence. It is only when a person's innocence has been repeatedly robbed from them that they become jaded. It is the end result of having a steady flow of negative experiences, from which their disappointment turns into anger, and eventually an acceptance of disillusionment. Pain and disappointment are not the best evidence to try to prove or disprove any theory. I had plenty of that in my life but those are the things that eventually caused me to seek God.

◆ ◆ ◆

I remember years ago praying a prayer that began, "God *if* you're real..." You might think you have to have it together or have a lot of faith to come to the Lord, but that is the farthest thing from the truth. I was confused. I didn't know how to pray or who to pray to. Was I supposed to light a candle or pray to some saint like Catholics did? Did I call out to some odd looking, mostly naked, bald headed fat guy that I only saw in nail salons or Asian restaurants? Was it someone else? I had heard a little about Jesus, but I didn't know enough to make an informed decision. I had looked for truth in the occult side of things, too. I had only gone to church a handful of times as a kid, so I formulated a lot of my own ideas about who God was based on information I'd picked up in life. I really didn't know what to believe about God, and truth be told, I was still pretty angry with Him, whoever he was. I blamed him for every disappointment, every failure, and every loser guy that ever hurt me. I blamed Him for my younger brother's untimely death, my inability to do well in life and the fact that I felt so unloved and insignificant. I blamed Him for a lot of things that weren't His fault. I needed someone to blame because I just couldn't accept the pain of my own sin and shame. Certainly I couldn't be the one who had made my own life so messed up, right? I hated who I had become, but I was too proud to admit it to myself. I was too busy drinking myself to death and wallowing in my own self-pity and misery. I was incredibly bitter. I almost allowed all that bitterness to take my life. It poisoned me and all I could do is wallow in it. There were many times when I would overdose. Several times the doctors told me they couldn't do anything for me because I had too much in my system. They just left me on a stretcher to see if I would eventually come out of it. I had doctors and nurses ask me why I was on a death mission. They were the ones that got used to reading my charts week after week. When people would ask me why I didn't see value to my life, I couldn't answer them. I had surrounded myself with people that repeatedly told me what a loser I was and how I wouldn't get any better. I heard countless people tell me what I needed to do to straighten out my life; the problem was, I wasn't motivated to do it because I no longer believed in myself. My self-image was so negative that I despised myself. I *agreed* with the voices that told me I was no good for myself or my daughter. I agreed with the voices that said I would never be successful in life or that I had nothing to offer. I agreed with the voices that said I was unlovable, rejected, unattractive and a failure. I cut myself repeatedly from the frustration of life and the hatred I directed towards myself. I had demons that contorted my body and gave me seizures. There were times when my arms and legs would do strange things and I had absolutely no control over my body. Something else was in control, and that scared me. I was so full of darkness that I could not recognize the voices of self-pity and self-loathing were driving me right off a cliff. I didn't want to live but I was afraid to die. I often wondered why I would still be alive. What purpose could there possibly be to a person like me remaining alive? That was my life when I finally decided to see if God was indeed real. As messed up, defiant and angry as I was, I managed to find a moment of sincere honesty. I simply asked God to show me if He was real and save me. I told Him what I needed to get out of my situation because it was literally destroying every part of my life. I didn't know if He heard me, and I didn't know if He cared. I don't think I even had the faith that I would receive an answer, but I was desperate for something to get me out of my miserable situation. A couple of weeks later, a string of unexpected situations occurred that I absolutely knew was Jesus answering my prayer. Let me tell you, He knows how to send an answer to convince you He heard your prayer! He led me to a lifeline of hope and help and in the process, someone to lead me to pray a prayer of salvation. I didn't need any more convincing, and God had turned my confusion and unbelief into a little seed of faith. You see, everything we need, including the little seed of faith to get us saved is supplied by God. It's all Him. All you have to do is ask. If you're feeling like you don't have faith to get saved, just ask Jesus to supply the seed. He never asks us to do something without first making it possible.

The bottom line for me is God has given me a testimony. When I was killing myself with alcohol and drugs and had no strength to deliver myself, when I came to an end of myself and cried out to God, Jesus was there. It wasn't energy or some other god. When I had exhausted all other options of relying on myself or others, when all my other resources and answers failed, God was there. Let me tell you, if you're hanging off the edge of a cliff, you know what name to cry out! Jesus Christ was the name I called on when I got serious and wanted to know truth, and He was the One that answered. He was the one that was faithful and true. He will never be anything less than what He says He is. He is so holy and trustworthy that He cannot contradict who He is! The bottom line for me is no one can ever try to convince me that He isn't real, or that other gods are equal to Him or it's all from the same source because God has proven a very different reality. I know demons are real because I've lived with them. I've heard them talk to me. I've seen them, and I've experienced them trying to destroy my life. So no one can ever convince me that "other gods" have my best interests at heart and it all comes from the same place. Neither do I believe all roads lead to heaven. That's a lie straight from the pit of hell designed to keep people in rebellion and away from the truth. Satan gets to claim those souls for eternal trophies if he can take their life before they come to the truth and commit their life to Christ. You see, it's not enough to know the truth, there has to be a commitment to live by it. People are just as much at risk of ending up in hell not because they don't know the truth, but because they won't submit to it and worship God in Spirit and in truth.

No man comes to the Father unless the Holy Spirit draws them and reveals the truth about the Son of God. Jesus showed me the reality of the scripture found in Romans 5:8-11. While I was still an enemy to Christ, he had chosen to die for me. Because of His sacrifice on the cross, I could be reconciled to my heavenly Father. He loved me through my anger. Through my rage and pain, though I blamed Him for things that were not His fault, He loved me. I was the one giving Him those 39 lashes and I was the one nailing Him to the cross. And He just took it. He forgave me before I even knew to ask and He accepted me though I was a mess. Most people who feel there is no God usually deny Him as a result of deep disappointment or a feeling that if God existed and if He cared for them, certain circumstances would never have occurred. Most would argue that if God exists, the world would not be full of pain, suffering and disappointment or characterized by evil occurrences. Yet pain, suffering and evil are the result of what happens when people fail to trust in God or turn to Him for help. Sin causes suffering, disease, poverty and much more. Evil is simply the absence of God in the soul of mankind. Evil is the result of what happens when people reject and refuse the Lordship of God and choose self-rule instead. The existence of evil does not disprove God's existence; it simply proves what man becomes where God's love is absent. Even the prophet Jeremiah said, **"The heart is deceitful above all things, and desperately wicked. Who can know it?"** Jer. 17:9.

Our hearts *will* deceive us if they are not kept by a holy, loving God. How easily evil appears when people lose sight of the fact that they are created in the image of God and that is their true Father. How easy it is for evil actions to be released when people accept the lies that they are rejected, unwanted, unloved and believe their existence doesn't matter. We have all seen what can happen when people's minds are not in alignment with love and truth. We've seen hate crimes. We've seen innocent people slain at the hands of those that can only be described as demonically energized to carry out evil. We see an unstable world that has put their hope and confidence in the philosophies of man and other religions, and hope that the government will provide for their needs, yet they have no real peace. They have fear because they are not at peace with God. Their conscience is not assured that their sins are forgiven. They have fear that the world will end, fear that they won't have enough to take care of their families; fear that says they are unloved or unwanted, fear that they are inferior or inadequate in some way. Fear always comes with accusation and that spirit of accusation will accuse us to God, and speak accusations against God to us as if they are our own thoughts. Fear is at the root of many works of evil. It is the very opposite of Love.

Fear has a loud voice and we must learn to silence it by the word of truth. We live in a world of chaos because of so many people that have put their confidence in the wrong things. It is not difficult to see where these lies originate. It is from the dark and wicked heart of one that despises God and whose only mission is to kill, steal and destroy the object of God's affection. We know where evil comes from. It is unleashed from hell itself. By the same token, if we are to believe that there is any good in the world, then we must also agree that the origin of all good comes from a holy and pure source.

Let me bring you back to my main point. Truth is relevant only so long as it is actually based on truth. It can only be truth if it comes from a higher authority than us. If we are to determine what is truth, it must have its anchor in something proven and solid, something deeper than what appears to be sur-face knowledge. It must be anchored in bedrock. Psalm 18:30 says, **"As for God, His way is perfect; the word of God is proven: He is a shield to all those that trust in Him."** The Bible is proven through fulfilled prophecies, archaeological discoveries, and the unity and consistency of the many books of the Bible that were written over a span of over 1,500 years, and by many different authors from various continents and a variety of different languages. Hundreds of specific prophecies were given and recorded, some hundreds of years before they were actually fulfilled. No other religion can verify itself in this manner. This alone validates the authenticity of what it written in the Bible. It is not a book of philosophy; it is a book of holy thoughts and spiri-tual principles, inspired by the unction of the Holy Spirit and given through the penmanship of the Holy Spirit working through man. One thing that man cannot do, that Christ did, was fulfill the prophecy that he would die and three days later be raised from the dead. No man can fulfill that in himself. The scriptures are proven by many people throughout history. Though written by many different authors, the content is harmonious and consistent in what is written. Multitudes of those that believe in Christ have testimonies from per-sonal experience that God did in fact hold true to His word by the fulfillment of various promises found in scripture. So you see, the foundation of where we place our hope, and ultimately our faith, is proven. It is solid, and thus be-comes qualified to serve as an anchor for our soul.

If we try to define God by our negative experiences, we will miss the truth. If we try to define who we *are* by our own perception or the perception of oth-ers, we will always fall short because human perception is flawed. Everyone eventually does make a choice whose image they will allow to be formed in them. They may not be aware that is what they are doing, but that is the result of what we choose to believe. I would much rather identify with the thought that I am made in the image of a caring, compassionate, merciful and forgiving God than take on the attributes of a selfish, twisted, evil persona. Every area of our life where we deny Christ's ruler ship becomes a place where truth and understanding is twisted. Everyone does eventually make a choice who they will allow to be their spiritual father. Everyone eventually does make a choice who they will serve. All of mankind makes these choices daily. Every voice requires a response, and every choice determines what identity is formed in each individual. Attempting to put off the choice and ride the fence doesn't work either. Not giving an answer is still an answer. Not choosing Christ is still rejection of Him, therefore, it's the same as getting the wicked stepfather by default.

I suggest to you, dear reader, that there is a better way to solving the identity crisis issue. It is turning to a holy source; one that cannot lie and is full of unconditional love and acceptance. Only one who truly has our best interests at heart and has no other motive than love should be allowed to define our worth and establish our true identity.

There is a God that absolutely adores each one of us. He knows our sitting down and when we rise up. He understands our every thought. He is acquainted with all of our ways, and scripture says in Ps. 139 that He already knows every word on our tongue. He formed us in our mother's womb. Even before we were born, we were known by our Father and loved by Him. His thoughts towards us are precious and more than the sand of the sea shore. There is nothing that can separate us from His great love.

There are some scriptures in the Bible that are universal truths, meaning, they hold true for every person in every circumstance, throughout all time. Isaiah 49:1 reminds us of this truth. **"...before I was born the Lord called me; from my birth he has made mention of my name."** Jeremiah 1:5 is another example. **"Before I formed you in the womb I knew you; before you were born I sanctified you... I ordained you a prophet to the nations."**

Jeremiah was a young man at the time God spoke those words to him, but he understood that God had an intimate knowledge of him; a relationship existed between the two of them even before he was born. Did you know that your spirit was in heaven with God before you were formed in your mother's womb? Jeremiah knew that God had called him to speak a critical message to mankind at a crucial time in history. So it is with each of us. We may not be called to the office of the prophet but we are born for just such a time as this, with a vital message of hope for mankind. It is critical for each of us to fulfill our purpose.

If you don't know who God is, you will never discover the real you, because you came from God. People can end up thinking that either He doesn't exist or doesn't love them, or sadly many give up and accept the lie rather than search for the truth. Both are completely false perceptions that are fueled by negative emotions, disappointments and rebellion. That is why so many people fail to discover the truth. It takes faith to please God and come to Christ. The most wonderful thing is if you sincerely want to know truth or take that step of faith, God will honor it.

Before we continue, I would like to insert a little prayer of salvation. I pray that the Holy Spirit will convince you of truth as you read throughout these pages. I pray that truth will indeed cut through the lies, the deception and the confusion that the enemy has led you to believe - about yourself, others, and about God. If this has spoken to your heart and you would like to receive Jesus Christ as your Lord and Savior, you can do it in your own words. All you have to do is to confess Him as the Son of God that died for your sins, and ask Him to receive you unto Himself. Thank him for taking all of your guilt, shame and penalty for your sins upon Himself and enduring the cross for you. Thank him for your salvation and adoption into His Father's kingdom. It's that simple. If you would like a little sample prayer you can also use the one provided on the next page. Pray it out loud as you make your confession of faith.

Dear Lord Jesus,

I thank you for the seed of faith to believe unto salvation. I choose to place my trust in You right now. I confess my belief in You, that You are the Son of God, that You took my sin, my shame, and all my guilt upon Yourself. Thank You for enduring the pain of the cross for me. Thank you that you died as me, in my place. Please receive me unto Yourself. I thank you, Heavenly Father, for adopting me as Your child. Let this be revelation in my heart. Thank you for the forgiveness of sin, eternal life and salvation. Holy Spirit, please fill me with Your Spirit and enable me to live for you. In Jesus name, amen.

CHAPTER FOUR

The Fatherhood of God

A father is responsible for the well-being of his family. He is not only a provider and head of the household, but by God's design he has a responsibility to provide spiritual and emotional protection and a role model of righteousness. By doing so, he provides his family with a sense of safety, security and stability. Children look to their father as an example to show them how to model certain responses, feelings and behaviors. They also receive their sense of self-worth, identity and values. When a father fails to meet these essential needs, a person lacks what is vital to their fundamental health and emotional development.

People that feel orphaned or fatherless struggle with deep feelings of rejection, abandonment, resentment, fear, anger, shame, insecurity, inferiority and much more. This is why society cannot effectively address the issues that affect culture, community and the needs of our nation without first addressing the urgent needs of the heart and soul. My husband and I have done a great deal of ministry to the homeless and we have seen a tremendous amount of brokenness that stemmed from broken and dysfunctional family dynamics. One particular day three men came walking up together and began to pour out their hearts to my husband. These men were probably in their mid to late thirties. Each one began to tell a story of their father's rejection and abandonment. They were angry, hurt and broken. By the end of this encounter with them we were all in tears. Norm prayed for their healing and restoration. It is devastating to see what a lack of fatherly love and acceptance has on not just the individual, but on society. If those men had fathers that truly cared about them, I doubt if they would have ended up homeless. We simply have no idea how rejection and abandonment affects the human heart. It shapes a person's feelings about themselves and their outlook on life. Healing is the first answer, not the last. We will never produce change in society, reduce the crime rate, see the reduction of runaways, people delivered from drugs and prostitution, break people free from generational poverty and other important aspects of transformation if we do not first focus on the healing and restoration of people's hearts. God wants to heal the heart of our families and heal the heart of our cities, but it's not going to come only through social welfare programs. We must sacrifice our brokenness and allow the Lord to heal us. As we do, He will break our hearts again in compassion for those that are hurting. Until we invest something of ourselves in others, we will never receive the beauty of a transformed soul. This is the beauty of Christ formed in us that reaches out to heal the hopelessness in others. We all have a responsibility to help heal and minister to the needs of others. Many people consider the broken and the outcasts to be invisible members of society, but they are not expendable. All human life has value! Real change is produced when a person's belief system is transformed and restored. Transformation is a process by which God changes a person and heals a broken life through the power of His love. Again, it comes back to the issue of identity, the Fatherhood of God and how it impacts each person's life.

I will never forget the day when God visited me suddenly and unexpectedly to give me a revelation of His Fatherhood. It changed a lifetime of hurts, religious misconceptions and lies the enemy had introduced into my belief system and brought me to a place of repentance for years and years' worth of believing the wrong things about Him. I believe this understanding of the Fatherhood of God is a key factor to initiating the salvation of many, the end of the religious spirit and vital to this next move of God.

> Until we invest something of ourselves in others, we will never receive the beauty of a transformed soul.

I had been a Christian for many years and gone through some great trials, had many great victories and testimonies of how the Lord had moved in my life. I had prayed for this particular revelation many times. Yet, for whatever reason in the heart and mind of God, the answer to my prayer to have deep revelation of the Father/child relationship eluded me until the Holy Spirit showed up with a personal encounter. It's important for us to realize that we don't get to pick and choose how we experience God. He chooses the timing and the way He releases the moment. It is different for everyone. I believe part of the reason I had to wait so long is because of the many, many people that are in this fatherless generation and need to be set free from religion; set free from many painful experiences and disappointments, and receive deep healing for their souls. Prior to this particular revelation, I had known Him in many other aspects, such as Deliverer, Savior, Lord, Healer, Provider and Friend; but I do believe that understanding the FATHERHOOD of GOD is key to this particular time in the kingdom. This incredible moment was the experiential reality of Galatians 4:6 being poured out into my heart in a way that I had never known before.

Galatians 4:6-7: "And because you are sons, God has sent forth the Spirit of His Son into your hearts, crying out, "Abba, Father!" Therefore you are no longer a slave but a son, and if a son, then an heir of God through Christ."

There are many things we know and understand *intellectually,* but we can still lack personal revelation of it. Hearing the same thing over and over again can reinforce something as truth whether that particular thing is actually a legitimate truth or not. Yet, when it comes to spiritual understanding it is a personal emotional experience that connects us to the heart of our Father. Defining moments between us and the heart of God have the potential to change us forever; and unravel every lie that affects our belief system. I cannot fully explain my own experience with God except to say that nothing I had experienced impacted my perception of God's Fatherhood as powerfully as it did when He suddenly showed up and birthed a cry of "Abba, Father" into my heart. Strong waves of emotion flooded my heart as I realized that I have a dad who loves me and will do anything for me. My Father has always loved me; I just couldn't foster a relationship with Him because the lies from the enemy hindered me. Different aspects of my broken childhood prevented me from entering into an intimate and meaningful relationship. Holy Spirit revealed spiritual things present in my family that were already present at the time of my birth. Two powerful demonic spirits, Fear and Lust, began to oppress me from a very early age. The Lord showed me that the rejection, the insecurity and the fear I had always felt were not indicators that I was rejected; they were evidence of the enemy's torment and presence. It was so freeing to finally understand *it wasn't me. I wasn't defective or unlovable, but that's what the enemy told me all my life.* Sometimes there are things waiting to destroy us that we don't understand and those things are present and active in our lives, even from before our birth. In a later chapter I will explain more about generational curses. The enemy had seeds of mistrust that were buried so deep I didn't know how to get them out, and he used those seeds of lies to bring me back under condemnation and guilt whenever it seemed convenient to him. Those lies also told me I was orphaned, uncared for and rejected. Inferiority told me I could never be 'good enough.' Many, many people, especially women, struggle with similar feelings. Daily challenges can, in what seems like a mere moment, strip us of confidence, self-esteem, and in an instant turn our thoughts to those of guilt and self-condemnation. These things strip away our peace and rob us of sleep. *"The thief comes only to steal and kill and destroy..."* (John 10:10). Do you see the thief at work? It wasn't until recently that I started to see all these things wrapped up in the whole identity issue. Why do we always seem to be on shaky ground? Why is our peace so easily robbed from us, and where lies the victory? Could it be that women don't really believe they are capable, strong, compassionate world changers? Could it be that we don't really believe who God says we are? Because I think if we did, we would snap out of it and shut down all those negative voices in one authoritative word, *"Enough!"*

In one moment, my heart was changed forever. The most powerful thing about this defining moment in my relationship with "Dad" is that this revelation suddenly shattered lies that had been intricately woven by the enemy since very young childhood. The enemy lost his grip that day. The seeds of lies that had operated in my belief system began to unravel. Every lie was ultimately an accusation against my identity in Christ. Every lie was tied to feelings of rejection. As far back as I can remember, my own father was mentally ill. He fathered me, but he was never a dad. He was absent mentally, emotionally and physically most of my life because of his condition. One simply cannot have a healthy, emotionally fulfilling relationship with someone that is not healthy and stable. When it came to trying to relate to a heavenly Father, it was completely foreign to me.

There are many other people in the same boat. Many people for one reason or another need this powerful revelation in order to feel truly whole. God wants to radically change our perception of Him so that we receive the deep healing that will reconnect us with our heavenly Father, change the perception of ourselves, and transform our identity. My prayer is for those that have felt abandoned, misunderstood, rejected, unwanted and orphaned to experience God in a fresh, new way. I pray that the Spirit of Sonship would be poured out into *your* hearts, thereby settling, establishing and reaffirming the faith and confidence you have towards your Heavenly Father. This is the perfect love that casts out all fear!

God gave me a personal point of reference to be able to connect with His heart. It all started with a word study related to a portion of scripture in Micah chapter 7. In verse 19, the word compassion is used. It is the Hebrew word *'racham'* which means to love from the womb. It depicts the tender love of a mother for her own helpless child and it speaks of the depth of compassion associated with this expression of love. This is where the revelation flooded my heart. I could not relate so much to the whole father relationship because mine was lacking, but I *could* relate to how a mother deeply loves a baby in her womb. I'm a mother and I understand what it feels like to bond with a child that you anticipate coming into the world. Over and over, waves of God's love poured out as He healed the deep issues of my past. Broken areas of my emotions, my heart and understanding were restored and made whole. I cried rivers of tears as I was filled with joy, relief and gratitude. Holy Spirit poured in the revelation of my Father's love and so much more that day. The moment He did, the struggles from my past, the lies, the religious misconceptions and even the understanding of how prosperity and formula preaching had defiled my heart all made sense. All those things had only added to the misunderstanding I had of God in my belief system yet never knew were there. Lies and faulty perception of a person affect how we think about them. So it is in our perception of God. Fear often exists where lies and deception are at work. When our love for God is perfected through revelation, it casts out the fear that was once there.

Some people have absent parents for whatever reason, or those relationships have been broken or estranged. Those things affect people deeply and can produce feelings of abandonment. The other reality is that religion also produces a sense of being orphans and fatherless because it substitutes rules, traditions of men and legalism for trust, intimacy and personal relationship. A person whose heart is bound by religion and people pleasing feels insecure and unstable because their acceptance is tied to performance. While the opinions of others may change as frequently as the wind blows, God's heart and acceptance towards His children is steadfast and certain. His love never fails us. His word is certain and trustworthy. Religion, performance and people pleasing keep a person's heart from truly connecting with their Father. This may be a blind spot in people, but again, I encourage each person to search their own heart and ask themself if their relationship with God is one of intimacy, trust, faith, and confidence. Do you feel secure in your Father's love or do you fight feelings of inferiority, fear, insecurity and condemnation? Do you feel that you have to work for acceptance or are you resting in His complete grace and what the blood of Jesus has made available to you? It is He that justifies. It is He that sanctifies. Jesus did it all. We can add nothing to the gospel or take nothing away; otherwise it becomes perverted with a mixture of man's beliefs and traditions, impure and diluted of power.

None of us will ever be able to love others unconditionally and purely without the revelation of the Fatherhood of God. We will never be able to free ourselves from fear or insecurity. We need to experience the passion of the Lord with a deep understanding that releases the love of God *from our heart to His*. 1 John 4: 18 tells us that he who fears has not been made perfect in love. It's not God's love that needs to be perfected, it's ours. When you receive the revelation of His deep, unconditional love towards you, it really will cast out all fear. Would you like to become fearless before the enemy? Set free in your mindset? Bold in faith? Absolutely convinced that God is on your side and will do anything to insure your victory? Ask for a deeper revelation of Him, because you will never move from where you are now to where you need to go without the faith to get you there. Ask for the Spirit of His dear Son to be poured out in your heart by the Holy Spirit and fill every part of you to make you whole. We love Him because He first loved us, and it's the personal revelation of this deep, sacrificial love that gives understanding to every other scripture. He who did not spare His Son for us, but delivered Him up as a living sacrifice for us all (Rom. 8:32) is YOUR DAD and He will do anything for you. How could He not? This is the love that is spoken of in Romans 8:38 which assure us that nothing can ever separate us from this love of our Father who is found in Christ Jesus our Lord.

◆ ◆ ◆

God wants us to dream with Him, and one of the very first things He does is to help us discover the beauty He has placed within us. For all the little girls who never got to sit on their daddy's lap and hear the tender words, "I love you,"...and all the women who still long to discover a close, meaningful relationship with their heavenly Father, daydream with me for a moment. Imagine yourself climbing up on your Father's knee, snuggling into the crook of his arm. You are safe, loved and He has all the time in the world for you. He is my Daddy now, and yours, too. Forgotten are the memories of days long past. Abba and I are playing a game. He has a big golden jar in His hand. I see something colorful and sparkling, radiating the most beautiful light and reflection within the jar.

"Reach into the jar, child," He said softly, as He gently peeled off one of my labels I'd been wearing. "Here," He whispered, as He brought the jar closer. "Choose one."

I reached in and pulled out a beautiful red sardius. It was breathtaking. "Oh!" I gasped, "It's...it's so beautiful!" I looked into the deep red gem. I studied the magnificent precision cuts. It was exquisite. I had never seen anything so captivating in all my life! Somehow, gazing into the depth of the blood red stone made me feel...*clean.* It was more than that, though. It made me feel...*special.* I sat back against Daddy and sighed. My Papa always had the best gifts.

"Thank you, Daddy," I said. "I love it!' "Oh, that's a great choice," Daddy said. "I've got a gift for you that I've been working on, and this will be the perfect addition to it. Let's see how it fits," He said, as He pulled a dazzling gold crown out from behind His back. He set the gem in place and put it on my head. I lifted my hands to touch the heavy metal crown sitting atop my head. I suddenly noticed that my old shabby clothes had been replaced with a gorgeous shimmering new dress. "Wow! Look at that!" "It sparkles!" I marveled. I look like a real princess! I gave my Daddy a puzzled look, wondering when my garments changed, but I was beginning to realize that every time I climbed up on Daddy's lap there were always incredible surprises in store! He gave me a knowing little wink and a smile.

I took off the crown for a moment to study the intricate design. I had never seen anything like it. I looked at the lovely red stone again. Wait! Something was written in the stone. What did it say? I peered closer, trying to make out the letters. How could I have missed that? R-e-d-e-e-m-e-d. No wonder I felt brand new! I turned over my Daddy's hand to see what was written on that label He had taken off of me. "Papa, what did that label say?" I asked.

"Oh, that old thing?" He asked.

"Yes." My forehead wrinkled in displeasure. I looked at the crumpled piece of paper with the familiar bold writing. "***Not-good-enough.***" All of a sudden I felt sad that I had agreed to wear it for so long.

"Now, now, little one," my Father said. "Don't fret. You never have to wear that label again." "And you don't have to wear these, either." He showed me all the other labels He had picked off while I had been looking through the jar. He sure had a lot of words in His hands. Words like, Fearful, Unattractive, Victim, Failure, Rejected, Unlovable and Unwanted. All of them were now crumpled in His hand. He leaned in and said, "You don't have to wear them because that's not who you really are!" Suddenly a little twinkle appeared in his eye. "Hey!" he said, with a big smile on his face. "I've got a great idea. Would you like to pick something else from the jar?"

This time I squinted to see if I could make out any words written in the stones, but I couldn't see anything. "It doesn't work that way, child," my Father said gently. "These are identity stones, and the names only appear once you take them as your own." Each stone is resplendent and unique, just like you. So is your crown. No one else has one just like it. I reached in, wondering what I would pull out next. *Overcomer.* That one was a luminous white stone. It glowed with shimmering, reflective light rays that seemed to glow even stronger as it came closer to my Daddy. Streams of light reflected off of Daddy's face onto my own and danced all over the room. He skillfully placed it into my crown. One by one, I watched as Daddy adorned my crown with precious stones and beautiful jewels. Then I noticed that with each new stone he set into my crown, He added a matching one to His crown as well. We had matching crowns! Those really made me feel special. I chose another one. A beautiful golden chrysolite that was absolutely stunning. This one said *Warrior.* Yes, that was a good one. It made me feel strong. I chose another, bluish purple jacinth stone. *Beloved.* It felt so good to know that I was loved! I pulled out a gleaming purple amethyst and it said *Royalty.* I was beginning to see myself in a different light! Then another, this time an exquisite emerald etched with the words, *My Father's Praise.* My Father is so proud of me! I like that one a lot. I reached into the jar again and pulled out the most dazzling apple green chrysoprase. Oooh...*Anointed Healer.* Wow, that's an interesting thought. I'd never thought of myself like that before. One by one, Daddy let me choose handfuls of stones, each one breathtaking, dazzling and brilliant to behold. Each one had a new name on it. Reaching into the jar was like picking out a prize every time! Papa and I laughed as we talked about the meaning of each new stone. He tells me all the time how special I am to Him, and that it is His joy to bless me with His goodness! As I open my eyes, it is like the fog has lifted. I can see the person Father created in me, and if I can see it, I can achieve it. This truth empowers me and you to become the person that exists inside of us. Once we see the future, each one of us can be empowered to endure the metamorphosis of change.

Dear reader, you are a child of God. The redeemed, His bride. You are the righteousness of God in Christ Jesus. It is time to discard all the hurtful words and labels that have shaped your identity into someone you were never created to be. It's time to listen as He tells you a new story, and wear the crown your Father gave you. You are destiny. Royalty! Your true identity in Christ is far more beautiful than anything you can imagine. Today is a day when you can choose to let go of the false labels, the regret, and the pain of your yesterdays.

Today, let's sing a new song. Sing a song of *victory*! Declare: I choose to believe the truth, and reject the lies I've allowed myself to believe. I am wearing my crown of victory, and I will *dance*. I am my Father's praise!

I'm the saved, the redeemed
I'm a child of the King,
I'm a weapon in Your hand O God!
I'm Your beloved and Your bride
Overcoming darkness with every stride
I'm a weapon in Your hand O God!

I'm the jewel in Your crown
I'm Your praise, Your renown, tearing the enemy's kingdom down
I'm a weapon in Your hand O God!
I'm the scepter in Your hand,
An ambassador in this land
I'm a weapon in Your hand O God!

The Spirit of the Lord has anointed me,
With His power and His might
To proclaim freedom to the oppressed
And give the blind their sight
I preach the gospel, heal the sick, and cast out demons with a word
I'm a weapon in His hand; it's the Spirit of the Lord!
I've been fashioned in the secret place
Covered solely by His grace
Hidden in the cleft of the rock...

I'm seated with Him high above
Covered by His strength and love
Hidden under the shadow of His wing
Created for His glory, His praises will I sing!

Your past, no matter how painful it may have been, has no authority, power or ability to influence your future. Your future does not rest in the hands of your enemies; your future is secure in God's hands. **"No weapon forged against you will prevail, and you will refute every tongue that accuses you. This is the heritage of the servants of the Lord, and this is their vindication from** me," declares the LORD. (Is. 54:17) No weapon will succeed against you, unless you give it power over your life. Doubt is a greater enemy than any failure. God can handle our failures but we must deal with our doubt. Doubt and double-mindedness will leave us confused, frustrated and with a lot of unanswered prayers. It also causes hopelessness. Fear is at the root of all the doubt and uncertainty. We must learn how to take authority over the spirit of fear and give it no place in our life. May I tell you something? You are fearfully and wonderfully made. God has put His name over you. His favor is for life. Nothing you do can stop Him from loving you. Jesus is your biggest fan! Your Father is your strong tower. You can run to Him at any time and feel safe. He has put His authority in you, and given you dominion over every manner of evil. As a child of God you are destined to change the world because you have received a commission from the Lord to heal the sick, cast out demons, open blind eyes, heal the lame, cause the deaf to hear and speak in a new spiritual language given by Holy Spirit. You are to *re*-present the kingdom of heaven right here, right now, everywhere you are, and God wants to equip you to do it! Your Father understands the enemy's tactics to try to intimidate you in order to keep you from inheriting your promise land, but He has said, "Fear not!" In other words, don't let fear hinder you! Get in the presence of the Lord. ***Fear is not evidence of truth; fear is a response of our emotions when we allow our thoughts to dictate a perceived outcome to a situation.*** Confront it, whatever it is, and cast down that vain imagination! You are not rejected, condemned or abandoned. You are not forgotten. You are accepted, given a pardon of 'not guilty,' and you are adopted as God's dear child. You are a joint heir with Jesus Christ. Everything that He has, you do too! Angels are waiting to be put on assignment to assist you, protect you and keep you in all of God's ways so that you can be successful in life. Isn't that great news? Let your confidence be renewed today!

It's time to rise up and take a stand against anything that would try to strip you of your royal garments. You are highly favored of the Lord! Rise up and confront that spirit of intimidation. **"For God did not give us a spirit of fear, but of power, love and a sound mind." (2 Tim. 1:7)** God's peace will cast out your fears!

Every wrong behavior in a person is the result of them believing a lie about themselves. Our behaviors don't have to be the result of how others respond to us; instead, we can learn to honor ourselves and others because someone honorable lives in us, and He never changes. We have been crucified with Christ, which means our old nature is dead. If there is some habit or behavior that we cannot seem to get rid of, something that does not reflect our true identity and new nature in Christ, then there is a lie rooted in our belief system that is at war with the spiritual reality of our true identity in Christ. It is literally holding our redeemed nature in captivity until the lie is displaced with truth! If you are trying to change a habit or something about yourself that you do not like, ask Him to uncover the lie and show you what is causing the war between your flesh and the spirit. When the lie is revealed and truth displaces it, you will have peace, and peace allows one's nature to change. God does not speak to our sin nature because the old 'us' was nailed to the cross along with Christ. He simply works in us, revealing who we are in Christ. As He does, truth replaces the lies that we have taken in about ourselves. God's grace is what allows His image to be formed in us. Today I offer you a prayer for inner transformation.

Father God,

Today I pray for a fresh perspective that will transform me from the inside out. give me eyes to see with clarity in the Spirit. Help me to see the opportunities rather than the obstacles. Holy Spirit, please reveal the fatherhood of God to me. I pray to know the depth of my Father's love. Let shafts of revelation light be shed abroad into my heart as You reveal my position as God's child and the beloved of His heart. Reveal the lies that are holding my redeemed nature in captivity. I renounce and forsake the unloving spirits that may have attached themselves to me, and the lies the enemy has told me. Lead me into Your truth by Your Spirit. By faith, I receive Your love, faith, and assistance to understand Your purpose and to cooperate with You as You change me from the inside out. Lift up my eyes to see things from Your perspective. In Jesus name, amen.

CHAPTER FIVE

You Are the Dream of God

Did you know that God has put a dream inside of each and every one of us? He has a dream specially created just for your life! We know according to Genesis 1:26 that God had a conversation with Himself and said, **"Let Us make man in Our image, according to our likeness…"** and when God created woman in Genesis 2:21 He said, **"And the Lord God caused a deep sleep to fall on Adam, and he slept, and He took one of his ribs and closed up the flesh in its place. Then the rib which the Lord God had taken from man He made into a woman, and He brought her to the man. And Adam said, "This is now bone of my bones and flesh of my flesh; she shall be called WOMAN, because she was taken out of man."**

The name Eve is from the Hebrew name *pronounced Chawwah,* (derived from the Hebrew word *chawah),* which means "to breathe," or the related word *chayah,* which mean "to live." Eve is the mother of us all, and her name literally means 'to live and breathe.' I love that the distinct identity associated with Eve as a woman is contained in her name. God's intent for women to be life givers and breathe life into everything around them has never changed. So, woman came from man, but she's made in the image of GOD. That's quite an interesting concept, isn't it? Woman is distinctly female, yet has inseparable qualities of both man and God within her. Think about that for a moment! We are so fearfully and wonderfully made! Can you just get inside the mind of God as He was dreaming about creating woman? What an absolute *genius* mind God has... yes, man is wonderful, and man is made in the image of God too, but one of the ways women are made unique is that we are made with both male and female qualities. We are the female counterpart to the Godhead because we mirror – or we're *supposed* to mirror all the qualities of Holy Spirit. Gentle, kind, loving, tender, yet absolutely the voice of authority in our sphere of influence.

Woman was taken out of man's rib, his side. She is not beneath him nor is she above him. God did not create woman to be inferior so there is no need to feel intimidated or insecure about our identity. We do not need to feel competitive or struggle for equal rights. People fight for their rights when their identity is compromised. A woman never needs to usurp authority from others in her life because whatever role she fills is a vital one to those she loves and serves. We can feel comforted in knowing that when we are submitted to God, He guards and protects His own. This is what releases us into grace. Our Father will deal with those that treat the bride of Christ unlawfully, unjustly, with disrespect or dishonor. If our safety is in jeopardy or if someone rises up to oppose us in something God has called us to do, He will step in on our behalf. He will turn the tables on those that warrant a rebuke. We don't need to feel as though we have to fight for ourselves. We have an advocate and judge on our side! As I write this, I am reminded of the wedding procession of Prince William and his lovely bride, Catherine, the Dutchess of Cambridge. As they took the honored customary carriage ride after the ceremony, "Kate" could be seen lowering her eyes as they passed by the Queen's Guards. It was a sign of respect but it was also significant in the fact that the new bride would never again have to defend herself. The entirety of the Queen's Guards is available at a moment's notice and will instantly come to her aid, should she require their assistance. *This is the benefit of being in covenant.* Kate Middleton was no longer a commoner; she was elevated to the position of royalty and trained in royal protocol. She understood what it meant to feel secure in her position as the bride of a royal. How much more should we, as daughters of the Most High God, heirs to the throne, and the beloved bride of the King of Kings feel secure in our position?

God created man to provide, protect and establish a role model of righteousness for the family. By God's design man is the head of the household and as we demonstrate respect towards the position God gave to man, we honor the Lord. (This is never to be misinterpreted as saying that women should submit to abuse or mistreatment). Men are created to be the head of the household but women are the *heart* of the *home*. When a woman carries unhealed wounds from her past, she will bring it into her family; but when she is healed, she will reproduce life and health. When a woman gets healed on the inside, she becomes the catalyst for healing her entire family. Sometimes we have a hard time doing the best thing for us because we fail at loving ourselves. Part of loving ourselves is surrendering what continues to cause us pain and toxic emotions. Most of us are great at encouraging others and we know what to say to them. It's time to talk to yourself the way you would talk to a friend. For the sake of our own well-being and those we love, we owe it to ourselves to trade in the ashes of our yesterdays, all the hurts and lingering memories of painful events, and allow the Lord to heal the areas of our brokenness. It is the only way to recover true strength. Women are designed to fulfill a feminine role but also one of strength, confidence and authority. When God formed a suitable mate for Adam, He took from the bone out of Adam's side, the rib. It is interesting that the rib is the protector of the heart. Women are to function in the grace, compassion and authority that allow them to be a spiritual shield around their children, husband, and loved ones. God's bride is humble and full of grace, but she is also a warrior bride. She has a sword of God's word in her hands and the shield of faith in the other. A woman is just as much a shield of protection to protect the heart of her family as is her husband.

There is power to keep evil away! It is ours by birthright. It is the power of a praying woman. Please let me stress the importance of prayers of agreement. When two are in agreement prayers get answered quickly! **"Again I tell you that if two of you on earth agree about anything you ask, if will be done for you by My Father in heaven. For where two or three come together in my name, there I am with them,"** (Matthew 18: 19,20). Faith is more than just a belief or an action; it is a spiritual law. Agreement is another spiritual law. If we want Kingdom results, we must first agree to live by the laws of the Kingdom. We cannot expect to enforce the laws of the kingdom if we do not first agree to live by those laws. Our prayers serve as a protector, nurturer and safeguard to those around us. Ever since woman was created, God has been trying to get woman to let the man out of her. (Let me clarify that statement as I don't want the reader to misunderstand what I'm saying). When I say "*man*," I'm referring to the voice of male authority that is found in Christ. It's the GOD-MAN in us.

God wants to see us live the reality of His word that says we are made in His image and likeness. That means we need to look like God. We need to sound like God. When we're walking in the dominion, the power, the author- ity, and the confidence of knowing who we are in Christ, the enemy shouldn't be able to tell the difference between us or Jesus. I wonder how you would feel if you could see yourself as heaven sees you. Do you think it would change your opinion of yourself? If we could see ourselves the way heaven sees us, as the finished work of Christ, we would all stand amazed. We would not doubt the authority we have as God's blood-bought children. Male or female, child or youth; if a person knows the authority that is available to them in Christ; they would turn the world upside down. They wouldn't fear the devil. When a person who knows their identity in Christ speaks, the devil has to shut up and take orders. We would make room for Holy Spirit to birth what is in the heart of God. Holy Spirit is the one that creates; He is the one who impregnates and conceives the dream of God. He is the very womb of God. He is the one that gives birth. He hovers over those He loves like a mother hen. He is the one that comforts, encourages, lifts up and nurtures those He loves.

Dear woman, you are Mary, whose submission delights the heart of God and thus becomes impregnated with the dream of God. You are unrelenting like Hannah, travailing to see the birth of the promise. You are Ruth, a gentle woman who understands the importance of devoted loyalty even in the face of personal sacrifice. You are Tamar and Rachel, tenacious women that wrestle with God and others, not dissuaded by circumstances but spurred on by injustice; women that bring forth a promise named Breakthrough and generations of great fruitfulness. You are Deborah, contending for the justice of God and one who compels others to rise up and fight the good fight of faith. And, you are Esther…a woman who has come into the Kingdom of God for such a time of this; a woman who will lay down her life to confront the enemy and decree life to those that have been targeted for destruction. You are a woman that knows what it means to wear the robes of royalty with gratitude, confidence and humility. You understand the great responsibility before you, and wisely consider that you are an extension of the King's scepter of authority. Heaven hangs on every word you speak, waiting for instruction. Regardless of what your thoughts and feelings may tell you, and regardless of what life has made you; there are seeds of those qualities living inside of you. Every woman that I mentioned is a different picture of who God is and what the Spirit of Christ in us yearns to do. So ladies, let Him out. This is who you really are!

"You will be called by a new name, that the mouth of the Lord will bestow. You will be a crown of splendor in the Lord's hand; a royal diadem in the hand of your God." (Is. 63:2,3)

YOU ARE THE DREAM OF GOD!

Don't be afraid to dream big, to be a woman of influence. God has spoken words of destiny over you and He wants His dream for you to come to pass! Do you believe that? Do you know He's had conversations about you in heaven that you know nothing about? He's spoken to the Godhead; He's spoken to the angels. He has words of destiny that are waiting to be fulfilled!

Some of us need divine surgery on our hearts in order to see that happen. You see, sometimes we have a filter on our ears, and it affects how we hear. Sometimes we have a filter on what we see, and it affects our perception. If we have unresolved offense or unforgiveness, everything is affected because of that filter. If a person has insecurities or fears, they've got a filter. Satan wants control over our ears. The enemy uses those filters – whatever they are – to manipulate a person's hearing so that he can manipulate their belief system. When the enemy manipulates an individual's belief system, it transfers over to their actions. *It has a ripple effect.* The Bible warns us to beware of anyone that has a root of bitterness lest it defile the hearts of others. Offense poisons others and multiplies greatly. The Bible admonishes us to be "wise women," and compares the wise woman to the foolish woman in Prov. 14:1. The foolish woman tears down her house through negative speech and unloving actions. A wise woman heals through love. A wise woman promotes wholeness and health in her family with sound speech, love and wisdom of God. Let me encourage you today to examine your own heart for places where you need the Lord's healing.

Is there someone that makes your emotions rise when think of them? Are you carrying offense towards someone that hurt or disappointed you? If you haven't dealt with the root of your issues, the enemy has an open door to continue to spin his web of lies. That's how he keeps that blind spot there, because that's where he has a hook in his victim. The next question is what do you give yourself over to? That misfortunate vice or area of spiritual weakness might be the thing that keeps you from your next door of opportunity. We may not even realize we have a blind spot. We might not stop to think that it could prevent us from receiving a blessing God wants us to have, but God doesn't want us to be vulnerable before the enemy. He knows the enemy will try to exploit it at some point. Do you know why it is called a blind spot? *Because you can't see it.* You have to trust Holy Spirit to do the assessment for you.

Our assessment of our emotional and spiritual development is absolutely irrelevant because the way we judge ourselves is not equivalent to God's standard of measurement. God's word is our standard, not our biased assessment of us or others, and not our personal opinions. Sometimes there are things that are too painful to admit; things that we're too ashamed to confess to ourselves much less to God.

God wants to go deep. We can't expect to go into our future carrying around all our baggage from the past. Think about the attributes of the Holy Spirit: Life-giver, nurturer, comforter, encourager, protector, mediator, peace-maker and so much more! Women are a huge key to families being healed, which is why the enemy has tried so very hard to destroy them and keep them from entering into their destiny. Women have a vital role in marriage and family and as anointed women of the kingdom. Women are also a key to healing their children and their children's destinies, because if a woman is walking in peace, joy and the love of the Lord – everybody around her is going to get a touch. Each one of us has the ability to change the destiny of our entire family and generations to come. A woman who has been healed will get up and go change her neighborhood. Women are gatherers. They draw people into their lives. They also go out and seek ways to make a difference in the lives of others. A woman who is healed will go change her city, one life at a time. It's wrapped up inside of us; it's in our destiny.

Fear and lack of understanding of our true identity can persuade people to try to do things by using guilt or manipulation, but that is called *witchcraft*. Witchcraft can be a lot of things and it's a very broad topic, but what it boils down to is forcing the will of one person upon another against their will. Fear, anger, control and bitterness are driving forces behind the spirit of witchcraft. That is why God equates witchcraft to a spirit of rebellion. They are opposite of the spirit of love. Love does not violate another person's will and love does no harm to others. That is why it is so important to give our heart a main-tenance check from time to time, to make sure we are not praying or doing things with an ulterior motive. Women often feel insecure that they are not be-ing taken seriously or their voice heard which can make them tend to want to control the responses of others and the outcome of certain situations. The key here is to take your concerns to the Holy Spirit and ask Him to speak to your loved ones. PRAY. Let God have a little time to work in the situation and influ-ence others so that you don't feel the need to be overly insistent, nagging and frustrated. Remember, fear produces anger, and anger causes people to want to control. Faith believes the best about others and releases them to make their own good decisions. The love and grace we receive from the Lord are keys to godly influence. When we flow in grace and love, the gifts of the Spirit allow wisdom and anointing to influence others.

The first step to walking in a greater anointing and sphere of influence is to embrace the reality of who God created us to be; not the identity the enemy has tried to mold us into. A person will conform to whatever they believe about their self, whether positive or negative. Every thought produces an action and every action is born out of a belief system. Change requires work. We have to be willing to let go of who we are today, because God continues to call us up higher. He changes us from glory to glory. It may mean letting go of certain behaviors, social activities or even certain relationships. We have to be willing to let go of things that don't line up with the person God wants to transform us into, because those things will keep us from entering into the destiny God has for us. Wrong influences will hold a person back in character development, integrity and keep them confused about their identity. God wants to pull up the spiritual weeds. Not every person in your life is there for your best interests. Some may be there by the plan of the enemy in order to derail you. In many people's lives the enemy has done everything possible to cause them to conform to some twisted, misunderstood, rejected piece of work and signed his name to his handiwork. TODAY is the game changer. It's the day when you can get the upper hand over the enemy.

There is a line from a little book called the Prayer of Jabez that has stuck with me throughout the years. The author, Bruce Wilkinson, gave an account of one particular man of God and wondered what made him so different from other men. Then he walked down the hall and overheard him praying. He said, *"Ahhh...Now I know. Great men pray different."* I'm telling you, to reach a place of influence...to see the power of God move the mountains and be big in your life; you have to get to a place where you pray different. Don't just hear a message and leave thinking what you heard was a great message. You have a personal responsibility every time you hear an anointed word. *Your life is the message.* We are living epistles read of all men. Our lives become the prophetic message to those around us. What sign are you wearing? What do others read from observing your life? The Holy Spirit inside of the believer is a healer, a reconciler, a restorer. He is the one who encourages us to forgive, be gracious and victorious. The God inside of us and inside of others seeks to encourage, lift people up, and nudge us, even push us towards mending relationships. We can't just talk *about* God. The question is, "Can others see Christ *in* us?" If we really believe we are made in the image and likeness of God then we should be so hidden in Christ that the enemy cannot even see us. All he will see is Jesus shining through. When Jesus shines through it will create divine appointments so that others stop and ask us for directions.

The Bible tells us to overcome evil with good and that love never fails. When we pray out of a pure motive - a heart moved by compassion and selfless, sacrificial love - This is true greatness, and this is the God that lives inside us. This is what He wants to create in us; the capacity to LOVE GREATLY. Until we are willing to be emptied of ourselves, we cannot be filled. If we are not willing to be humble, we will never be able to receive the grace that awaits us. Unless we surrender the false perception of ourselves and agree with how God sees us, we remain unchanged. If we cannot surrender our fears, we will have difficulty trusting Him and our faith will not grow. Until we surrender our hearts, we won't know the intimacy of fellowship or what moves His heart. He wants to take the filters off; the ones that the enemy uses to make our love grow cold. The ones the enemy uses to distort what we think we're hearing or perceiving. God wants to rip the veil off the blind spots and give us clarity. He wants to take every deficiency and fill it with power, authority and anointing to help us take back our families and our inheritance. We are not weak or helpless and we are not victims! We are more than conquerors through Him who loves us. The devil cannot have any promise that God has said is mine. He cannot have my marriage, my family or my future. He cannot have my children or grandchildren's future. Dear woman, what do you say? It's time we put our foot down on the devil's head and take it all back. It's time for recovery! It's time for every daughter of Eve to walk into her rightful inheritance and fulfill her purpose. You are a woman of grace and beauty; an incredible woman of destiny. God is calling you up and out of the ashes of your yesterdays. Never give up on the brink of your miracle! Put on the robes of royalty. Dare to believe, because God is restoring His dream in you!

Father,

I submit myself to You, Lord Jesus, and your Holy Spirit. I thank You that I am made in the image and likeness of God. I surrender the false perception I have had of myself. I thank You that You put your greatness inside of me, and that You have a dream in Your heart you want me to fulfill! Holy Spirit, if I have any blind spots, reveal them to me so that the enemy cannot exploit them. Show me how to get free. I give You permission in advance of any situation that may arise, that You have permission to change my responses so that they honor You. I give You permission to help my heart yield to Your desire and Your will in any given situation. You may change my words and responses so that the enemy cannot receive any glory or any gloating. Please reign and rule over my emotions and help me to have self-discipline over my thought life. Show me how to partake of your power, outwit the enemy and bring healing and wholeness to myself and my family. I thank You for helping me be an agent of healing and reconciliation. Fill me with Your love, grace and mercy so that it can be used for the good of healing others and glorifying You. In Jesus name, amen.

CHAPTER SIX

The Truth that Frees Us

People demand truth in every aspect of their daily lives. We insist on reading the details of legal contracts because we want to know what's outlined in the fine print. We look for truth in those that provide mechanical service to our vehicles, those that are potential candidates for political office, and those that interview for employment. We look for truth from those that handle our finances in the banking industry and those that uphold the law. We expect truth to be given to us when we go to the doctor or have our health evaluated. We expect and even demand truth in so many different situations because we know how valuable it is. We know that it can make all the difference as to how it could potentially affect our lives if we were not to examine truth.

In the examples listed above we have no problem using logic and reason to make an informed choice of the things we feel are in our best interests. We examine the evidence and make a rational, objective decision. A person can be absolutely convinced in their knowledge of facts, yet still be absolutely mistaken in regards to the truth. There are times when people choose to discard the truth because it challenges everything they've believed. There are times when people become willfully blind because they don't want their illusion shattered, or they avoid truth because they don't want to be accountable to it. Truth does have the capacity to make us uncomfortable at times. It could be about someone or something we admire, respect or love. Sometimes the truth we resist knowing is not even about others as much as the fact that truth reveals what *we* are *not*. We don't want the illusions of ourselves shattered, or we are trying to avoid accountability to the truth that we already know. (*Ouch.* That hurt, didn't it?) Hit the stop button for a moment. *Pause, think about it.* Truth is important. There are definite consequences for ignoring it, yet people will still avoid, dodge, deny or wiggle away from truth when it comes to matters that hit close to home. Do we really think we will be any better off for trying to avoid the conviction of something we need to face? Avoiding truth keeps a person stuck in a state of emotional and spiritual immaturity. Embracing truth propels us into growth. Relationships tug at our emotions and our loyalties. Our values reflect our ideals. People tend to filter in information that allows them to uphold a particular value or esteemed ideal and filter out the information that could potentially shatter the illusion.

Take, for example, the woman who so esteems the institution of marriage that she refuses to acknowledge her spouses infidelity, his reckless spending, lack of respect towards her as an individual or numerous other ways that he devalues the institution of marriage. "Shelly" would have done anything to turn a blind eye away from the truth just so that she didn't have to admit failure or go through a divorce. Her parents had gotten a divorce when she was young and it was the source of great pain to her. It wasn't just an emotional letdown, she looked for someone to blame for the failure. Her need to find someone to blame had broken the relationship with one of her parents. It brought such an unsettling to her heart that she lived with fear and insecurity. The broken family dynamics of her youth caused her to do anything within her power to try to preserve her marriage. Her attempts to make her marriage work were a noble endeavor, but it became less honorable when it risked her safety and the well-being of her children. In order to preserve her ideal there became a continuous need to lower her standards of expectation and what she would tolerate. Shelly willingly submitted herself to the degradation, but the children were innocent victims of the circumstances. She would have tolerated anything from her husband in order to preserve the illusion that the marriage and family were ok. They were separated for a year before she could bring herself to admit that he no longer lived at home. She was willing to turn a blind eye to his infidelity. She could live with the fact that he didn't love her; she was willing to live with anything so that she didn't have to go through a divorce. In every other aspect of her life Shelly was a strong and capable woman, yet the issue of her broken marriage was her Achilles heel, and that is where the enemy chose to hit her hard. He knew her weakness, and everything that he did was to keep Shelly and her family in captivity. If he could keep Shelly in bondage he would have control over the children and future generations as well. She was willing to tolerate captivity for the sake of an ideal. The judgments she made towards her own parents had caused her to make a vow in her heart that she would never find herself a statistic of divorce, and her anger and attitude towards the parent she felt was responsible for the marriage failure blinded her to her own need for humility and healing. Yet, the truth of the matter is that her husband had already divorced her in his heart. He didn't want to be married and he did everything in his power to force her to make the decision for him. She forced herself to smile and put on the appearance of a happy family, until one day she couldn't. Her world bottomed out when she could no longer deny the reality of her situation. She had prayed for God to heal her marriage, but then it got remarkably worse. Her husband left her for another woman. He took all the money in their bank account. He changed the locks, threw her belongings in the trash and told her it was over. By all apparent indicators, the marriage was dead. She finally succumbed to the truth that had been there all along. Her marriage and family were an illusion she set up for herself in order to preserve an ideal that she held dear, but it wasn't her reality. Then, and only then, was she willing to face the truth.

"Maggie" was another woman who was loyal to a fault. Maggie was loyal to her husband, but it was loyalty to the point of idolatry. The moment she met this man Maggie began to change. He was her world. The warning signs were there from the beginning. This man caused division and discord within the family. He lied about inconsequential things, was controlling, short tempered and he isolated her from others. He displayed many of the trademark indicators of an abuser. He was jealous and possessive. He was hyper-critical towards her and verbally abused her. He took an authoritarian role and insisted that his way of seeing things was truth. Maggie's whole belief system began to change as he insisted that she conform to his version of reality. Her husband intimidated her with fits of rage and anger and withheld love and affection in order to manipulate her emotions. Maggie constantly worried about how he would react to things and she lived in fear of her husband's responses. Yet, to her family, friends and others Maggie tried hard to present a different picture. Others could see what she refused to acknowledge. Maggie's willful blindness was a defense mechanism in order to help her uphold her fantasy of being in love, and a certain sense of safety in the midst of fear and conflict. Her world was so fragile that she willfully became blind so that she could avoid confrontation and even more instability. Her self-esteem was so battered and bruised that she did not feel strong enough to survive on her own. Truth had been re-written so often by her abuser that she believed what she was told. She *wanted* to believe everything was ok, and so she exchanged the truth for a lie because it seemed easier than trying to break free and start over.

Why is it that when others try to present information that suggests someone or something is not what we want them to be we immediately file a silent 'Motion to Suppress Evidence' in our head? The truth is too painful to acknowledge. Preconceived ideas and judgments can cause us to make idols of falsehoods. When people consciously avoid the truth it requires the person to filter truth out and make a decision about what they will allow themselves to hear. This editing process allows them to feel safe or protected from things that pose a threat to their beliefs, ideals, values and illusions. Although it is human nature to try to preserve our ideals and values, to do so by suppressing truth leaves us fearful and captive to our own fragile illusions. We go through life handicapped instead of healed. We trade strength for weakness. Loyalty is a quality that God honors, but He also does not want us to take part in our own deception and ignore reality. Fear will cause people to go through life in constant denial. When we deny truth, whatever that truth may be, and embrace willful blindness, we make room for more deception in our life and that is dangerous. We must be able to discern the difference between truth and falsehood so that we don't get taken in by the enemy. Learning to love ourselves requires being able to embrace the truth about us and then be willing to change. Love for others has its eyes open to reality and makes an informed choice to love and stay in relationship with someone, knowing there are certain risks – or, walk away from those that do not take responsibility for their actions and refuse to change. A refusal to acknowledge and repent from wrongdoing is something God calls evil, wickedness and iniquity. It is unwise to continue relationships where these things exist because eventually it will cause additional hurt and disappointment. We can all be stubborn to a fault when it comes to trying to protect our own heart at all costs. The reality is we only hurt ourselves more the longer we allow deception to override truth. We become vulnerable to even deeper emotional pain when the illusion is finally shattered. When truth comes knocking it doesn't always come with a prosecuting attorney handing us evidence marked 'Exibit A.' Sometimes it's a gut feeling, a hesitancy in our spirit or a nagging feeling that something isn't the way it should be. We surrender ourselves to the chains of captivity because we refuse to read between the lines and extract the truth that is there staring us in the face.

Procrastination may work for a time, but avoidance over the long haul can have serious consequences. Some problems only get worse with time. In order to get down to the bottom of the issue we must ask ourselves exactly what we are attempting to avoid. Disappointment? Confrontation with another individual? Will we be required to take another action that makes us feel uncomfortable, and if so, how can we best handle it? You are strong enough and resourceful enough to come up with a solution, even if you do not feel that way in the present moment. Courage is not the absence of fear; it is the conviction to act in accordance with one's belief regardless of danger, difficulty or other people's criticisms. The opposite of courage is cowardice. **"For the Spirit God gave us does not make us timid or fearful, but gives us power, love and self-discipline,"** (2 Tim. 1:7). Confrontation of us or others *does* require change. If we're not willing to take a stand and confront the issue, then fear becomes our master. Wisdom considers all known possibilities of the situation and formulates a plan on how to address potential issues. We are more likely to take action when we feel empowered. The reality is that procrastination is simply putting off the inevitable. The truth we refuse to deal with will one day create a situation that forces us to deal with it whether we want to or not.

In the previous examples of Shelly and Maggie's lives, the events of their lives culminated to a point where truth could no longer be avoided. Shelly and her husband both had to surrender control, judgments and fear. Shelly learned how to lean on God even more and trust Him to do what she could not. Her own marriage failure taught her not to judge others and released her anger towards her parents. She learned to see things from a different point of view rather than holding on to the judgments she formulated from the standpoint of an insecure, wounded child. Her husband learned some very difficult and humbling lessons and through it all came to appreciate the wife and family that he had all along, but took for granted. They were so used to being at odds with one another, each struggling to control the relationship that God had to bring the circumstances to humble their pride before He could go to work to heal the marriage. He waited until the marriage and the illusions were all dead, and then resurrected it and put new life into it. They weren't the same people anymore, and that family got a miracle.

Maggie was also forced her to face the reality of her life. Her husband's abuse escalated until one day she was forced to choose between living the lie or protecting herself and her children. She formulated a plan, took her children and went to a women's shelter. She went through therapy and turned her life over to Christ, and through it all, learned to embrace truth. She volunteers in various crisis centers where she shares her testimony and speaks to other women. Maggie is no longer a victim and has become a source of faith and encouragement to empower other women to change.

When a person desires truth it is an indicator that they have admitted to themselves that they are ready to face their illusions being shattered. Uncomfortable as it may be to face the truth, the person no longer desires willful blindness. They are ready to receive the truth because they know it has the ability to set them free and release healing.

One of the most difficult things to face about God is the fact that sometimes He strikes us in order to heal us. **"Blows that hurt cleanse away evil, as do stripes the inner depths of the heart,"** (Prov. 20:30, NKJV). Several other scripture references in regards to this thought are found in Isaiah 19:22, Deut. 32:39, Job 22:23 and Hebrews 12:11. I want to be very careful in expounding on this thought because it is not intended to imply that God is angry with us. His wrath against the sin of mankind was expended upon Jesus, who took the full weight of the penalty for our sin upon Himself. God is not angry and does not react as a man; He is a holy, loving Father. But, He does allow affliction and the pressures of increased trials in our lives in order to purify our hearts. Sin hurts. It doesn't just hurt us, it hurts others, too. It causes all manner of mental torment, sickness, disease, loss, broken relationships, and painful events to take place in our lives, and those things affect the lives of those close to us. These things come as a result of the enemy doing what he does best: he comes only to kill, steal and destroy. Satan inflicts pain and suffering and there are times when God allows it. Discipline cleanses the heart. Father's desired end for all people is repentance that restores us to right relationship with Him and others and also releases healing. **"For whom the Lord loves, He chastens, and scourges every son whom He receives."** (Heb. 12:6). The word scourge literally means to be lashed with a whip. Now, that doesn't sound very pleasant, does it? It was not an enjoyable experience for Jesus to take the lashes upon His back as the penalty for our sin; yet God struck His precious Son so that through Him the world might be healed. **"Surely He has borne our griefs and carried our sorrows; yet we esteemed Him stricken, smitten by God and afflicted. But He was wounded for our transgressions; He was bruised for our iniquities; the chastisement for our peace was upon Him, and by His stripes we are healed."** (Is. 53:5)

Perhaps the best analogy I can compare it to is this: When God wounds, it is along the lines of a doctor that must open an infected wound in order to cleanse it and thus prepare the wound to be healed. Our wounds are in the form of pricked consciences that are heavy with the weight of our own sin. Father wants us to recognize that willfully insisting on our right to retain sin in our life is selfish. Spiritual wounds such as these cause people to turn to Him so that the guilt and stain of sin can be cleansed. The fruit of cleansing and repentance is a change in behavior. **"No discipline seems pleasant at the time, but painful. Later on, however, it produces a harvest of righteousness and peace for those who have been trained by it."** (Heb. 12:11).

"Bless the Lord O my soul, and forget not all His benefits: Who forgives all your iniquities; who heals all your diseases; who redeems your life from destruction; who crowns you with lovingkindness and tender mercies; who satisfies your mouth with good things, so that your youth is renewed like the eagle." (Ps. 103: 2-5).

◆ ◆ ◆

Answers to prayer often look far different than what we might imagine. We ask for strength, and God gives us opportunities to depend on Him and develop strength through trials. We ask for discernment and we get confronted with spiritual warfare. We pray for an increase in faith, and we are given miracle needing opportunities. We pray for an enlarged heart, and our heart is broken so that we may learn compassion. We pray for one thing and then it seems as if lightning strikes the thing we hold dear. God understands the things that really need to be healed, and when He puts His finger on something, it isn't just to be cruel. The blows that strike fear or pain deep inside of us produce ripple effects, and those ripple effects touch every single aspect of our heart, emotions and belief system. He causes us to examine truth so deep that we have to acknowledge our fears, insecurities, judgments and areas of unhealed offense. He puts His finger on things like pride, stubbornness and resistance to truth but in His mercy He shows us *why*. He shows us the lies we entertain so that truth can prevail and, once the lie is extinguished, the enemy can no longer deceive us in that particular area. We all have blind spots, but God is so full of mercy that He doesn't leave us blind. He opens our blinded eyes and sets us free. The truth that we are least likely to want to receive is often the one that brings about our healing.

In Mark 1:40-42 A leper came to Jesus and said, **"If you are willing, You can make me clean."** Then Jesus, moved with compassion, stretched out His hand and touched him and said, **"I am willing; be cleansed."** As soon as He had spoken, immediately the leprosy left him and he was cleansed. This passage of scripture demonstrates several important truths. First of all the leper came humbly with a request to the One that could resolve his problem. In biblical times, leprosy was a result of sin. There was no known cure. The man did not directly ask to be healed; he asked to be cleansed. In other words, he had an understanding that his current issue of leprosy was a result of sin, and that the remedy was to be cleansed from his sin. Jesus responded, **"I am willing; be cleansed."** Once the sin was removed, the man received his healing. When the issues of our soul are healed, our physical body can receive healing as well. God wants us to not just be healed, but cleansed of the thing that made room for the disease. Sometimes God in His mercy heals individuals regardless of whether or not their sin has been dealt with, but I don't think it is wisdom to expect Him to do this every time. God is sovereign. He knows each person's heart and life. Perhaps that is one answer why some people receive healing and others don't. I can't explain why some people are healed and others are not, but doesn't it make sense to come to the One who has all power to forgive our sin, heal us, restore us and make us whole again? If you knew He was willing, able and compassionate towards you and desired to heal you, would you be willing to surrender your sin, no matter what it was? Isn't that a better way to receive your complete and total healing and restoration?

Ezekiel 36:22-35 contains a beautiful promise of restoration. God's promise is that when we are cleansed from the things that make us unclean, He will restore our losses. His promise is to give us a new heart after cleansing, reverse the famine that has robbed from our lives and bring multiplication of blessing. Now that is motivation for the pursuit of holiness! The truth that frees us is the truth we must admit to ourselves and God, and perhaps another individual. It's the confession of wrongdoing so that we may be healed. It removes the guilt from our conscience and restores a right alignment with our heavenly Father. **"Therefore confess your sins to each other and pray for each other so that you may be healed. The prayer of a righteous person is powerful and effective.** (James 5:16, NIV). Notice that the scripture instructs us to confess our sins to one another. This sort of confession requires honesty and humility. Without honesty or humility, we cannot have fellowship with Him. God cannot fellowship with those that desire their own sin, self-deception and darkness of heart more than they desire Him. **"Behold you desire truth in the inward parts and in the hidden part you will make me know wisdom."** (Ps. 51:6). He is the light shining in the darkness, but the darkness cannot comprehend Him. When Jesus shows up, He is fully aware of all the things that have prevented us from seeing Him for who He really is. He also knows the things that have prevented us from seeing ourselves in our true identity in Christ. He wants to heal our fractured soul! He simply asks, "Do you *want* to be healed?"

The truth that we need to be free is what has been with us all along. Truth speaks. People know when they have sin in their life because their conscience tells them so. How often they try to hide from the conviction of their conscience! The conscience is that inner voice within a person that helps them distinguish between right and wrong. When a person violates moral values or integrity, their conscience will produce feeling of remorse and guilt. Unless, of course, a person has repeatedly, deliberately rejected the voice of their conscience so often that they become hardened to truth. Some people are so good at rejecting truth that they honestly don't feel convicted to change. They are convinced they aren't guilty of wrongdoing. That is a terrible place to be because once a person has so hardened their heart in rebellion, God may not be able to reach them at all. Don't ignore your conscience! Your conscience is there to protect you and keep you in the ways of righteousness. No one likes to feel guilt, but the truth is, we need it. It is the only proper response to sin. Guilt is what eventually leads us to confess our sin so that God can cleanse us from that unrighteousness. It unlocks the door to forgiveness. In most people, truth that they know but don't necessarily want to accept will continue to rise to the surface, especially if God is trying to communicate something to them. It's a funny thing about truth. A person may try to run from it but truth will always follow them home. It demands a decision. We can make excuses to try and avoid dealing with it, but at the end of the day truth is still quietly staring us in the face.

There have been times in my past when some of my mistakes were so painful to admit to myself that the temptation I fell into was trying to re-write the truth in order to make it easier to bear. It was far easier to blame others than to accept responsibility for my own actions. It was a very difficult day indeed when I was alone with God and had to admit my failures to Him. Though unjust things had occurred in my life and others had contributed to my hurt, I was still responsible for my own actions. It felt unfair to have to take responsibility for my own pain. I felt so vindicated in blaming others, but one wrong action does not excuse another. We can argue our case all we want but the Judge isn't necessarily going to agree with us. That is the nature of pride and accusation. Those spirits always help people find someone else to blame. God never refuses a heart that is truly broken over our own wrongdoing. He steps in and offers us comfort, reassurance and love. He draws us to Himself. It is the comfort of knowing that we are not rejected even when we admit our wrongs that allows us to offer up the things we hate to face about ourselves. We can freely admit our failures to God; accept responsibility for where we went wrong, and face the reality of our situations. We may still have to walk through something difficult as a result of things we've done, but humility is what allows us to receive healing from the Holy Spirit.

God knows when we resist truth. He knows if a person is resistant to hearing truth because they simply want to do their own thing and try to avoid submission to Him. So, no matter how many lies we may try to tell ourselves; we still can't avoid accountability. There is a saying that one lie always leads to another. It's true. Once a lie has been told, it will require more to keep it in place. Truth, on the other hand, needs no excuses. False truths will be inconsistent and create a troubled mind. They whisper to our conscience, disrupt our peace of mind, and pull us back into mental questioning because there is a nagging sense that something is not quite right. If you don't have peace with God and your conscience is agitated, then it is a good indicator that your conscience is trying to tell you something! As long as the answers which we seek remain unanswered, our spirit will continue to search for truth. Deception creates doubt, while truth just stands there waiting for us to receive it. Truth won't go away even when we want it to! We can run but we can't hide. Truth is very patient. It just stands there knocking at the door of our heart until we are ready to open the door and face it. Do you know why truth is so patient?

Truth is the person of the Holy Spirit. We know it in our inner man because if we have Him, He is our witness. **"It is the Spirit who testifies because the Spirit is Truth. For there are three that testify: the Spirit, the water, and the blood; and the three are in agreement."** (1 John 6-8). Jesus told us in John 16:13-16 that the Holy Spirit would reveal the truth about God and He would lead us into truth. He doesn't just reveal God; He reveals other truth, too. Jesus said further: **"When, however, the Spirit comes, who reveals the truth about God, he will lead you into all the truth. He will not speak on his own authority, but he will speak of what he hears and will tell you of things to come. He will give me glory, because he will take what I say and tell it to you. All that my Father has is mine; that is why I said that the Spirit will take what I give him and tell it to you"** (John 16:13-15). Jesus identified Holy Spirit as a person and the one who reveals truth. **"And I will ask the Father, and he will give you another advocate to help you and be with you forever— the Spirit of Truth. The world cannot accept him, because it neither sees him nor knows him. But you know him, for he lives with you and will be in you."** (John 14: 16,17). Jesus also said, **"The Helper, the Holy Spirit, whom the Father will send in my name, will teach you everything and make you remember all that I have told you, "** (John 14:26). The Psalmist cried out In Ps. 25:5, **"Lead me in Your truth and teach me, for You are the God of my salvation; on You I wait all the day long."** If we truly belong to God our soul cries out for understanding and yearns to be led into truth. **"All the paths of the Lord are mercy and truth…"** (Ps. 25:10).

And in Ps. 33:4, the scripture says, **"For the word of the Lord is right and all His ways are done in truth."**

John 1:17 tells us that truth came through Jesus Christ and in John 10:27 Jesus declared that His sheep hear His voice. Again in 1 John 4:6 it says, **"He who knows God hears us; He who is not of God does not hear us. By this we know the Spirit of Truth and the spirit of error."** Those that identify with Christ through His cross and resurrection have his Holy Spirit and the certainty of God's witness within them either confirms or denies truth. So, it stands to reason, if we want to know the truth about a matter the person we need to consult with is Holy Spirit, for He cannot and will not lie.

Truth doesn't always knock on your door to announce itself. The way God shows us truth is to first remove the barriers that have been constructed to keep truth out. In order to get us to face truth, sometimes God has to take a sledge hammer to the walls around our heart. He knows exactly what it will take to open our blinded eyes and get us to see things from a different perspective. Remember that God's gifts often come in odd packaging. That obstacle in your path is an opportunity in disguise. Your problem is a possibility waiting to happen, you may just need eyes to see it in a new light. Every impossible situation is simply there for you to receive. Difficulties exist in order to position us in teachable moments; teachable moments exist to guide us into truth. When we know the truth, it will open our eyes to see things the way they really are, and not some false reality we've painted for ourselves. It allows us to shed the baggage of our past, unload other people's version of truth, and even our own twisted stories we've told ourselves. It allows us to see ourselves in light of the truth and discover who we really are, what we believe and be able to live freely. Once we're free we can love ourselves and others without constraints.

Dear Lord Jesus,

Forgive me for any areas where I have resisted truth. Forgive me for unknowingly making room for deception in my life. I'm sorry I have not wanted to acknowledge certain faults and sins about myself or others. I am ready to have the truth revealed so that it can make me free. Give me courage and acceptance to face the things I may not want to deal with. Help me not to resist You any longer. Holy Spirit help me be willing to yield. I give You permission now to remind me that I asked to know the truth so that when it comes, I will be able to receive it. Holy Spirit, please forgive me for resisting You. I am sorry if I grieved You. Please unravel the lies the enemy has used to deceive me. Let discernment and sensitivity to Your Holy Spirit return. I thank You for helping me face truth and to also know the correct response when you reveal it. Thank you for exposing the lies, revealing the truth, making me free and leading me into my healing. In Jesus name, amen.

CHAPTER SEVEN

The Power of a Virtuous Wife

God wants to heal marriages and families. The divorce rate among Christians is just as high as non-Christians. If there is one thing the enemy will fight hard against, it's the power of two in agreement. He is after marriages, families and covenant relationships. Trust in a marriage is what holds the bond of covenant together. It's not the marriage license. It's not the ring, the kids or even the law. It's the power of covenant that is built on mutual trust and loyalty to one another.

It takes faith to trust in the Lord and do things His way, but the strength of any marriage is dependent upon the weakest place where the two are joined together. If trust is broken or shaky, the marriage lacks strength. It's like a shaky leg on a table; if trust is broken you don't have a leg to stand on. _Trust is the very foundation of covenant._ This is true whether it is in a marriage between a man and a woman, or the relationship between us and God. Obedience to the law alone does not put us in covenant. Anyone can have a contract that states they are "married," but if the heart is not in the marriage, then it lacks the very elements of love, respect, honor and loyalty upon which covenant is made.

Real strength in a marriage is built by trust and truth. The enemy will bring a variety of temptations to either spouse but it's important to keep in mind that often it's not so much about the actual temptation to do the wrong thing as it is about secretly working to destroy the foundation of trust between two people in a covenant relationship. When trust is eroded, offense is created and all things become suspect. Satan's temptations are to undermine that loyalty, trust, and mutual submission one to another. Loyalty is the bond by which the covenant is held together.

What exactly are the trademarks of a virtuous woman, and what effect do those characteristics have on marriage? Let us look at what scripture tells us.

The Wife of Noble Character

[10] [a]A wife of noble character who can find?

>She is worth far more than rubies.

[11] Her husband has full confidence in her

>and lacks nothing of value.

[12] She brings him good, not harm,

>all the days of her life.

[13] She selects wool and flax

>and works with eager hands.

[14] She is like the merchant ships,

>bringing her food from afar.

[15] She gets up while it is still night;

>she provides food for her family

>and portions for her female servants.

[16] She considers a field and buys it;

>out of her earnings she plants a vineyard.

[17] She sets about her work vigorously;

    her arms are strong for her tasks.

[18] She sees that her trading is profitable,

    and her lamp does not go out at night.

[19] In her hand she holds the distaff

    and grasps the spindle with her fingers.

[20] She opens her arms to the poor

    and extends her hands to the needy.

[21] When it snows, she has no fear for her household;

    for all of them are clothed in scarlet.

[22] She makes coverings for her bed;

    she is clothed in fine linen and purple.

[23] Her husband is respected at the city gate,

    where he takes his seat among the elders of the land.

[24] She makes linen garments and sells them,

    and supplies the merchants with sashes.

[25] She is clothed with strength and dignity;

    she can laugh at the days to come.

[26] She speaks with wisdom,

    and faithful instruction is on her tongue.

²⁷ She watches over the affairs of her household

and does not eat the bread of idleness.

²⁸ Her children arise and call her blessed;

her husband also, and he praises her:

²⁹ "Many women do noble things,

but you surpass them all."

³⁰ Charm is deceptive, and beauty is fleeting;

but a woman who fears the LORD is to be praised.

³¹ Honor her for all that her hands have done,

and let her works bring her praise at the city gate.

The Proverbs 31 woman is an ideal picture of a wife that possesses excellence, moral worth, ability and nobility. She exalts dignity, integrity, and virtue. She doesn't just care for her family; she cares for others, too. She remembers the poor. She is humble, kind and everything about her displays her confident assurance of her worth and value, to her family, her community and God. Her very essence releases the lingering fragrance of a beautiful spirit. She displays the unmistakable characteristics of royalty.

Scripture tells us that a wise woman builds up her house. She fosters an environment in the home that makes for peace, love and respect. She demonstrates respect and honor towards her husband which nurtures trust and encourages communication. The house built with wisdom is likened to a gracious hostess that takes care to attend to every detail of a lovely banquet. She prepares the atmosphere of her home to be welcoming and inviting, hospitable, well-mannered and pleasing. Her home is pleasant because she is characterized by a gracious spirit. She is known as one who is kind, generous and conducts herself in good taste.

A foolish woman, in contrast, tears down her house by sowing seeds of destruction. You might think, "What woman would dare do that?" Yet, it can be easier than you might think. A foolish woman is an undisciplined woman that lacks understanding. She is indifferent to the wisdom of God and unteachable. She is easily vexed and refuses to submit herself in love and respect to those around her. An undisciplined woman is impolite, ill-mannered and is outspoken to the point of being careless and inconsiderate of others. She is disingenuous and indiscrete. She does not think to use her words carefully. She may get a lot of attention from being loud or brash, but she does not understand what it takes to make a home feel comfortable, peaceful and enjoyable. She releases strife and discord rather than love and grace. In doing so, she tears down her own house.

One of a woman's biggest challenges in a family can be letting the frustrations of daily life pull at us until we get caught in a cycle of negative responses. My heart is grieved every time I snap at my kids or feel resentful of things I know I need to do for them, yet there are times when I feel stretched so thin that my responses run away with me. I bark instead of bless. I display a look of irritation instead of lighting up when my loved ones come into the room. I relive the failures of the day and despise the careless manner in which I sometimes let negative words hurt the ones that mean so much to me. I wonder why I do the things I do and why change is so incredibly difficult when I want it so much. The truth is I am not as virtuous as I'd like to be. I admit it. I look into the mirror of God's word and I know what the goal is, but I'm not all there yet. I have been greatly challenged while writing this book. We are always tested on the things we try to impart to others! Some days I do feel like it's an exercise in futility but living without pretense allows me to admit my struggles without feeling like I am any less a woman of faith. We are all a work of grace in action, and there's the key we need to understand. We are *in process.* Some days I feel like God ought to put up orange construction cones and yellow flashing lights as a warning to others to tell them: "careful: work in progress!" In other words, proceed with caution! Do you ever feel like that? God is the one that supplies the grace we need to change. It comes by trusting Him and leaning on the grace that He has made available. I think sometimes we just need to remember to ask for it before we need it. We also need to learn how to give ourselves a break before we break under the strain of guilt and self-condemnation. Condemnation is a tool of the enemy to cause discouragement, while conviction draws us closer to God with a desire to change.

It can be so easy to have answers for everyone except ourselves. Implementing lasting change is *hard.* It's difficult to change myself even when I know I need to choose a different response than the ones I've grown accustomed to, but the important thing to remember is that it's the work of God's grace that leads us into greater measures of sanctification. We can't do it on our own strength! Every day I fail in areas where I've prayed for change. Every day I fall short of the good things God wants for me. I often feel guilty for it; many women do. Sometimes we need to take a step back and pray for ourselves. We need to pray that we would be blessed with the grace to modify our behavior and have it be a permanent change. We need to renounce those familiar spirits of condemnation, unloving spirits, criticism, fault finding and shame, and command them to leave us. We have not because we ask not, so ask and receive the grace to change. Ask for and receive a spirit of faith and love. Every day is an opportunity to make a choice to not focus on what we can find to criticize in others. It's not them that need to change; *it's us*. We cannot live with the expectation that the only way we will have peace is for the world around us to change. It doesn't work that way. Change must come from within, and that includes both our expectations of others as well as our own responses. Today we can make the choice to pray for the grace to overlook things that aren't really necessary to criticize. Today we can pray for the grace to know when to keep silent, grace to know how to handle things that do need correction and when to simply acknowledge and bless the positives. Today we can ask the Lord to give us new eyes to see what's good and reward those things with praise. This is the prayer from one woman's heart to yours. I know that as much as I want to be able to break bad habits and replace them with new ones, so do you.

If the heart is defiled, it will infect others with bad fruit, and those seeds of gossip and discord will be replanted elsewhere in other people's lives. *Love covers* a multitude of sins. Our home is like a garden, and whatever we plant in our garden will grow. *Plant wisely.* Plant seeds of faith. Faith treats others as though they are already the finished work of Christ, walking in that transformed character. Faith believes that what is unseen will come forth, and love never fails. Build others up by sowing seeds of positive affirmation, honest communication, love and demonstrating good character.

God made marriage to take two individuals and bind them so tightly to each other that they actually become "one." Somewhere along the way it would seem that many marriages have lost that bond of unity. Many people are entangled in power struggles, emotional conflict and fight because the enemy is really good at knowing how to push all the right buttons. Your spouse and your other family members are not your enemies. You love them, and they love you. Never lose sight of that! The ENEMY is your enemy. How often we surrender ground to the evil one simply because he knows what triggers will set us off and what buttons to push, knowing it will bring division. When we are divided we don't have the prayers of agreement that will release answers to prayer.

In a previous chapter I mentioned that if we want Kingdom results, we must first agree to live by the laws of the Kingdom. We cannot expect to enforce the laws of the kingdom if we do not first agree to live by those laws. Faith is a spiritual law and so is the power of agreement. The power of two in agreement is something the enemy absolutely hates, because he knows the multiplied power it brings into a couple's prayers. When God finds two in agreement with His will, nothing can stop the prayer from coming to pass.

- It was the witness of 'two' or more in the Old Testament that testified to guilt or innocence in legal proceedings (Deut. 19:15);
- Two are better than one because they have a good reward for their labor and can withstand an enemy (Eccl. 4:9-12);
- Where two or three are gathered in the name of Jesus, He is there, and He has said "Again, I say to you that if two of you agree on earth concerning anything that they ask, it will be done for them by My Father in heaven." (Matt. 18:20)

If a couple is not seeing answers to their prayers, then it is time to step back and investigate the cause. Is there a place where your relationship is out of alignment? Here are a few things to consider:

1. The husband and wife are not in agreement. Both God and the devil know when lips say one thing but the heart is not in agreement. People can say one thing but still be wrestling with the inner struggles of their heart. The result is wavering convictions. Divided loyalties, uncertainty and fear produce double-mindedness. According to James 1:8, a double minded man is unstable and receives nothing from the Lord. God is not the author of strife and He will wait until spouses resolve their differences.

2. We are not in agreement with God. Now that can be a tough one. Sometimes people spend all their time struggling because they think they're fighting the enemy but they are really fighting against God. Wanting something is not the same as it being God's will. Never presume you already know the will of God for any given situation. What is God saying to you? Do not assume that common sense or

knowledge of scripture automatically tells you what to do. Ask God for clarification.

3. The answer to your prayer requires a step of faith on your part. The principle of faith works against common sense, practicality and reason. The results of our prayers can only be received by faith, which will always contradict the ways of natural man and our carnal thinking.

4. It is not yet time for the answer to be fulfilled. Patient endurance is required until the time for fulfillment comes to pass.

5. Lack of obedience, respect or honor towards one another hinders the answer to prayer. Seek God to find out if there is an area of obedience or repentance that needs to be fulfilled so that He can release the answer to your petitions.

6. This depends a lot on the nature of your petition, but it worth considering the thought that it may not be the right time for the fulfillment of your request. Or, it may be that God is taking you through a process of purification and the experience of the journey has not yet produced the lasting change God desires in the individual(s) nature. The right questions to ask Him are: What process is He taking you through and what is His goal? What does He want you to learn? What is He trying to produce through this process? How can you cooperate with Him in the process of sanctification? What is the action or word that will bring the breakthrough?

When you pray in agreement with the conviction of knowing His will, you can confidently declare the word of God into the situation. The enemy's job is to oppose you; your job is to enforce the laws of the Kingdom of God. The word of God is like a hammer, crushing and breaking down the mountain of resistance that stands opposing you. As long as one or both spouses are outside the principles of obedience, faith and agreement, the enemy can withstand them. Even so, many times God still answers our prayers. That is how good and gracious He is! But, the enemy knows that if he can get people to waiver in their conviction to sanctification, then he has access to many areas of a person's life. The mountain must move when the spiritual laws of faith and agreement are working together. *Faith is a force.* The force of applied faith is more powerful than any resistance.

There can be many challenges and differences in a marriage, but if both people truly want to save their marriage and see it healed a great majority of the struggles can be resolved peaceably. One thing the enemy does is to set off silent triggers that cause people to immediately experience heightened emotions, which in turn almost always can trigger an anger response. When the enemy pushes "old buttons," he knows that the emotional hot buttons he sets off are often those that remind people of previous experiences in former relationships when they didn't feel respected, valued or validated. Perhaps it is another painful emotion, like shame, fear, injustice or something else. He "pulls the trigger" on emotional issues so that without anyone having to say it, a person will automatically draw the connection between a former relationship or situation where they felt some negative emotion and then pull that experience into their current relationship. These sort of responses should be an indicator that there are old issues that need to be healed. Forgive those that made you feel hurt and offended from the past. It's not worth it! Offended people reproduce the same negative relational dynamics that they experienced before. We must break the cycles that set ourselves up for failure. If we carry the bricks from the past relationships to the new one, we will build the same house. These disappointing responses can be broken, but we must be willing to change.

Unhealed offenses and judgments against those that have hurt us in the past can cause us to hear things in such a way as to magnify feelings of insignificance. Offense, unforgiveness and judgments against others serve as filters that cause other things to be seen through the eyes of fear, anger, resentment and suspicion. Anger is a response of both fear and pride. Anger is a voice that drowns out the voice of God. It also drowns out the voice of those that want to communicate with us and causes them to feel unheard or their feelings invalidated. When people stop listening, they start fighting. The first step to healing any relationship is forgiveness. The Lord knows your hurts, but you must be willing to let go of them and allow Him to come heal you. No matter what someone else may have done to you, and no matter how painful a situation, God holds each person accountable to whether or not they will choose to forgive. The Bible is clear: If we do not forgive others, our own sins are not forgiven. Unforgiveness will block our prayers and cause God to withhold revelation until we are obedient. It will also block us from going to heaven. God has a prescribed order for restoration. He resists the proud but gives grace to those that are willing to be humble. God's strategy is to outwit the enemy through humility and disarm those you've been at war with through the acts of kindness, love, affirmation and forgiveness. Lay down your weapons, take yourself out of the fight and humble yourself. It is the only prescription to restoration and healing. How many times has Jesus humbled himself in order to reconcile people to Himself and His Father, when He did nothing wrong? Jesus may have finished it on the cross but He still takes our pain, blame and anger even today. Every time we falsely accuse Him of not being fair; every time we bristle against truth, rage against another brother or sister or loved one; every time we scream, snap or blow a fuse, we elevate our emotions against the example of humility He modeled. For as we do it unto others, we have done it unto Him. Humility is the key to surviving and thriving.

The Bible says, in Ephesians 5:22-33 says, [22] " **Wives, submit yourselves to your own husbands as you do to the Lord.** [23] **For the husband is the head of the wife as Christ is the head of the church, his body, of which he is the Savior.**[24] **Now as the church submits to Christ, so also wives should submit to their husbands in everything."**

[25] " **Husbands, love your wives, just as Christ loved the church and gave himself up for her**[26] **to make her holy, cleansing**[a] **her by the washing with water through the word,** [27] **and to present her to himself as a radiant church, without stain or wrinkle or any other blemish, but holy and blameless.** [28] **In this same way, husbands ought to love their wives as their own bodies. He who loves his wife loves himself.** [29] **After all, no one ever hated their own body, but they feed and care for their body, just as Christ does the church—** [30] **for we are members of his body.** [31] **"For this reason a man will leave his father and mother and be united to his wife, and the two will become one flesh."**[b] [32] **This is a profound mystery—but I am talking about Christ and the church.** [33] **However, each one of you also must love his wife as he loves himself, and the wife must respect her husband."** My husband and I had a great conversation one day early on in our relationship. He explained that although men do have a need for love, friendship and companionship, respect rates an even higher priority. Women need love and understanding, but men need respect. If you want a great marriage, do all you can to keep respect and honor at the top of your priorities.

Notice that the scripture does not emphasize the husband's authority, but focuses on sacrificial love. This is what it means to walk in genuine humility. It's laying down our lives for one another, esteeming others better than ourselves and not always fighting for our rights. The husband is the head of the household and as such is granted God-given authority over his family. It is not to be used to oppress, but to cover the family with safety, protection and loving guidance. Many women are waiting for the men in their lives to rise up into their rightful place of spiritual leadership in the home and family. Even the strong, capable woman longs to be understood, nurtured and affirmed. (If you are a male reader, please know that your encouragement and words of

affirmation go a long way in pleasing that special woman in your life!) This includes encouraging them as women of faith, lifting them up and helping them
fulfill their dreams and aspirations, their calling and destiny. Your relationship
will be so much richer for it! If either person feels that their significant other
does not have their full support, it can cause the other person to feel deval-
ued and resentful. This is where we must guard ourselves against seeing our
loved ones through the eyes of familiarity, for familiarity breeds contempt.
Familiarity can be perceived as a lack of confidence towards the other person.
Men have a great responsibility to oversee, protect, and guide their spouses
and family in all of God's ways and they are greatly needed to insure that
women and children have a sense of destiny, identity and self-esteem. When
a man treats a woman with love, a woman will have no difficulty submitting
herself in respect to his authority and role as a husband and leader in the family. It is a beautiful partnership when a marriage comes into divine order! 1
Peter 3:7 also reminds husbands to honor their wives so that their prayers will
not be hindered. Respect and honor are keys to maintaining a sense of *loyalty
and trust* in a marriage, and are essential to protecting the very foundation of
covenant.

It's not always easy for someone to lay down their rights or humble themselves when they may feel as if they have to deal with trust issues; perhaps they
do not feel their voice is heard or they do not feel respected by their spouse.
These can trigger responses of fear, but it's faith that moves God's hand. Each
person has to decide for themselves whether or not they believe God is bigger
than their current challenge. Both spouses degree of willingness to demonstrate humility, honor and respect will determine the health of the marriage.

Fear or anxiety motivates people to try to control and manipulate others.
These tactics rarely achieve the intended goal. Control most often incites rebellion and gets the opposite response of what a person wants. Let me give a
gentle reminder that it is not our job to be the voice of the Holy Spirit to others.
It is not our job to convict others of sin or convict them of *our* convictions!
Guilt, anger, harsh words or withholding love doesn't work. Frustrations come
from trying to carry burdens that are not ours, and trying to do a job that is not
our job description. When we exceed our bounds of authority we step over the
line into transgression. The role of the Holy Spirit is to convict others for their
need for change. (John 16:8). Our job is to be a loving wife, mother, help mate
and friend. Our role is to point our family to the God that can convict them for
the need to change through our responses of love and grace. It is not always
easy to remember that our spouses and our kids have a heavenly father outside

of our relationship with them. We have to leave room for their Father to *be* their Father and teach them how to be a man or woman of God. It is so easy to extend grace to a stranger, but the more familiar we are with others the harder it can be to extend grace to them. We want those in our life to understand truth and how their actions affect us and others. When we are emotionally invested in others it can be difficult to extend the grace that they need. Hammering them with truth will not produce the change we'd like to see. It will probably only cause resentment and hurt feelings because what they need is love and acceptance. The same kind of love and kindness that you would freely give a way to a stranger is what we need to give our loved ones, too. Jesus is grace and truth according to John 1:17. He gives us both; truth about ourselves and the grace to give us room to change. Instead of trying to change others, we must learn to focus on changing ourselves. How often we want God to change someone else so that their behavior pleases us, when the person He's trying to change is us! Take yourself out of the battle. If you have to go for a walk, sit in the Wal-Mart parking lot and pray for an hour until you feel better, just do it. Go for a walk. Go to a coffee shop or find a place to pray, but get with God and let GOD BE GOD over your marriage and your family. If you're going to battle with anyone, go to battle with the enemy. Do something so that the enemy is shut out of your marriage and family. You'll get the victory and God gets the glory.

When kids are involved in a marriage, whatever affects the parents also affects them. God has unlimited power, ability and creative ways to bring healing to marriage. As painful as some offenses can be, forgiveness needs to be a starting point. When relationships are broken, both parties have to examine themselves in light of what contributed to the problems. Getting wrapped up in the blame game is not profitable and bears no good fruit. If you need to disagree, then agree to fight fair. Keep it respectful and on the issue at hand. Don't bring up old issues that you have been simmering over. Love does not ambush others with painful words to make a point. If you're hurt, say so, but work through to a resolution. Don't punish each other with unforgiveness and cold love! Agree together to forgive one another and let God work on the communication and other issues. Forgiveness allows the Holy Spirit to work in both of you, and understanding will come. Forgiveness shuts the door to strife so that together you can begin to pray against the enemy. It takes faith to trust in the Lord and do things His way. Most marriages have difficulty because of selfishness, pride and an inability to surrender control. I'm not just talking about how spouses deal with each other; I'm referring to the degree which they fail to trust God and surrender their selves to Him. A marriage will turn around when people begin to put aside their own selfishness and begin to love and serve their spouse with unconditional love.

Some behaviors must be examined in light of spiritual root causes. When there are generational issues of parents that committed sins such as adultery, or they broke trust, vows and covenants, the enemy finds a legal right to revisit the next generation and try to produce the same results. Spiritual roots that come from unclean spirits of lust, addictions, or rebellion also greatly affect the condition of a marriage. Spiritual doors remain open until people bring those issues to God and ask His forgiveness for those sins, and then renounce them. The fruit of generational curses can cause divorce to run in families as well as barrenness and miscarriage. Those things are the result of familial spirits that attempt to reproduce the curse. When people begin to realize that there may be spiritually rooted generational curses that have set them up for failure, they can then come together in agreement to do something about it. Instead of fighting against one another, they can begin to unite in a common cause against a common enemy: *Satan*.

It's time to help recover the strength and grace that brings healing and unity back to marriage so that the "two" can withstand the enemy. Truth be told, it's not just the marriage the enemy wants; it's the children. He is thinking way ahead. When the enemy devises a plan, it is always with multiplication in mind. He wants to devise a plan to hurt and destroy as many people as possible. Children are vulnerable and greatly at risk of the enemy attacking them when there is no spiritual covering or unity between the parents. When a household is divided and out of order, the enemy has a legal right to come in and bring all manner of problems and spiritual plagues. The encouragement to every couple is to examine their issues and ask themselves, "Is any of this really worth being divided over, considering the enemy has a well thought out plan how to get to your family and children?" If you can agree to table your differences, forgive each other, and allow God to deal with you both, He will bring your marriage back in order. Your spouse is not your enemy; Satan is, and you don't want your family to become his prey.

One of the biggest problems married people face is power struggles over who gets to be right on what issues. It's not worth it. *Apologize.* God honors humility. It brings peace back into the relationship. Anger, strife and stubbornness grieve the Holy Spirit. When the Spirit is grieved it chokes the life out of any relationship. We never want that. The presence of Holy Spirit is so precious! We must guard it and honor His presence in our lives and in our home.

When people have relational issues, most of the time they have taken Holy Spirit out of the equation and disregarded God's counsel and wisdom.

The Bible gives each person a responsibility in marriage. Read 1 Peter 3:1-12. Wives are to be submissive, showing their husbands respect. Don't usurp their God-given authority in the household, especially in front of the children. Kids learn honor and dishonor at home. Husbands, show your wives you understand them and honor them so that your prayers will not be hindered. Christian husbands are to demonstrate that they are intimately aware of their wife's needs as well as her strengths and weaknesses. He should support and encourage her in her goals and desires, and he should pray for her regularly. The wife should do the same for her husband. Each person has a destiny and a calling ordained by God. They have dreams and aspirations. That does not cease to exist when people get married. It's also important to realize that God does not call husbands and wives in different directions. He calls them as a team. One thing I think worth mentioning is the issue of ministry in a marriage. One or both partners may feel a calling towards ministry, but if their marriage is not healthy and in order they should really consider waiting. The enemy will take advantage of every weakness and target them for an even greater destruction. If you are not in one accord with your spouse, ministry can have disastrous results because the enemy is after more than just the two; he wants to defile others that have accepted ministers as their role models. He wants to reproduce offense and take down as many as possible. Though ministry may be in a couple's future, it is wisdom to consider the impact that your marriage may have on others. A divided marriage is no longer just a marital issue when people are in ministry; it becomes an example that others will follow. The relationship between spouses must be healthy before it is the appropriate time to accept a role to minister to others. God will not call two that are divided into ministry just because one or both people want to fulfill a desire. He will wait until they are in one accord. Love is patient, and mature growth comes through learning how to wait upon God's timing.

A couple's strengths and weaknesses are there to add balance to their spiritual gifts, calling and aspirations. They should complement, not compete with one another. The husband and the wife must realize that as unique individuals, each person has a responsibility to God and themselves to honor their calling and purpose for which they have been created. Spouses should always support and encourage each other to put God first and honor Him. God is tolerant of a lot, but one thing He doesn't take lightly is when people disrespect and dishonor the Holy Spirit, and that is applicable in marriage, too. Familiarity that causes disrespect and dishonor towards other brothers and sisters in the body of Christ are sins against them and the Holy Spirit and should be avoided. When a married couple humbly acknowledges that their lives serve a greater purpose than only being there to serve one another in selfishness, they help keep a right perspective towards each other and the Lord. They have an anointing and gifting that is there to minister and serve others in order to release God's kingdom on earth. Servant hood is serving the Lord in humble service. Keep God first and honor the presence of the Holy Spirit in each other's lives. It keeps the marriage in proper alignment and it releases greater blessing to the entire family.

1 Peter 3:8 says, **"Finally, all of you be of one mind (there's that power of two again!), having compassion for one another; love as brothers (agape love), be tenderhearted, be courteous; not returning evil for evil or reviling for reviling, but on the contrary blessing, knowing that you were called to this, that you may inherit a blessing. For He who would love life and see good days, let him refrain his tongue from evil, and his lips from speaking deceit. Let him turn away from evil and do good; let him seek peace and pursue it. For the eyes of the Lord are on the righteous, and His ears are open to their prayers; but the face of the Lord is against those who do evil."** I inserted a couple of comments to stress the point. The Apostle Peter is still speaking about marriage.

If you haven't done so, invite the Holy Spirit into your marriage. Make a fresh commitment and a covenant to Him and your spouse. Take time to worship and pray together. Let God be God over your marriage, and put your relationship with Him *first*. When God is in the midst of your marriage, He fights for you. A threefold cord cannot easily be broken. He is there to gently nudge you in the right direction, to take the right course of action and resolve your differences peaceably, but you must invite Him in. Holy Spirit is a gentleman. He won't interfere where it is obvious that you still want to be in control. If you want a successful marriage, surrender control to Holy Spirit and honor that vow. Let Him help you. It takes godly wisdom to make a marriage work and raise your children to understand the ways of the Lord. It takes a conscious effort to encourage one another, build each other up with positive words and affirmations, and serve each other out of love. When couples stop building each other up it's easy to slip into less respectful ways of communication that begin to erode the relationship. Please understand I'm not referring to ego stroking that just builds pride or vain glory - but reaffirming what God has said about them. Wisdom builds their house with life giving words. Take communion, talk with your spouse, agree to put your differences under the blood of Jesus and begin fresh any time you need a do-over. Put the excuses aside and make time to do it. This is powerful and will once again bring the power of two in agreement back to your marriage. It will help you to stand instead of falling. It will help bring your marriage back into godly order and alignment and shut out the enemy. Protect your family and your children's future. It's time for a spiritual lock down! It's time to lock the enemy out and secure your home! Commitment to being a woman of virtue is not an easy thing but the rewards are worth it. This is a prayer you can do with your spouse.

Dear Heavenly Father,

Help us shut the enemy out of our marriage and family. We repent for anger, power struggles, poor communication and dishonoring one another. We repent for any ways that we have rejected or disrespected one another. We chose to forgive each other of the past and we will not bring up old issues. We will not continue to blame each other for things that happened in the past. We repent for any sins of ourselves or others in our family line that led to adultery, jealousy, broken vows, and betrayal of trust or broken commitments. We ask that the sins of the past be broken off of us and forgiven. We ask You, Lord Jesus, to receive us as Your own. We believe You can heal our marriage and make it healthy. Let this be a brand new day.

We renounce fear, unloving spirits, anger, condemnation and criticism. We repent and renounce any ways we have entertained fault finding. Today we ask for grace to modify our behavior, to know when to remain silent, and appropriate ways of addressing issues. We ask for a release of Your love and grace to help bring lasting change. Give us eyes to see the positive things and help us bless those things deserving of praise. Help us to replace bad habits with good ones.

We come together now in a prayer of agreement, asking that you help us recover trust, love, honor and respect. Holy Spirit, forgive us for grieving you and not honoring Your authority over our marriage. We make a covenant with You now, and ask that You speak to us, bless us with wisdom and counsel from above. Help us to remember to honor You and ask You for help. Please protect our marriage from the plots and schemes of the evil one and workers of iniquity. Come and refresh our marriage. You can make all things new. You can resolve issues that on our own strength we cannot. Let the hurt feelings be washed away by the power of Your love. Breathe a fresh wind into us individually, but also into us as a couple, and let your love wash over our children, too. Fill us with Yourself, Holy Spirit. We need You. We cannot revive ourselves. Please, help us come back into divine order in all things and shut the enemy out of our thoughts, our responses, our family and our future. In Jesus name, amen .

CHAPTER EIGHT

Liberated From Shame

Many women seem to carry the guilt of past events, failures and emotional baggage as if they don't understand that they can let go of them. Jesus took them upon Himself at the cross. They don't belong to you anymore! It's time to release the weight of these burdens instead of carrying them around with us. God wants to break all false yokes of condemnation!

What we see throughout the gospels is the ongoing theme of two worlds colliding. The kingdom of God challenged kingdoms of men. This was true in Jesus' day and it's true now, in every nation, tongue, tribe, and culture. That is why the gospel message as well as the scriptures remains just as relevant today as when they were written. It's important to understand that this is what sets the tone for the gospel accounts. It was the power struggle between the existing religious order and the message of grace as Jesus came on the scene. In almost every place or situation, power encounters and struggles for control are at the heart of many spiritual battles.

In the gospel accounts, there was a tremendous amount of tension because the old order did not want to make room for grace. Jesus knew the real matter was about power and control. With the Pharisees, it was always about who would control the people. They wanted leverage, and entrapment was the method they choose to try to fulfill their agenda. When hearts are wrong, judgments will be skewed. They weren't interested in justice or truth, they were interested in getting rid of the anointed one (Jesus) that could see through their motives and free those under ungodly control. God gave people a living example of His grace because their belief system was rigid and unyielding. Their hearts were bound by fear and pride; extending grace to a sinner offended them. Jesus knew their judgments were predisposed to judgment and fault finding. What is interesting is that when Jesus was in the wilderness being tested and tempted by the enemy, one of the first things Satan did was challenge His identity. In Matthew 4:6 Satan said, *"If you are the Son of God..."* Satan was appealing to Jesus' humanity and trying to create doubt. Satan knew if Jesus didn't know who He was, He would not be able to fulfill His purpose. (If you don't know your identity, you will never be able to stand in the face of opposition). The interesting thing is, once Jesus began His ministry, He was the one that challenged the religious crowd on *their* identity issues. He told them they didn't know what spirit they were of and they didn't know who their father was! He knew who He was, and who did not belong to His Father! Identity issues are at the heart of many problems, and it was no different in Jesus' day. The balance of power was shifting! Prophecy was being fulfilled before their very eyes!

Jesus was always clear about the fact that He was a messenger sent to reveal a Kingdom and a different reality than what they had known. Jesus said if a person saw Him, they saw the Father. John 1:17 says **'grace and truth came through Jesus Christ.'** The people needed someone to demonstrate the reality of the message of grace, so Jesus showed them how it was done. He gave them grace when they didn't deserve it. He didn't fight back when people wanted to kill him, mock him or spit angry words in His face. Instead, He demonstrated real concern over their welfare by speaking truth in love and showing them in practical ways how the Father really loved them. He healed them, fed them spiritually, multiplied food when they were hungry, and cast out the demons that tormented their souls with fear. He encouraged them, spoke kindly to them, and didn't condemn them for their sins. Love wants others set free, healed and restored to God. Love wants relationships restored, healthy and moving forward towards the good plans that God has for people's lives. Jesus, in His own words, proclaimed that the one that came to Him would by no means be cast out. (John 6:37) God's heart is for restoration, not condemnation.

The Encounter with the Woman Caught in Adultery

John chapter 8 gives us the story of a woman caught in adultery who was dragged to Jesus by a mob of angry Pharisees. Nothing was said about the man she was caught with, of course. There were those that knew that he was equally guilty of the same sin but they did nothing to hold him to the same standard of judgment. In perhaps one of her worst moments of shame this woman found refuge and forgiveness. The enemy only has power when his schemes are covered by the cloak of darkness, and when no one stands up to defend those he attacks. This woman found a defender and a liberator in Jesus Christ. The Pharisees wanted to test Jesus by challenging him to a duel of the law. They thought they could force him into a corner. Instead, Jesus reminded them of things that pricked their own conscience and brought such conviction that the crowd dropped their stones and walked quietly away. *"He who is without sin, cast the first stone,"* He said. Perhaps he wrote the 10 commandments in the sand, or perhaps he wrote things pertaining to their own sin that only God would know, but it was enough to convict their consciences and shut down the attack of the mob. Condemnation is a tool of the enemy which he uses to strip us of our real sense of identity. Legalism thrives on condemnation, finger pointing and people comparing themselves to others. If we want to get down to the truth, their accusation probably wasn't even about the woman. It was the fact that Jesus touched their sacred cows of religion. Jesus knew this. This is why He never backed down and he didn't let others control him. He stood his ground. When the accusers left, Jesus asked the woman, *"Woman, where are those accusers of yours? Has no one condemned you?"* She said, *"No one, Lord."* And Jesus said to her, *"Neither do I condemn you; go and sin no more."* (John 8:10,11)

The Liberator Sets a Woman FREE from Shame

Religious spirits aren't afraid to make a public example out of others in order to exercise fear and intimidation as a means of controlling others. Jesus didn't condone the woman's sin, but He didn't condemn her, either. The amazing thing is, He extended grace without her even asking for it. *Before* He went to the cross. *Before* she prayed a "sinner's prayer" or demonstrated repentance. Nothing speaks more of the Father's intention to extend forgiveness and grace than this verse. This woman didn't know Jesus personally, but she was about to. She met Jesus when she met Grace and Kindness. Who *doesn't* want to know a God like that?

Jesus' heart is full of mercy. He could have condemned this woman in her sin; instead He chose to take the opportunity to rescue her. That is the beauty of His love and acceptance. It transcends our unworthiness and sin, and looks beyond our current state. God's mercy lifts us up and points us towards the future He has for us. God did not curse the woman. If He had cursed her, he would have to curse us all, but He sent His Son to deliver the world from condemnation and judgment. We are all guilty of being the adulterous woman. We are all guilty of elevating judgments and criticisms more than we have loved others. We are all guilty of sharing our affections with worldly lovers. We've loved materialism, greed, ungodly attitudes and allowed other masters to divide our loyalties to the One who came to save us. Many people have had one foot in and one foot out of God's Kingdom, wondering why they haven't experienced more from life. Yet, even when we were still sinners, Christ laid down His life for us. The answers we need are found in Him. The very purpose for which He was sent to this earth was to demonstrate God's great love, mercy and kindness to a world that had no idea of their true identity as sons and daughters of the Most High God. Over and over in the scriptures we see GOD humbly taking our rejection, anger, betrayal, as He watches and waits for people to realize how much He truly loves us all. He won't break covenant with us, but so many times we have broken our vows to Him, even when we told ourselves we would live to honor Him. When we may be tempted to judge others we must stop to remember the adulterous woman lives inside all of us. If we judge others, we reap that same judgment into our own lives according to the principle in Matthew 7:1. **"Do not judge or you too will be judged. For in the same way you judge others, you will be judged, and with the measure you use, it will be measured back to you."** (NIV)

Jesus was there to liberate her, and He is here today to liberate all of us. Jesus didn't condemn her, He consoled her. This is a wonderful example of how Jesus stepped in and became her advocate. He took the position as her defender, her attorney. This is the power of the cross of Christ and the cleansing power of His blood! This is the message of the gospel! Jesus stood between those that saw no value to her life and the Father's desire to have her experience the goodness of God. The Pharisees cared nothing about this woman's life, her feelings or her future. To them, she was expendable. They wanted to stone the woman but Jesus wanted to set her free. He saw great value to her life and wanted to restore her. They looked for someone to accuse and to blame; Jesus looked for someone to forgive and exonerate. The truth is hard heartedness blinded those that thought they could see, and the kindness of God allowed a sinful woman to experience an encounter with Divine Love. Her eyes were opened to see Him in Spirit and in Truth. The mob mentality was anger and hatred from people who weren't interested in knowing Grace; they were only concerned about being right. A bunch of angry, offended people presented the facts, but they weren't living in truth, at least not the truth of the scriptures they seemed to hold in such high regard. Fear is at the root of religious legalism. A religious spirit looks for ways to manipulate and control others. It withholds acceptance and approval until demands are met by those wielding control. A religious spirit is *exclusive* rather than *inclusive*, and it divides rather than unifies. A religious spirit will try to make people's judgments sound biblical but often completely miss the heart of God. If a person tries to interpret God's word without understanding His heart, they will always come up short! God <u>always</u> acts in mercy before He is willing to execute judgment. That is just who He is! He extended forgiveness of sin and acted in this woman's defense. He didn't demand brokenness from those that were already broken. He comforted them, spoke kindly and reassured them that as they came to Him, (an act of faith) - their sins were forgiven. What graciousness! What love He displays that releases peace to the lives of those that desperately need Him! The important thing for each of us to understand is that God expended His wrath upon His Son; He hasn't held it back to unleash it upon us. The price for the sin of all mankind has already been paid in full. It wasn't a down payment. The BLOOD of CHRIST is sufficient! We can't earn any part of the grace that Jesus paid for with His blood. The bridge between sinful man and a Holy God has been made through a relationship of love. God's intention is not to condemn the world but to save those in the world. *If the message isn't the good news of forgiveness, grace, restoration and relationship then it's not the gospel.* It's somebody else's message, but it isn't the message the Father sent by His Son.

It is the kindness of God that leads men to repentance. How often we forget! And when we forget to be kind, how can people possibly see or understand the kindness of the God that Christians profess to serve? We are messengers of a different reality, a different kingdom than what people are accustomed to. Jesus was an ambassador of His Father's kingdom. He was sent to model the kingdom to us, and so are we to model the kingdom to those around us.

Jesus confronted heart issues and what motivated people to exalt their judgments above the law of love. Jesus told the Pharisees in John 5:39, **"You search the Scriptures for in them you think you have eternal life; and these are they which testify of Me. But you are not willing to come to Me that you may have life."** Jesus was trying to get the religious leaders to see beyond the physical aspects of teaching to the real issues, that if they believed on Him they would have eternal life. Pride blinded them to their own need for grace and so they rejected the God that came to save them. Perhaps they didn't even do it knowingly, but they still denied the mercy and forgiveness that could have been theirs. The law that they used to judge others became the law that was used to judge them. They exalted their knowledge of the law to the point where it completely blinded them to their own need to come to God on His terms. No one can come to God on their terms and be justified. They must come on His.

In the story about the adulterous woman there were people that were convinced they were righteous, but weren't following God at all. The hardness of the Pharisees hearts caused them to make judgments that did not represent God's heart. Here we understand an important spiritual truth: a heart that lacks love and mercy will fail to truly understand the heart of God and misunderstand the intent of scripture. The Pharisees followed a god of their own understanding and clearly missed the boat entirely when it came to understanding Father's heart. The irony of the situation is that they accused the woman of adultery but they were equally guilty of spiritual adultery. They weren't having a relationship with God. They loved their judgments more than they loved Him. If they had really known and loved Him, they would have understood Jesus' decision to show mercy. Instead, they loved their false gods of judgment, religion, control, pride, unforgiveness, anger and hate. That is why Jesus warned the disciples to beware of the beliefs and doctrine of the Pharisees and the Sadducees. (Matt. 16:6,11-12). They were full of spiritual hardness, hypocrisy and political opportunism. They failed at the first and greatest commandment, to love God with all their heart and love their neighbor as themselves (Matt. 22:38). Jesus did not come to condemn the world. He came to judge the works of the enemy. There is a big difference. **"For God did not send His Son into the world to condemn the world, but that the world through Him might be saved."** (John 3:17,18)

This story in John 8 reminds us that no one is above being tempted by the enemy, no one is above failure. Jesus judged with righteous judgment because He did not judge by the flesh. (See Isaiah 11: 3,4) He took all things into account, including heart attitudes, motive and intent for people's actions. Our position is not to act as judge or juror against others, but to show grace and mercy in hopes that kindness opens the door for people to be reconciled to God. Release words of life or share a testimony. Tell someone how God met you with love when you didn't deserve it. Encourage others the way you would want someone to minister to you. It is so easy to judge someone else without having to walk in their shoes or live their life. Sometimes failure is life's greatest teacher, and failure is the thing God uses to bring people to Himself. The God of compassion meets people at their lowest point. Even when He brings correction, He is gracious and kind.

The story about the adulterous woman carries a profoundly deeper message of hope for every person. The Book of Matthew chapter one lists the genealogy of some very notable women among the catalog of names. Four women in particular are mentioned and given extraordinary emphasis: Tamar, Rahab, Ruth and Bathsheba. Each one was notorious for having a disreputable reputation and carried the stigma of being "unclean" or "unworthy" in every sense of the word. Even Mary, a young virgin girl who would become the mother of Jesus - handpicked by God because she said yes to His greater purposes - bore the burden of being falsely accused. She bore the reproach of a disgraceful reputation for many years. Do you think that others believed she was impregnated by the Holy Spirit? Did they even know who that was? She said yes to God but His favor meant that she had to carry the stigma of being marked by God. **God is not afraid of shame or reproach on a person's reputation.** He allows it to be there for a reason. Each of these women had a strength, determination and tenacity that refused to give up. Against all odds, they overcame. They wrestled with God and man and prevailed. This is the quality that God looks for in those that will give birth to His promise.

God is not put off by people's sin. Jesus took care of our sin issues. God Himself provided the solution for our redemption, sanctification and justification. God supplies the grace and uses the scandal, accusation and pressure to birth what He wants to release into the earth. He chooses people that the religious cast out, deem unfit and despise because it causes them to be jealous for His encounter in their lives. He loves His bride but He is jealous for the world, too. He will win them to Himself using vessels the church has rejected and cast off. **"But God chose the foolish things of the world to shame the wise; God chose the weak things of the world to shame the strong. [28] God chose the lowly things of this world and the despised things—and the things that are not—to nullify the things that are, [29] so that no one may boast before him."** (1 Cor. 1:27-29) God is outrageous in the ways He chooses His servants. His ways are incomprehensible and far above the thoughts of man! *What good news for all of us!* There is no sin or bad reputation that is beyond God's ability to redeem and restore. His arm is not too short to pull those who call on His name out of the deepest pit. He can lift the lowest of the low out of the ash heap, out of despair and shame, and place them in royal lineage just as He did with Tamar, Rahab, Ruth, and Bathsheba. He can use the woman that is the outcast, the rejected, and the least likely to win the spiritual Miss America pageant. What these women could probably not foresee was the bigger picture of how their life would impact generation upon generation of those that would come after them. This is the truth that we all need to understand. *It's not all about us.* God's love for mankind is so deep. He wants no one to perish. He wants all people to be saved. **"The Lord isn't really being slow about his promise, as some people think. No, he is being patient for your sake. He does not want anyone to be destroyed, but wants everyone to repent,"** (2 Pet. 3:9, NLT). He is willing to go to great lengths to restore each of us because first and foremost, we belong to Him. We are His children. God uses our lives and our testimonies to reach more people, all with the intent purpose of winning them back to Himself so that others can enjoy the blessing of knowing their sins are also forgiven, and share eternal life with Christ and our Father in heaven. He rescues us from the flames of hell.

The question each of us must answer is, *"Can God forgive so completely that the stigma of a scandalous reputation is no longer a sign of rejection?"* The answer is yes. God is able to do exceedingly greater than anything we can imagine! Will we be people that are so transformed in our minds that we see the reproach and stigma of a tainted reputation in a new light? Will people stop to consider the fact that God remakes our human vessels? I hope so. I believe God can use anyone to do amazing kingdom work. The very things that might offend our sense of propriety could in fact be the very mark of God that indicates an individual has received His approval and acceptance. If we are able to be offended, God will bring it to light. He will challenge the self-righteous attitudes in all of us. This is the decision all will come to when God chooses to work through ordinary, earthen vessels that have been redeemed, refashioned and made honorable for His purposes. He is the Master Potter. Praise God that He never throws away the clay! Praise God that He sees people through eyes of faith! He knows exactly where to find something worth redeeming in us - *because He put it there!* Praise Him, because your life is not outside the grasp of a loving God that has good plans for your life. He thinks thoughts of peace and not of evil. His ways are not our ways; they are so much higher than what we can imagine! God's wisdom turns the kingdoms of men *upside down.*

Lord Jesus,

Thank you for liberating me from shame. Thank you that even when I fail, Your love and acceptance are constant and assuring of my place in the kingdom. No one can take that from me. Thank you for standing as a shield and a protector from the voice of condemnation. I love You, Lord. Please continue to unravel the lies I have taken into my belief system so that I can be truly free. In Your name I pray. Amen.

CHAPTER NINE

Scandalous Grace

I love the fact that God is willing to risk His reputation of what others think of Him just so that we can be restored. He doesn't care if others get offended. Your healing and restoration are *that* important to Him. Talk about a knight in shining armor! But Jesus is not just a knight...He is the King of Kings, and He won't apologize to anyone about how committed He is to loving you. You are the apple of His eye, His bride! Have you ever had anyone love you like that?

There are times when God will seemingly break all the rules just to re-store a person's hope and future. He isn't called the King of Kings for nothing! He is the master of flipping the script and turning the tables on those who thought they could get away with treating someone else with injustice. In the midst of contriving evil, people tend to forget that the Lord sees into everyone's hearts. He knows why people do the things they do. He never sides with injustice. God will take what someone else says or does unjustly against another person, and turn it around so that the one who is victimized becomes the one who triumphs in the face of injustice. **"The lowly he sets on high, and those who mourn are lifted to safety.** [12] **He thwarts the plans of the crafty, so that their hands achieve no success.** [13] **He catches the wise in their craftiness,   and the schemes of the wily are swept away.** [14] **Darkness comes upon them in the daytime; at noon they grope as in the night.** [15] **He saves the needy from the sword in their mouth; he saves them from the clutches of the powerful.** [16] **So the poor have hope, and injustice shuts its**

mouth," (Job 5:11-16). God did something special in the life of one woman named Tamar. She was an unlikely candidate for a breakthrough. What is amazing about this story is that God was willing to disregard something considered taboo in order to give this tenacious woman hope for her future. The story of Tamar is found in Genesis 38. Something that is taboo is considered absolutely prohibited or forbidden by social or customary beliefs, tradition or law. It is something considered absolutely improper or unacceptable, and breaking a taboo will definitely cause strong personal reactions from others. Tamar's story is an unusual case of a woman who broke all the rules and yet God showed her mercy and pardoned her sin, so let's take a look at *why*.

This is an aspect of God's character people may not stop to think about and many probably don't like. They would say it doesn't fit with their ideal that God has to "play fair." But God's standard of "fair and just" is not based on human standards or opinions. It is based on His ability to see every aspect of the situation, taking everyone's heart, motive and actions into consideration. He takes into consideration everything the enemy has done. God is not concerned about offending people because He doesn't need anyone's approval. Jesus offended people all the time. We all need to be prepared for the chance that God will do something to deliberately offend us at some point in time. God can be pretty shocking at times!

The scandalous side of God includes the fact that sometimes He will mess with our theology. We don't always have to agree with God but we do have to keep ourselves from touching what He's doing. The ways of God often challenge what a person thinks they understand about Him and His word. Offense is pride that feels man knows better than God. Jesus challenged not only his disciples' way of thinking, but the religious and those with hard, judgmental attitudes as well. They could not understand this God-man that was unsafe, uncontrollable and unpredictable, but it was also the reason why they missed the time of their visitation! God will break a taboo in order to personally see to it that the person He has chosen to carry out a particular task is able to fulfill it. He will disregard protocol, opinions and preferences of others so that those He has chosen to bear His name are able to do what they were commissioned to do. God will do just about anything to restore a person's hope for the future. He will always see to it that a seed of hope is there to carry on the promise. And when the enemy tries to kill that seed of hope, God can be even more inclined to seemingly break the rules that man thinks God should follow. *Expect Him* to turn things upside down. We may not understand why He is doing things a certain way, because God won't fit in the box of anyone's expectations.

When we think of Tamar, we must realize that social customs were far different than what we know today. There were different roles and expectations from women in biblical times. I wonder though, about the young woman who grew up and perhaps dreamed of love and the happily ever after story that so many girls dream. Her life certainly did not mirror that reality. Her life took a terrible turn from one disappointment to another. She married a wicked man by the name of Er. Wicked men are not necessarily pleasant to live with. I can imagine that Tamar must have felt like she was living a nightmare, but it was about to get worse. God's opinion of this man was so poor He decided to end Er's life early, which left Tamar a widow while she was still quite young. Hope for the future was dashed upon the rocks of despair. There would be no prince for Tamar, no tender romance, no happy home life with babies jabbering and playing beneath her feet. When her husband died, hope for the future died with him, and she became the responsibility of her father-in-law, Judah.

Judah promised to take care of Tamar through Levirate marriage. The Levirate marriage was more of an honored custom than the law, but people in that society were expected to adhere to it. It was obligatory when a brother's widow had no children. Levirate marriage was practiced in societies where marriage outside the clan or tribe was forbidden. The next son in the family would marry the widow of his dead brother in order to make sure that the name of the family line was perpetuated into the next generation. Judah's second son, Onan, was to fulfill his brother's duty of marrying Tamar and provide an heir for his deceased brother, but he was selfish and spilled his seed on the ground. He refused to honor the Levirate marriage, and God called him wicked. Onan lost his life also because of his evil deeds. He intentionally deprived a widow of descendants. It's important to understand that a woman at that time could not directly inherit wealth or property; only the children could serve as inheritors, but a woman did have a right to be able to bear children and have descendants. For a woman in that day and age to be barren was a disgrace. People considered it to be a curse or a punishment from God. It was extremely important to have someone to continue the family name. The third son, Shelah, was much too young to marry but Judah deceptively convinced his daughter-in-law to be patient, leading her to believe that when he got of age, the youngest son would marry Tamar and give her an heir. Tamar put all her hope in this promise, yet Judah had no intention of fulfilling his part of the deal. Perhaps he became too afraid of losing another son. Both his previous sons had died, and no doubt he blamed Tamar rather than the wickedness of his own sons. Tamar's situation was not just a case marked by a lack of integrity within the family dynamics. Her case was an issue of social justice. She was denied her rights. Tamar understood the reality of her situation, and Judah's disingenuousness towards fulfilling his word. By this time, she had grown significantly older and her chances of marrying and having children were slipping by.

Tamar was spurred on by the injustice of her situation and decided to take matters into her own hands. She devised an unorthodox method of fulfilling her plan. She took off her robes of a grieving widow and posed as a temple prostitute. During this period of time Judah's wife passed away. After a time of mourning, he was more than likely feeling a bit lonely. Just as he was feeling a need for female companionship, he came across Tamar disguised as a woman for hire. When he bumped into Tamar, he didn't know it was his daughter-in-law. Thinking she was a prostitute, Judah propositioned her to have sex. Judah's act was more than just lust for sex. Sex with a temple prostitute implied a pagan or cult prostitute which was an act of worship of pagan gods. It was absolutely forbidden by God. Judah may have made the offer for prostitution without knowing it was his own daughter-in-law, but he was far from innocent. He knew what that act constituted. It was an act of disloyalty to God. Tamar wasn't innocent either, but her motive was different. Her actions were intended to reclaim her rights and secure hope for her future. She was not going to be denied her inheritance of children. Fruitfulness was that important to her! A key part of this story is the fact that Judah left Tamar with his staff and signet with her as a sign of good faith that he would send payment for her services. Tamar wasn't interested in payment. She had something better. She had evidence of his sin. This woman caught a glimpse of encouragement in her troubled circumstances. She understood the weakness of her enemy, saw the opportunity and recognized when she had the upper hand!

We need to pause here just for a moment. Many people can read the weaknesses of their enemies, just as your enemy, Satan, understands yours. He gives our opponents eyes to discern our areas of weakness and vulnerability and that is where the attack is aimed. But, God wants to give us wisdom to outsmart the enemy. As followers of Christ, we don't do things the way the rest of the world does. I would never advise anyone to take the sort of action that Tamar contrived. We need to trust God to work out the details of our injustices and act on our behalf. *When the time is right, He will.* Everyone that does wickedness or injustice towards others will encounter a day when God sets matters straight and turns their wrongdoing on their own head. What I do want the reader to understand is that there is a set time for your enemy to fall, but even if you recognize the inevitable, let God work out the details. Even David recognized that King Saul would eventually fall by his own hand, but David didn't do anything to deliberately make it happen. In other words, he didn't taunt Saul to make those unfortunate events occur any sooner. David did his very best to act in good faith towards Saul, and even when he had the opportunity to do him in he respected Saul's position as King, knowing that God established his authority and God would have to take him out. In time, Saul's actions put an end to him and David inherited what had belonged to his enemy. God prepares the character of those He chooses for promotion and to inherit a blessing of great proportion. No matter what is occurring in your life or what others may do to treat you unfairly, keep your perspective by holding on to God's promises. His character is trustworthy and His word will not let you down. Do your very best to keep your heart pure, for God judges us by the intent and motive of our actions. Now let's resume the story of Tamar.

As a result of her bold act of faith, Tamar conceived twins. When it was reported to her father-in-law that she was pregnant, everyone knew she had not remarried. In the eyes of society she was guilty of an immoral act that warranted punishment. Judah, seizing the opportunity to rid himself of Tamar, commanded that she be brought out to be stoned for her sin. Tamar, however, sent a message back to him, saying, "By the man who owns these, I am pregnant with his child." She presented the staff and the signet that identified Judah as the father of her unborn children. Confronted with his sin, Judah was convicted in his heart and declared, "She has been more righteous than I, because I did not give her Shelah my son." What had been a private injustice became known publicly. God saw it all and decided to bless her actions that were birthed out of pain and injustice. Never let it be said that God does not see or understand what happens in secret. He knew what Judah had promised, and He knew Judah never intended to make good on his vow. He understood what motivated both Judah and Tamar. Although it might not sit well with our concept of "righteousness" or even our understanding of God's word, God chose Tamar and put a blessing on her life. The key to understanding why God did not punish Tamar is the fact that her determination to adhere to the Levirate custom seemingly took precedence over the law of incest or adultery. It is interesting that through her tenacious determination to obtain what was rightfully hers, she chose the stigma of being known as a prostitute over the shame and stigma associated with barrenness. I am sure that if we had lived in her day, many people would have some very choice words to describe Tamar and her actions. Many, including Judah, were probably offended at the thought of this woman. She lured her father-in-law into bed under the guise of being a prostitute just to get impregnated. Many might say that she should have received the death sentence for her impropriety and unabashed, shameless way that she conducted herself. It would have been customary to have her stoned. However, this is *not* what going through God's mind or heart as her story was being played out! God always, *always* looks at the motivation of people's actions. Man may judge by outward appearances but God looks at the heart. He knows why people do the things they do. God disregarded what was taboo in the minds of others and gave her not just one child, but two: a *double* portion. Twins were considered a special blessing from the Lord. Perhaps the nature of the blessing was in fact a statement of her vindication.

While Tamar was giving birth, a midwife tied a scarlet thread around the hand of the child that was about to be born first, because his hand had already come out of the birth canal. Zerah had the scarlet thread around his hand in order to mark him as the firstborn. Then, *what should have been physically impossible* occurred. The other twin, Perez, suddenly moved into place, displacing his brother, and was born first. If you know anything about the tight constriction of the birth process, it would seem as though nothing would move that particular child out of place. Yet, by the election of God, and the perfect time and placement of God, this child came forth first and became the one to inherit the promise. Tamar was not from the tribe of Israel. She was a Canaanite woman. Even though she was an outsider of God's chosen people, she became a heroine in the Bible and in the lineage of the Messiah. Despite where she came from and the nature of her actions, she gave birth to a son named Perez, which means breakthrough.

◆ ◆ ◆

How often we can see only what concerns us, and we fail to recognize God has a bigger plan in mind. God's plan was so much bigger than this one woman. She did not know and could not have known that the deliverer of all mankind and the Savior of the world would be coming through her bloodline generations later. The great, great, great grandmother of Jesus Christ was a scandalous woman! I doubt if she ever thought that she would someday resort to the desperate act of prostitution, but she did. I don't even have to wonder how she felt. I believe her self-image suffered even more after that. Perhaps she looked at her life and assessed it as a big failure. I'm sure it didn't all turn out quite like she hoped, or even what she may have dreamed about as a young woman. What would she have thought if she knew that someday she would be listed among the heroes in one of the greatest books ever written? What would she have thought if she knew that her story is still being told to this day? Do you think she could have forgiven herself a little bit easier? What makes her a heroine is the fact that she didn't give up in the face of deep disappointment.

The child that came forth from her union with Judah was in the lineage of the son of God. God used the life of a woman driven by injustice and labeled from those around her as immoral to bring forth a royal bloodline. I think there is a lesson hidden for all of us as we examine the lives of others from a broader point of view. First of all, we can't reduce God to the size of our biggest failure. Disappointment in life and disappointment in us does not make God small. Secondly, maybe we should not try to sum up the impact of a person's life based on what we observe from our perspective or timeline. Perhaps the extent of how a person fulfills their purpose can't be fully seen unless it's looked at through the wide angle lens of an eternal perspective. When we look at things in review of what transpired throughout generations, it is clear that God chose Tamar, and he chose her son, Perez. He could have chosen Perez's twin brother, but He did not. This shows us the evidence of election according to God's predetermined choice. God saw something in this woman that he approved of, even if others couldn't see it. She had a scandalous reputation, but God showed her scandalous grace. Once again, we are reminded that our lives are not just about us. It's about who is to come, and who we will touch through our lives. God has the eternal perspective, and He has chosen certain things to come from the events of our lives, no matter how awful or disappointing they may appear to us or others. He has a bigger plan than what we can possibly understand, and our purpose is intricately interwoven into the lives and destinies of others that are beyond our understanding. What hope it gives to all of us! No matter where we've come from or what we've done, God can put a special blessing on our life, too. He moves the mountains of impossibilities to make room for hope to be birthed again. Our promise may be delayed for a season but we have a hope that will not be cut off. God has a plan to bring it all to completion. **"For I know the thoughts I think about you," says the Lord, "thoughts of peace and not of evil, to give you a future and a hope."** (Jer. 29:11).

This is the God we serve; a God that isn't predictable and or able to be controlled. This is the God that loves us so incomprehensibly and so dearly that He is willing to break what others may consider taboo just to bless us and give us hope for our future. He doesn't care who it offends as long as we continue to believe. He will never leave us or forsake us. He sets things right. And when the enemy comes to kill the plan or promise of God, He has a seed waiting that will spring forth and bear fruit to birth His promise at the appointed time. It is already appointed and set in place. Dear one, your hope will not be cut off. God sees. He understands, and He has a plan with all of this in mind. *This* is the God that loves *you.*

Heavenly Father,

I give You all the pain, sorrow, tears and injustice from my yesterdays. I sow them all as seeds to reap a bountiful, supernatural harvest of blessing. Lord, I forgive everyone that the enemy used to hurt and betray me, and those who wanted to try and deprive me of justice. No one can outwit You, for You see and understand everything. I thank You for restoration and that it has already been written into your plan for my life. All I have to do is trust You and it will come to pass. Thank you that You think good thoughts towards me to give me a future and a hope. You said that when I search for you with all my heart I will find You, and when I pray, You will hear my prayer and answer it. Give me ears to hear You, Lord Jesus, and sensitivity to recognize your Holy Spirit. Even when Your answers do not come packaged as I might expect, help me to accept the things I don't understand and trust that Your plan for my life is still at work. Transform the ashes of my disappointments into ornaments of beauty and grace. In Jesus name, amen.

CHAPTER TEN

Dealing with Failure

Did you know that every time you share your testimony of what God did for you, an anointing comes over you for breakthrough? It's true. When you tell your story, people listen, and as they do, the walls they've had up in their own heart begin to soften. The power of the Holy Spirit works on them so that they can receive something to heal their life, too. Every time we share honestly about what we've gone through, how God intervened, and what He has done for us, God is at work creating an elevated expectation of hope and faith.

Through our testimonies, God breaks yokes off of others and sets the stage for their own breakthrough. I've seen it happen when people share about God healing them in some way. Someone will rise up and claim that testimony for themselves and receive their own miracle of healing. Miracle breakthroughs are not limited to just healings, though. It can be anything. This is how we overcome the enemy, not just for our own lives but it helps others overcome, too. That is why it is so important for people to share their testimonies of what God has done for them, no matter how complicated, messy or embarrassing it might be. Your greatest failure might just be one of your greatest victories, if you can learn to look at it from a new perspective. If we allow the enemy to steal our testimonies, others cannot benefit from them. Sometimes the very things we're afraid to share are the very things that will release God to do greater than we've ever imagined. The gallows the enemy constructed to kill you can be turned around to launch you right into the purposes of God!

For many years I have had a hard time sharing my testimony about a certain situation. It is not so painful anymore to share about God saving me from alcohol and drugs, wanting to die, cutting myself, deep depression or years of bad relationships and how they almost destroyed my life. I can do that one now, although there was a time when sharing that part of my story was tremendously painful. There are things about other aspects of my life that I haven't wanted to share, because, quite honestly, most people wouldn't understand. Failures before a person becomes a Christian, well, those are a bit more forgivable. People tend to frown upon those that fail after they've been a Christian for a while because they hold Christians to a higher standard. Christians *should* be held to a higher standard. We represent the King of Kings and a kingdom characterized by holiness and power. The problem is, many people do not automatically achieve a state of being free, healed and delivered upon conversion, and so, they are labeled hypocrites. I don't think the majority of people want to live hypocritically. I think they want to be true to their faith and the convictions they find in God's word but struggle to do so. The reality is many people haven't yet received all the answers they need in order to live victoriously. The world is full of judgmental people and no one wants to feel judged and rejected, which is why people have such a hard time being transparent. Some of my biggest failures happened after I became a Christian. I'm not proud of it, but it's true. My story is complicated. It's messy. It's scandalous. I wanted the shame of those events to go away. As much as we may want to bury our skeletons six feet under, God wants us to take a look at them and not be afraid. He wants to heal us from the pain of our past and learn to share our stories that can help set others free. We will never be able to release healing to others if we can't get past our shame.

I got tired of a spirit of fear trying to steal my testimony and lock me up behind a wall of intimidation. I used to think that if others knew how badly I failed, they wouldn't see anything credible in me. Then I realized that my story isn't for everyone. It's for those that want it as a lifeline of hope for their own life. I just want people to see Jesus and understand that we're all a work of His grace, and we're all a work in progress. Identifying with Christ and calling yourself a Christian doesn't mean anyone has attained perfection. It means He is perfect and we are just sinners saved by grace, trying to keep moving forward one day at a time. Fear has tried to block my ability to share my story in a lot of different ways, through fear of rejection, shame, insecurity, condemnation and much more. I know that I'm not alone in that struggle. There are a lot of people that are disconnected from others for just those reasons. Many have been hurt or disappointed by the lack of love from people they care about and even those in the body of Christ. Perhaps they have been hurt by family, friends or others that they thought would love them instead of pass judgment on them and make them feel unaccepted or condemned. A fear of shame, rejection or betrayal makes people afraid to trust. Fear of being judged by others is huge among many people, but we have got to get past that because we can't fulfill what God designed for us to do on our own. If these words are ministering to you right now, please know that you are not alone. Maybe you're also a woman with a complicated story. You need to know that what you've been through and even what you've done is not who you are. There is always a reason to hope again because your story isn't over yet.

There is a place for each of us in the Body of Christ and in His kingdom. We are intricately designed to fit in a specific place just like a puzzle piece. What we've gone through won't be wasted. It will be used to help others. Don't give up just because you've been hurt, labeled or betrayed. We can't afford to give up just because we might have gone through something painful or failed in some area of our life. Some people might not receive us, but there are others that will. We need them just as much as they need us! When a person comes out the other side of failure what they have is grace. *Abundant* grace. It enlarges a person's heart to show love greater than they could before they experienced failure. When God shows us His unfailing love and mercy there is such a deep appreciation for it. Grace is never just for us; we have a responsibility to extend it to others as well. To whom much has been given, much is required. I never really understood that phrase until I went through some difficult things. We have an obligation to give away to others what we have received from the Lord. Grace gives others the benefit of the doubt even though we may feel they don't deserve it. None of us deserve it, but grace treats others the way we would want to be treated. God has a people prepared that will not let personal judgments taint the gospel or distort the message of grace. God's kind of love and grace confounds those that are wise in their own eyes. This is the amazing grace God has shown me. I know He wants others to know of His great love. He will restore anyone that is willing to come to Him. Jesus said in John 6:37, **"Those the Father has given me will come to me, and I will never reject them."**

The truth is no one is defined by a moment of weakness or a personal failure. There is a quote that says "Every saint has a past, and every sinner has a future." Aren't you glad we have a future in Christ? We are not defined by what others may say about us or the labels they might want to apply. We are defined by what we do when we force ourselves to get back up after failure and try again. We are defined by what GOD says about us! In the whole span of our life, the painful things are but mere moments, or chapters in our life.

We overcome by the Blood of the Lamb and the word of our testimony. First of all, the enemy cannot argue with the shed blood of Jesus, for it overcame all the power of hell. The blood of Jesus speaks on our behalf, no matter how scathing the accusation. All of heaven must listen and acquit when it comes to the blood of Jesus, for His atoning sacrifice was not in vain. Romans 8:33 says, **"Who will bring a charge against God's elect?"** Hebrews 10:17 is another wonderful reminder that God himself has said he will not remember our sins and lawless deeds. The accuser will try to remind us of our past, but when he does we can turn it into an opportunity to share what God has done for us.

Everyone has a story or maybe several testimonies about times when they've gone through something really hard. Believe it or not, rejection, accusation, failure, betrayal, pain and loneliness are often part of God's plan. If we never experience trials, injustice and betrayal, how can we identify with the sufferings of Jesus and understand what He went through for us? Who else understands the deep pain and bitterness of these sufferings than one who has gone through it themself? There is one thing I know for certain. Every person will face the purifying process. All people will be sifted, tried and their faith tested before the King returns for His bride. Everyone will face a day when their life encounters a crisis, their faith fails and life falls apart; and in that day, they will seek people that have answers for the questions of their heart. They will need the testimonies and experiences of those that have gone through the fire and come out healed. They will not care about what religion has branded different individuals. They will not care what stigma a person has on their life. People will cling to the lifeline of hope through our stories. They just want to know what God did for us in our time of need. They will want to know how we got through tough times, and that is when you will have a captive audience hanging on your every word. God wants us to have the answers that give others hope. He wants us to be able to identify with the pain of others and have the keys to unlock their hearts. A person that has been hurt has two options: They can keep themselves locked up behind the walls of pain, distrust, fear and rejection and hold on to their pain; or, the person can unlock the door to their heart and let God in so that He can heal them. God is a gentleman; He will knock, but He won't enter unless He is invited in. Only you can open the door. **"Look! I stand at the door and knock. If you hear my voice and open the door, I will come in, and we will share a meal together as friends,"** (Rev. 3:20 NLT).

I want to encourage others in the fact that sharing our experiences is what makes our Christianity authentic. People are so afraid of being judged that they have a hard time being honest. Some people will never admit their disappointing moments to others, but just about everyone has experienced failure. The problem is people fear rejection so they often only want others to know the parts of the story they're comfortable with. The reality is we will never set anyone else free if we are too afraid to share our stories. People don't care so much what made someone else a success. They want hope to get through the difficulties of their own life. People want to hear about our problems, broken hearts and shattered dreams. They want to hear about the God that doesn't give up on us when everyone else has walked away, or when life has gotten so difficult they don't know where to turn to for answers. Because they're sitting on the edge of their seats, waiting to hear what came next, when the Lord of the impossible showed up to change the situation. People want to hear about the God that can turn *their* mess into a miracle. There is a God that I have encountered that is so big He can handle any problem you have. He doesn't get intimidated, frustrated or fearful because He can create whatever is needed to fix your mess. Isn't that wonderful news? That ought to give you something to smile about!

The painful times allow us to examine deeper issues of our heart and begin to ask the right questions. What made us vulnerable to failure? Are we going to throw in the towel when everything seems to be against us, or will we continue to be faithful to the Lord? Will we trust Him when we've been mistreated by others? Will we take justice in our own hands or allow Him to oversee retribution of justice? Will we abandon our integrity when we feel that He has abandoned or forgotten us? Until we know the answers to some of these questions we will never be ready to fulfill God's greater purposes. Tough times cause us to grow and learn from experience. Failure was God's plan for me and my husband. Without going through the things we have, we would not be the people we are today. So I own every part of it; the good and the bad. And now, this brings us to my story.

◆ ◆ ◆

Some years prior to my coming to a particular church, the founding pastor left and the church was given to his son-in-law and daughter. Behind the scenes the influence of the founding pastors was still very strong. Some of it was good, but other things were not so good. Religious control put a veil over people's understanding. Their eyes became focused on man rather than on God. The older pastor had a great emphasis on prophecies and Old Testament stories which were wonderful to listen to; however, the emphasis was put upon the law rather than grace, and that legalism permeated the church mentality. Whether people understood it or not, that was where the root issues began. Legalism is rooted in control, not faith. Whenever a church gets away from the gospel of mercy and forgiveness, trouble is not far away because the doctrine is compromised and unbalanced. A spirit of error brings deception. It twists truth and uses it inappropriately, which also makes room for a perverse spirit. One wrong spirit will always bring more with it. Wherever there is legalism there will be a misuse of authority, and use of intimidation to control the people. What the church lacked was the revelation of Jesus Christ and the message of love and forgiveness. The foundation was laid upon prophetic revelation and good teaching of Old Testament stories. And so, it made room for the curse to come in.

When the founding pastor turned over the church to his son-in-law, many people who had been following the man began to drift away from the church. Some left because they sensed it was unhealthy. The church was overextended financially as well and in many ways it was like a slowly sinking ship. Although grace began to be preached more and more from the pastor who took over the church, the Old Testament mentality of legalism had infiltrated the heart of the church and began to quench the Spirit. There were many other things that were spiritually out of balance. Every time the new pastor made an attempt to do something different it was met with resistance. A religious spirit refused any variation of the form established by the founding pastor. The numbers were still diminishing by the time I started attending the church, and it seemed to be a gradual process that continued for years. It had become a small, ingrown church stuck in the wilderness. Many people were really not ready to grow spiritually.

Going back several years before "the big failure," there were some things going on that were huge factors to what would happen later. One of those things was the fact that I had taken a position at my church as secretary. There wasn't much that I wasn't involved in. I worked in the church office, assisted on the worship team, organized outreach activities and led Bible studies. I loved what I did but it was my position that also allowed me to be privy to a lot of sensitive and confidential information. It didn't help that I was a single woman that worked directly with the pastor, and it made me a target for a lot of gossip, speculation and eventually, accusation.

A short time later it became apparent that the enemy was creating an uprising from within. Jealousy, competition, and insecurities allowed wrong spirits to operate through others. Their perceptions were influenced by false judgments and wrong attitudes. I don't think they fully understood how much the enemy was whispering accusations in their ears and creating more issues. Many were led by emotion rather than praying and seeking God for wisdom. It was those same wrong spirits at work that influenced people to try and manipulate others, including the leadership. The enemy was at work long before people realized it, and he tailored his bait to each one's weaknesses. To some, it was the suggestion of coming into a new place of power, authority or influence in the church. For others, it was the thought of getting rid of those they were jealous of; and others, it was the desire for a feeling of importance and acceptance by gathering others to them through gossip. What people either didn't seem to recognize or didn't seem to care about is how they played right into the enemy's hand, and how they contributed to the rebellion, slander and fault finding that tore the church down from the inside. Nothing prospered and a growing number of people were busy pointing fingers, trying to find someone to blame. One night I walked into a mid-week prayer meeting and sat towards the back. I entered the room just in time to overhear some people in leadership and a few others praying about a certain matter that I recognized as a plot to remove the current pastor. Trusted intercessors that had been a part of the church for many years were involved. Several of those people had been a part of the church long before I ever arrived. I tried to leave as quietly as I could, unsure of what to do with what I had just witnessed.

To say I was shocked was an understatement. I was afraid for everyone concerned. Regardless of what people might think in their personal opinions, rebellion against God's authority is not a matter to be taken lightly because authority is established by God. Orchestrating an overthrow is never a good idea. I didn't know what to do and tried to slip out without anyone seeing me, but it was too late. I didn't usually attend those prayer meetings because I led a Bible study a different night of the week, but that night I did. They saw I was there and they knew their intentions were discovered. One of the things that was especially difficult for me to understand is that two of the people involved were people God used to bring me to salvation. One had been a spiritual mother to me. These women had been instrumental to me coming to Christ and getting established in the church. I felt like my heart had been turned upside down. From that moment on, growing opposition against both me and the pastor grew rapidly and there were whispers of a wrong relationship between us. Accusations quickly became very bold, confrontational and there were a series of meetings where people were taking their feelings, gossip and suspicions to a whole new level. At the time, there was honestly nothing between us except for a close working relationship and friendship, but the enemy had an agenda to fulfill and the gossip spread like wildfire.

Two of the main instigators pushed harder and harder to eliminate me from my position and take over in the youth ministry. They succeeded in gathering about a dozen people to go along with their rebellion. At this point the church was definitely in a much more severe financial state due to all the problems. Some of the people involved had pressed other people to withhold their offerings, which made things a lot worse financially. The enemy aggressively pursued his lust for power and control and was working through as many people as possible.

About 6 months later, we were ambushed. Someone had infected our computers with spyware. Without our knowledge, people had been silently monitoring the correspondence between the pastor and me. For almost 6-7 months and perhaps longer they looked for any information they could find to try to build a case against us. They had hand-picked selected emails in an attempt to frame us and prove to others that their accusations were justified. These people sent packages of the emails to others in the church. They also sent them to other churches and ministries within the network of pastoral relationships both in the community and at large. All of it was done anonymously, of course. We knew who was involved but we couldn't prove it. The enemy loves to hide behind secrecy and anonymity in order to avoid accountability. Every person has a Judas somewhere at some time in their life and we had ours. Those that received them shared them with others. When an enemy rises up against you it is always with the goal to destroy credibility and a person's ability to influence others. An enemy in your life causes division and forces people to take sides. It was an attempt to totally discredit us in the eyes of others and cause people to lose faith in us, which is exactly what happened. Subsequently, it allowed the enemy's influence to grow even stronger. The church was falling right into the enemy's hands of his plan to divide and conquer. A house divided <u>will fall</u> and eventually it did. What we found out later is the main instigators that started much of the rebellion had done this to another pastor and destroyed another church before coming to this one. They had left their former church while under church discipline. They had done something similar in this same church many years earlier, but the issues had been forgiven and they had convinced people they had changed. Their offenses had never been healed, though and eventually resurfaced. Their rebellion caused others to follow them and share the guilt of their sins. In the end, they left a path of destruction behind them.

It felt like we had been publicly raped. We were definitely on trial. Later I figured out there were people that knew what was about to happen but didn't say anything. There were others that were also indirectly involved, although we could never prove it. At the time a few stepped in and tried to shut down the attack but the seeds of suspicion were already sown. We had been set up and we knew it. Many people had already passed judgment against us. That was when the battle was really lost. From that point on, things continued to grow in intensity. The stress was becoming unbearable. More and more during this time of intense battle the prophetic anointing continued to increase in my life. When I looked at certain people, I could literally see demons as if they were staring a hole right through me. It is eerie to look at someone you know and see the hatred of hell starting back at you! Devils are not tormented by our humanity; they are tormented by the presence of the Holy Spirit in us. Devils are afraid of the authority of Christ and they are fearful of anyone that can see through their agenda and expose them. People feel the torment caused by their own guilty conscience and become a pawn for the enemy to work through. When the presence of Christ in a person's life causes others to feel convicted of their sin, persecution will always arise towards the object of the enemy's torment. It was clear that this battle was very, very personal. This was the first church I had ever attended after getting saved. I did not understand what it meant to be put in God's boot camp, but that was my training ground.

I think what surprised me so much is the blinding effect the enemy had on others. Truth is often found in shades of gray. It's not always what appears to be in black and white. Discerning truth takes into account the bigger picture and involves motive, intent, hidden deception and much more. No one can arrive at truth unless they are willing to look beyond what they see as surface issues and look to what motivates people's actions. The enemy enjoyed every moment as he created more and more illusions in people's minds, yet no one stopped to consider that it was simply a smokescreen for what he was really doing to take control of the church. In hindsight, I recognize how the enemy worked on people to get them to keep secrets rather than expose what he was doing, myself included. I feared confrontation and I mistakenly thought I could pray things through. Intimidation is a trademark of the Jezebel spirit at work. During the time that these things transpired, it seemed as if no one wanted to be the one to stand up against the workings of the enemy. And so, the enemy that was allowed to be there continued to wear people down and accomplish his goals. More and more people gave themselves over in one way or another to cooperating with the enemy. He exploited their fears and weaknesses. The congregation members were tearing down the church from the inside out. Fear and control, rebellion, gossip, backbiting and suspicion over ran the church. Criticism and judgments replaced love. The atmosphere was charged with bitterness, anger, offense and negativity. It seemed like the more I prayed, the worse it got. And just when I thought it couldn't get any worse, it did.

One day unexpectedly, I had an encounter with an individual that had a significant amount of influence in the church. She came into the nail shop where I was having my nails done. As we sat across from the table from one another, I knew the Holy Spirit wanted to minister to her. She had been retreating from fellowship and her responsibilities at the church for quite some time. I knew that something was not right although I didn't know exactly what it was. I was concerned for her and wanted to encourage her. I reminded her of her talents and how she could be a blessing to others if she would take the step of faith to get involved again, but she had been hurt in the past and those wounds kept her from moving forward with the Lord. Though she had walls up, I still tried to encourage her in her relationship with the Lord. Eventually we came to a place in the conversation where I asked her if she would trust Jesus to heal her and give her a fresh start to touch the lives of others. I could not believe the words I heard when she looked me right in the eye and said, "NO. I am not willing." I was shaken by her response. Neither of us spoke after that, and I left there knowing that something was very, very wrong. There were things she had spoken during our conversation that didn't sit well in my spirit. She insisted Jesus did not have to love anyone; He just had to fulfill his duty. I disagreed with her perspective, reminding her that He was full of compassion, and that it was love that compelled Jesus to endure the cross. She just shook her head and got very silent. Her heart was hardened towards the Lord.

In a moment of unguarded honesty, the mask slipped off and she revealed something deeply significant about the reality of her spiritual condition. A great deal was exposed about the spiritual dynamics at work within the church. Situations continued to escalate and many just looked for a scapegoat to blame for all the upsetting things going on in the church. The same people that had been present at that prayer meeting many months before were insisting that there was an adulterous relationship between the pastor and myself, and they insisted that I be removed from the church. We were friends, but not lovers. Only the pastor and I knew that their accusations were false, but others believed the rumors. There were many times I wanted to leave the church, but my pastor was not just my pastor; this man was my friend. True friends don't abandon one another just to save their own skin or make their own life more comfortable. There was a plot to overthrow him and set in the authority the enemy had in mind. I felt sick that the enemy was using accusations involving me to take him down. Many people were against him, but I believed in him, and I believed in the anointing in his life. I always have. When everyone turned against me, he was the only one left that seemed to believe in me. I was simply not going to bail out just because it was the easier thing to do. Although I wanted away from all the turmoil, I refused to abandon him.

There were many difficult decisions to be made all the way around. The betrayal ran very deep. Fear of how others would react was a big factor. The problem with fear is that it will keep people trapped in pride and pretense even when they know they need to take action. So many people are stuck because they fear being judged by others that may not understand their situation or offer compassion in a time of need. When ministers feel this pressure, their choices affect both their personal family as well as those in their congregation. Loss of security, finances, job, reputation and relationships are all at stake. It is a lot of pressure. Sometimes that fear seems so overwhelming that they try to keep up appearances rather than take the steps to resolve serious problems that require change. When people are in ministry, their marriage becomes an example for others to follow; if things are out of order, those spiritual dynamics become transferred to the rest of the congregation. What is evident in the head is reproduced into the body. When spiritual leadership has unhealthy relationships in their life, they have open doors to the enemy. Those same open doors affect those that have accepted their leadership. Whatever people are submitted to has authority over them and their family. This is what had happened in this church. The spirits operating in the leadership affected the health and spiritual dynamics of the entire church. Power struggles were in just about every home. Fear of being judged is a very real trap that many people fall into. They fear being misunderstood or pressured by others that will only give a religious answer. I don't tell you these things to make excuses but to help people recognize that we can never help others if we are busy judging them. People will never ask for help from those that judge them. A man that I cared for and respected was going through a very difficult time in his life. I was too. When you work closely with someone day in and day out, you can't help but notice some of the personal pressures and difficulties others go through. That develops compassion. Our friendship deepened in spite of - indeed *because of* - all the opposition against us. We each felt as though we had no one else to turn to. Without all the false accusation and stress from that situation perhaps things would have worked out differently, but those things served to forge us together.

Circumstances can make or break anyone, and the truth is, we had both reached a breaking point with all the conflict and opposition. The situations involved had reached a boiling point and demanded decisions. It seemed as if everyone had an ultimatum. We tried to protect one another from more of the onslaught and figure a way out of all the mess, but the whole ordeal had gotten increasingly worse over an extended period of time. When the enemy devises a plot, he is not impatient in calculating every move. Not everything was public knowledge. Many things occurred privately that others were not aware of, and rightfully so. It wasn't their business. When a person's life is in the public eye there are many things that are known, but there will always be things that are not. Sometimes the things that are hidden are known only by God and the individuals involved.

I don't know exactly how to explain what I felt back then, but there was a very strong sense of fear and evil, and that demonic presence managed to influence a lot of people. There were a few times I knew I was being followed. I was at a park one day and someone drove up and snapped pictures of me before getting back in the car and racing off. I would see car lights stop in front of my home at night and drive by slowly. I came home to accusing messages on my answering machine many times from people that tried to intimidate me. One couple followed me after church one night and blocked my car in a driveway while screaming obscenities and threatening to sue me because they felt I was responsible for them being asked to step down from their positions as youth pastors. They didn't see that it was their own behavior that had caused it, or the fact that they were inciting rebellion in the church and bringing division between the youth and their parents. I can't tell you the turmoil I felt from all of this. The enemy was doing his best to incite more and more fear. I did not know enough about how witchcraft operates at the time we were going through everything. Now I understand that people gave that negativity momentum and gave the demonic force power through destructive emotions. It was a very strong influence that assaulted us from every direction. When we went to church, it was there. Neither of us could escape it at home, either. Everyone has a breaking point, and we had reached ours.

Though there had been stressful opposition, accusation and warfare against us, we fell in love. Eventually, in spite of all our good intentions, we failed and fell into sin. It wasn't when everyone had already judged us and assumed we were guilty, but near the very end of all this we did have a serious fall from grace. I know that because the accusations and suspicions eventually came true, people felt it must have been true all along, but that was not the way it happened. Before anything romantic occurred between us there was a commitment of loyalty towards one another. We could see where things were headed but we were going to stand with one another regardless of the outcome. We knew we were going to end up alone and that was another reason we clung to one another. We had both felt starved for love and beaten down by people we thought we could trust. I realize others felt betrayed, but so did we. We felt abandoned, judged and rejected. The pressure was intense and brought great discouragement. The thing the enemy most wanted to avoid and railed against was us coming together; but somehow the exact opposite occurred. In spite of the many people praying against us, the opposition and warfare served to forge us together in a deeper commitment toward one another. None of it was done with intent to be rebellious. We sought comfort. That's not an excuse for sin or errors in judgment; it's just the reality of what we had gone through. One thing I learned though this is that it is so easy to be critical of other people's lives but if we fail to recognize their emotional needs we will never be able to help people through their difficulties. Lack of compassion causes human beings to be hard hearted but the love of God compels us to offer support. Emotional pain, grief and the feeling of being unloved can cause people to do things they might not do under different circumstances. The emotional, physical, social and spiritual deficiencies in our lives become the weaknesses the enemy targets, so these things deserve to be mentioned. If we want to be in a place of strength when the enemy pulls the trigger and forges weapons of mass destruction, then we need to examine our lives for places of weakness and vulnerability, for those are the areas the enemy will strike. Sometimes he hits us hard in the place where we feel strong and don't feel a need to pray about; at other times he strikes where he knows we have a void. Love began to heal us and give us hope for the future in spite of everything that was happening around us. Please understand neither of us are trying to justify wrong actions; I am simply trying to explain as honestly as I can our emotional and spiritual state when things occurred. It was never intentional to hurt or offend others. We didn't want to fail God or disappoint ourselves and others, but we did. The final point of confrontation came when certain people tried to force this man to choose their ultimatum, but it backfired. The people never thought he would walk away from everything, but they had no idea how much he had struggled to make things work with little success over the course of many years. Norm had planned on making an announcement that he was stepping down but things blew up before the announcement could be made. He had wanted to try to locate interim leadership but never got a chance to do so. The enemy was losing control and took one last strike: he thought he could force a man that had already been spiritually undermined, attacked and accused to do what others demanded. The decision to step down had already been made, so he left. God would have to settle the matter and reclaim the church His way, but it could not come by the forced will of others.

My husband and I take responsibility for our wrongdoing and admit we failed. There were a lot of areas in our lives where we were vulnerable to falling, and we learned many lessons from that experience. We both deeply regret the pain, offense and disappointment we caused others to feel towards us. In the midst of the battle, we all wanted to protect what we held dear. But for some it was not about love; it was about winning at any cost. It was also a difficult thing to grasp that people we once felt were family didn't stop to think that we were equally hurt, disappointed and grieved by their actions towards us. There were some very spiteful things done towards us that were completely unnecessary. We weren't the only ones tested. Others were too. There were days when it felt like it would never end. During the years we lived in Florida some of the harassment continued by those that had given themselves over to a religious spirit of persecution and demonic torment. For the longest time I did not understand why people continued to go out of their way to harass us. We were 2000 miles away! They even went so far as to contact people we were associated with in an attempt to persuade others to have nothing to do with us. They continued to broadcast our sin to others in an attempt to shame us and told others their reputation would be tarnished   if they associated with us. When we moved back to California, it started up again from some of the people that still nursed their grudges. They contacted anyone they thought we were connecting with and tried to discourage them. Random, offensive emails from individuals that were consumed with bitterness and unforgiveness continued for many years. Some people wanted to make sure we never forgot about our failures and desired to have us live under the heavy weights of condemnation, shame and intimidation.

Jesus said we would know what spirit people are of by their fruit. People are held accountable to the doctrine they live by as well as the spiritual fruit in their lives. God examines each person for the fruit of love. False brethren are wolves in sheep's clothing that try to blend in with other Christians but don't have the Spirit of Christ nor do they walk in love. They walk in offense, judgment, unforgiveness, pride and rebellion. They are unrepentant and will turn the hearts of others away from godly principles by twisting scripture and using it for selfish gain. Forgiveness, restoration and reconciliation always have demands and strings attached because acceptance is conditional upon meeting certain criteria. Jesus never responded that way. True believers walk in forgiveness, restoration and humility. Their love is made evident by the ways they seek to bring healing to others. The Spirit of God inside the believer always pursues reconciliation because that is the work of the Holy Spirit. The Spirit of the Lord is Love, and Love cannot deny Himself. He longs to reconcile broken relationships and make them whole. He longs to restore the lost back to right relationship with His Father. Sometimes people do not know what spirit others have in them until they encounter circumstances that strip away the mask of pretense. When people are tested, what's in their heart is made evident by their responses. Many people are tested every day without them knowing it! God calls us to be wiser than the enemy. Sometimes we need to examine the fruit of others in our lives. If we continue to make excuses for the bad fruit in the lives of others, it will eventually come back to bite us. It is like trying to keep poisonous snakes and thinking you won't eventually have to deal with snake bite. It doesn't work that way. Bitterness, jealousy and other negative emotions will bite you, and they will infect and defile others if they are allowed to have a place in people's lives. Sometimes relational changes are necessary, and at times, though it may come painfully, God separates us from others so that we *can* change.

Please do not judge other churches or Christians by what I've shared through my testimony. It's true that there were many things that went wrong in that little church, but that doesn't represent the majority of Christians or churches. Every one of us is broken to some extent. We all have flaws, feelings and experiences that have left some wounds on our heart. Everyone needs to grow in love and grace as they learn to walk with God. There were definitely those that gave themselves over to wickedness and had evil intent; but the rest of them got swept up in the wave of emotion contrived by the enemy. Many people allow their emotions to get out of control at one time or another and do things they might regret later. That is something we are all guilty of from time to time. Knowing this about ourselves and others should enable us to have compassion and extend grace and forgiveness to those that wound us. Granted, it often takes time, but we need to remember that the enemy is our enemy; not people. Hopefully everyone learned some valuable lessons just as we did. The Jezebel spirit is an enemy against Christ and His church. The enemy had an assignment against the people in that church and unfortunately, carried it out effectively. It has all been forgiven. I know the majority of those people were hurt, fearful, confused and offended by everything that occurred. The enemy took advantage of their weaknesses and blind spots just as much as he did to take advantage of ours. Those painful trials taught us both some very important lessons about human nature. Anything we fail to surrender to God becomes food for the enemy, and Satan waits to make prey of us. The enemy will use any open door we carelessly leave open, and he will use our unhealed wounds and offenses to hurt and offend others. It is easy to judge someone else's life and think, "Oh, I would never do this or that. I wouldn't let the enemy take advantage of me to do the wrong thing or cause pain to someone else." The reality is none of us can truly answer that because we don't know some of the things we're capable of until we're tested. Tests don't come when we feel capable of withstanding them. Tests come when we're off guard and vulnerable. Given the right set of circumstances, any one of us might do a lot of things we never thought we would do. If we judge others when they are being tested, that judgment is going to find its way back to us and boomerang back into our own lives. Satan has a way of making things sound so reasonable and justifiable when he's working a lie and baiting someone to cooperate with his schemes, and he exploits people's pain. The only thing we can be sure of is whether or not we choose to forgive things that happen to us and not allow bitterness to have a place in our heart. That helps keep the doors to the enemy closed so that he can't find something to exploit. The second thing we learned is that the old saying 'time heals all wounds' is a myth. No, it doesn't. Forgiveness is what allows people to heal. Offense creates more offense and those that carry unhealed wounds end up hurting others. Regardless of the reasons why people incur emotional wounds, the important thing is that we each surrender our hurts to the One that can heal us.

Though we offered to meet with people months later to put it under the blood of Jesus and work towards closure, it wasn't the closure others wanted. People were persuaded to have nothing to do with us, and only a few opened their hearts to us. We wanted to shut the door to offense but most did not respond. I know that some people felt as though God failed them because they prayed expecting God to change the situation and it didn't end up the way they hoped. The truth is there was no point in saving what everyone else insisted on saving. If God does not answer the way we pray and hope for, then He has His reasons. Sometimes we don't have the benefit of knowing those reasons, but our disappointment doesn't mean that God has failed anyone. It just means that God had a different plan. Our eyes need to be on Christ. When we put our trust in God, our faith can remain stable even though situations around us may be quite tumultuous.

> "The enemy will use any open door we carelessly leave open, and he will use our unhealed wounds and offenses to hurt and offend others."

Many people wanted to put all the emphasis on saving this man's marriage because they thought it would save the church, too. The church and marriage were a package deal. They would have been happy keeping all of it on life support but the reality is that both died a long time before. The church became a magnet for a demonic presence because the Holy Spirit was no longer honored or the spirit in control. People were full of fear and afraid of change and so many tried to control the outcome of the situation. Control is witchcraft. Everyone seemed to be so desensitized at being immersed in an unhealthy environment I don't think they understood how painfully sick and diseased it really was. There was a lot we didn't understand ourselves until we were broken free from it and experienced a healthy spiritual environment. The church suffered because there were open doors to the enemy. It needed new leadership and our failure caused that to occur. It removed some of those that needed to be removed and scattered the wolves. The church needed leaders without ulterior motives. The predators and opportunists needed to be removed. Deceitful individuals took advantage of people's vulnerability and trust. There was much more to the story that what a lot of people understood at the time. The main problem through a lot of those events is that people rode the wave of emotion rather than getting the mind of God through prayer. Gossip is a big tool of the enemy and he used it to his advantage. People judged by what they heard and what they thought they knew without really understanding that through it all, God still had a plan. It wasn't their plan, but His plan was to set His people free from a very toxic environment.

Sometimes we need to admit that failure is God's plan for reasons bigger than what we might understand at the moment. So many people think that when trouble occurs they can blame it all on the enemy. It isn't always the enemy. Sometimes God is involved in the demolition process, too. He cannot build on a faulty foundation. Any master builder knows that without a proper foundation, the rest of the building is unstable. That isn't just applicable to churches; it applies to individuals, marriages and other things, too. God will tear something apart in order to fix what needs to be fixed. He will tear up the foundation and start all over again. The foundation of any lasting relationship must be built on mutual trust, acceptance, humility, forgiveness, love and mercy.

We had been publicly humiliated and our names drug through the mud. I finally understood that no matter how many times I replayed it in my head, every possible variation of the story was bound to have the same ending. God could not and would not allow things to stay the same. The story was always going to end up with us cast outside the camp. It was the hardest thing either of us ever had to deal with, but it was far from over. The harassment didn't stop even after we left the church. I received hate mail, prank phone calls and people left ugly messages on my answering machine for many months. Another bombshell dropped on us about 4 months after we left the church when I found out I was pregnant. There were more rumors of course; that I had gotten pregnant on purpose as entrapment, but that was not the truth. We were committed to each other before that occurred. I didn't think I could get pregnant, so it was definitely a surprise when I found out I was. There I was, 38 years old, pregnant and unmarried. Everyone we knew had cut us off and wanted nothing to do with us. We had no job, church, friends and not one person left for a reference. Everything pertaining to our lives was connected to that particular church. We were out on the curb with no one left but God. It wasn't one of my greatest moments and I'm not proud of it, but there you have it. I told myself I'm going to surrender the secrets. I had to deal with a lot of shame and emotional pain. We married shortly after and then relocated to Florida.

Those events happened 10 years ago. I don't tell you about all the ugliness in order to glorify the works of the enemy, rather, to pull the covers off the enemy and expose his tactics. Recognizing his ways can help others be a bit wiser in the situations for their own lives. Maybe it can help save another church family from the ploys of the enemy to divide and conquer in their house. If you can learn from my mistakes and from what I've experienced, then maybe you can avoid putting your foot in a snare. I don't want anyone to have to go through the pain of failure, but in life we all stumble at times. When we do, we should stop ourselves from judging others and start asking each other, "Ok, so what happened, and what did you learn from it? What allowed the enemy to get one over one you? Because I don't want to be vulnerable to the enemy either. Tell me what you learned from your experience." When we learn to accept one another without judgments and tell our stories and testimonies, we can help each other heal. Honesty and acceptance of one another allows us to show compassion for one another and speak from a place of strength instead of shame. This is how we give courage to others to get back up again and get back into the Lord's army. We have to pick up our fallen soldiers, dress their wounds and get back on the battlefield. After all, aren't we all merely sinners saved by God's amazing grace? Where would any of us be without the blood of Jesus and His incredible love that restores our soul? Not once has He ever withheld His love, forgiveness and grace in our time of need. Freely we have received; freely we must give it to others. None of us can change our past, but we can all learn from it. That was the training ground God picked for me and my husband. God often trains His servants in the house of an enemy. Both my husband and I needed to learn discernment of what is commonly referred to as the Jezebel spirit of witchcraft. Trademarks of this spirit are very warlike. This spirit targets those that have unhealed offenses, power seekers and those that have issues with authority. It operates through a spirit of jealousy, pride, narcissism, rebellion and a hatred of male authority, specifically *Christ's* authority. The spirit is not gender specific; it looks for anyone that feels entitled to power, position or prestige and those that are willing to destroy others in order to take what they desire by force. You can read more about this evil spirit found in 1 Kings 21. It sows confusion, insecurity, fear and is unrepentant. It is a danger to the structure of families, churches and ministries, and to our nation. This destructive spirit isn't just in the church; it will thrive where ever there is a lust for power and control. It has an appearance of good but the spirit behind it is evil and self-seeking, and disguises itself in deception, hypocrisy and pretense. The Jezebel assignment always brings a perverse spirit with it, lying spirits, a spirit of murder, rebellion and much more. **"For where envy and self-seeking exist, confusion and every evil thing are there."** (James 3:16). God has a specific training ground for each person in order to help them learn and develop the understanding of spiritual things they need for the future. If I hadn't gone through the things I did there are many things I never would have learned. So for that, I'm grateful. God took me through those painful experiences that allowed me to grow through them. We need those experiences in order to understand what others feel, too. We also need certain confrontations with evil in order to exercise discernment and increase the anointing in our lives. I don't want anyone to have to go through the things I did, but I know there are many people that have also been spiritually abused. I have a message to those that have gone through spiritual abuse and persecution from the enemy: Forgive every bit of it. What doesn't kill you makes you stronger. *Once you're healed you have automatic authority and an increased anointing over the things you've conquered.* Staying hurt and withdrawn from others is the enemy's game plan to keep you from having authority over him. The ultimate victory is when a person surrenders their pain, unforgiveness, bitterness and offense and they let God bring healing and wholeness to their life. That's when they can recover all. It's when a person is no longer hurt from their past that they can share their stories without fear of how others might react. Failure can get embarrassing and messy, and the enemy is banking on the fact that if he can keep people intimidated by shame, he can keep them from telling their story. If he can keep people from telling their stories, he can keep them from entering into the strength of an overcomer, and others will never benefit from our experiences with the Lord.

No one is above being tempted by the enemy. No one is untouchable. The enemy can get to us all if God allows it. There are going to be times when we don't want to fail but we experience failure anyway. Instead of judging those that go through a failure, maybe we just need to understand that that is part of their personal journey. My husband and I had to ask ourselves some hard questions. One of the reasons we failed is because the enemy saw open doors of opportunity. Some were doors we didn't even know existed.

God wanted us to have the answers for our own lives, but He also wanted us to have the answers for others, too. He took us on a long journey to purify our hearts, motives, and pull out the weeds of spiritual error. We needed to be healed from a lot of things. It is amazing how many things people pick up along the way and accept as correct doctrine when it's really not. People justify a lot of things and hope God agrees with them. God took us through the wilderness to re-teach us things that had been accepted as doctrine but were rooted in religious pride and misconception. These things have a perverse spirit intertwined in them and it can be very difficult to separate truth from error. That is why there are certain things that can only be learned through experience. In the next chapter, I will tell you how God gave us a new beginning.

So, there it is. My big, bad, scandalous story of failure is out there for the entire world to hear. Whew! But you know what? There is such a sense of victory in overcoming the intimidation the enemy sets up in our mind. When we overcome our fear of what others will think and bring ourselves to be transparent about things we've gone through; when we tell others of our struggles and how God brought us through a difficult time, I have this feeling it gets the attention of heaven. The accuser, who stands by to slander our names and read off his account of our painful pasts, is put to an open shame and rebuked. "Silence!" Booms the thunderous voice of our Father. "You will not speak of this again!" He says. "The blood of my Son covers this child. I see no sin. Away with you, Satan!" And once again, Satan falls like lightning. The enemy may whisper his thoughts to bring fear in people's minds, but fear is ruled by pride. Fear of rejection, fear of being judged or what others will say is all rooted in pride. It's human nature to drive us towards self-preservation. I certainly understand that, because it had me over the barrel for a long time, too. This is how the spirit of Leviathan works. It uses the unhealed wounds, self-pity, rejection, shame and all the emotional entanglements to keep a person's heart tightly locked up behind the steel plated armor of pride. Of Leviathan in Job 41 it is said, **"He looks down on all that are haughty; he is king over all that are proud."** (Job 41: 34). The plated armor of Leviathan is literally impenetrable unless the person truly wants their freedom and healing. People must be willing to part with their excuses and their pride. God doesn't get the glory through our pride. The enemy does. It's what he uses to hold us captive. The last thing Satan wants is for people to share testimonies because he knows it actually empowers others to do the same. It releases faith into the atmosphere, and an increase in faith increases the potential for miracles, healing, deliverance and breakthrough.

I remember one church service we were in some years ago. A friend of mine got up and went to the front and took the microphone. She began to share something she didn't want to confess. She spoke of how she had sat there during the worship service resisting the voice of God because what God was asking of her would hurt her pride. Finally, she could not resist the deep conviction she felt from the Holy Spirit and that's when she came forward. It was an emotional experience to watch her humbly admit something that was embarrassing to her, but she did it in front of about 700 people. She told how her insensitivity had hurt a dear friend. Then she publicly asked forgiveness to the person she had offended. Her friend came forward and gave her a big hug. Let me tell you, it won the respect of everyone in the room. All of a sudden, people all throughout the church started confessing their sins and going to others to ask forgiveness. People were crying, hugging, and the Holy Spirit moved mightily. He was reconciling His body and mending relationships. NEVER underestimate what God can do with your humility! I wonder how many others He worked on that night before this one woman acted in obedience. Were there others He also tried to get a hold of that didn't respond? Sometimes we're not God's first choice, but He needs someone to act in obedience so that He can release His miracles. Never underestimate what He can do with your life and your story! Never underestimate what God can do through gut-wrenching honesty. The Holy Spirit can do more in a few moments of transparency and humility than we can ever hope to achieve through our own good efforts. Sharing testimonies is powerful. If one person can admit their failures, others are empowered to do the same. *Humility always conquers pride, and humility is what releases God to move.* That is why the enemy tries to shut people down. The angels know this, too. That is why heaven stands in awe when a person overcomes their fear and pride. Can you just see it? Angels look at one another in stunned silence. Worship is interrupted. Harps hang in mid-air. They glance at Jesus, and then quickly survey the expression of those around them. The look on their faces says it all: *She did it! She's not afraid anymore!* A roar of applause erupts as all of heaven worships and shouts in victory. They aren't chanting my name, oh no...They're praising Jesus. "*Jesus! Jesus! Jesus!*" They shout in delight."

That's *my* Jesus. *My* king. The One who stands beside me as I tell my story. He gets the glory and I get the victory.

And then, I notice my Father. He reaches towards me, and pulls another label from my shoulder. "Ashamed," it said. Not anymore. I see Him putting more jewels in my crown. He holds it up for me to see. "Grace and glory" is written inside a beautiful diamond. "Fearless," says one of the stones. "Bold-as-a-lion" is written on another one. "Compassionate and "The sword-of-the-Lord" is written on others, as He sets them neatly into my crown. My daddy smiles as he places it back on my head. "My child," He says, "I am so delighted in you!"

Holy Spirit,

I surrender the secrets. I surrender my pride, fear of what others will say, and a desire to protect myself. I have no self-righteousness on my own. Give me the Spirit of Faith to trust You with my life, my future and my reputation, and help me to be able to be transparent with others when it will help them draw near to You. I thank You that the god of self is dethroned in my heart. In Jesus name, amen.

CHAPTER ELEVEN

A Fresh Start

After many months God moved us to Florida. It was a tremendous shock all the way around, but shortly after getting there the Lord gave me a dream. It was interesting in that I knew I had been taken to heaven and in the dream I was on a gurney being wheeled into a vacant, yet very immaculate hospital. I saw no one, but I heard the Godhead speak. "What shall We do for her?" they asked. I heard one of them say, "Open her eyes that she may see Us." Then the same question again, "And what shall We do for her?" I heard a voice say, "Open her heart that she might believe in Us." I couldn't tell you which one of them was speaking, only that I knew I was overhearing the Godhead speaking about me as if they were right above me. They were about to perform divine surgery.

The Lord also gave me a song which came from that experience. It is a very simple song and I realize you can't hear the melody, but these are the words.

Oh He's the God of my wilderness
He's the God of my troubled soul
He led me by the brook
And He fed me so
That I might know His love,
That I might know His love

He came that I might know His ways
And follow after Him
And now I've tasted and I've seen
The goodness of His love

Oh He's the God of my wilderness
He's the God of my troubled soul
He led me by the brook
And He fed my soul
My well overflows with love,
My well overflows with love!

When you go through something traumatic and everyone you once knew rejects you, it is amazing to find out that the Lord does not treat us like those that relish the idea of our misery. He understands people's pain but He doesn't give his approval to acts of hate and vengeance. People that treat others with this sort of contempt will find themselves on the receiving end of God's discipline. He is with us through the fire and He promises to never leave us nor forsake us. What I've found is that there are a lot of people that want to tell others how God would respond in certain situations or how He feels about a matter when they have never personally walked through the same type of situation. It's so important not to leave people feeling condemned or put them at odds with a loving God. We need to be careful that we don't add to the discouragement of others by trying to tell them something based only on knowledge of scripture when we lack the experience. Our experiences with God are what breathes life into the word and releases life to others that hear our testimonies. The word without the spirit causes death of a person's hope, faith and trust in God.

Jesus was more real after our failure than at any time I had ever experienced up to that point in my Christian life. I remember waking up one night with anxiety over our future. I had just had a bad dream, yet when I awoke, I looked straight at the wall ahead of me and through the darkness of night I saw the name JESUS written in glow in the dark stars. I kid you not! I knew there were some of those glow in the dark stars in the room left over from some my daughter had put up a long time before, but I laid there for the longest time racking my brain as to how in the world they spelled out the name Jesus. And just when I needed a reminder that He still loved me, too. It looked like it had been written in cursive writing! I tossed and turned throughout the night but every time I opened my eyes I saw the name of Jesus before me lighting up the wall. All night long they glowed brightly and it brought me comfort. In the morning I got up and looked at the stars on the wall and in no way whatso-ever did anything come close to spelling anything legible, yet I had seen it so clearly the night before. He is so faithful to give us a sign just when we need it! Painful situations can either turn a person away from God or they can cause a person to run to Him. We chose to run to Him. His presence was real and His words of encouragement were powerful. His love was the glue that held us together.

A broken and contrite heart He will not refuse. **"A bruised reed He will not break, and smoking flax He will not quench."** (Is. 42:3) The Lord is always kind, even when we need correction. He will not crush the spirit of those that have almost lost their faith and hope in Him. Others may represent God in a different fashion, but religion is a poor substitute for the beauty of the Lord. Those that truly have the Lord's heart will come as a servant to restore the poor in spirit.

"But He was wounded for our transgressions; He was bruised for our iniquities. The chastisement for our peace was upon Him, and by His stripes we are healed." Is. 53:5

"He heals the brokenhearted and binds up their wounds." Ps. 147:3

I guess what puzzled me during and after that dream is why the Godhead said what they did. I thought to myself, "But I'm a believer. Of course I be-lieve in You." What I didn't know at the time is how little I actually knew of God's ways. I knew what others had preached and told me about God, and I had accepted the teaching of others as truth. Even though I had some previous experiences with the Lord, what I hadn't understood is how miserably short I fell when it came to truly understanding His heart. A soul that is wounded is prone to drawing the wrong conclusions. The Lord took us through the wilder-ness because of His great love and desire for us to truly know Him, and so that He could heal us. We had been bound by religion; bound by judgments and thoughts that came from other spirits. We were bound by people that wanted to see us fail; those that wanted to control us and bound by fear. It was literally choking out our faith. This is how a spirit of Pythos or the python spirit oper-ates. God broke us free from an environment that was toxic to our faith and growth. Failure was the tool God used to set us free. It hurt tremendously but sometimes God has to strike us in order to heal us and make the crooked places straight in our understanding. We needed to see Him for who He really is, and not what we were led to believe through our preconceived ideas, fears, insecurities and false perception. We needed to experience His miracles to learn His faithfulness and be able to trust Him. How often we feel that there are certain circumstances that we have to try and handle ourselves because we are afraid God won't take care of us. God stretches our trust level in order to increase our faith. If you cannot trust then *you don't have faith.* We had to learn that by repeated tests, trials and stretching. We think He needs to earn our trust yet it is us that need to earn His. I pray that you will find the same loving, faithful God that we did and know that no matter what you're going through, His purposes are always, always redemptive. You can trust Him. Jesus is your biggest fan, your greatest ally, and you will find Him to be your greatest encourager. He's in it to win it, and He will take you by the hand so that even when your knees are weak and you feel like you have no strength left to stand, He is there to hold you up.

"Fear not, for I am with you; be not dismayed, for I am your God. I will strengthen you; yes, I will help you. I will uphold you with My righteous right hand. Behold, all those who were incensed against you shall be ashamed and disgraced; they shall be as nothing. Those who strive with you shall perish. You shall seek them and not find them - those who contended with you. Those who war against you shall be as nothing, as a nonexistent thing. For I, the Lord your God, will hold your right hand saying, 'Fear not, I will help you.' " (Is. 41:10).

When we turn to the Lord and allow Him to comfort us, His presence is reassuring that our Protector is with us. Like a crying child running to their mother, He is there to put His arms around us and let us know His love will never leave us.

My testimony is messy. It's controversial. It's because it's controversial that I haven't been so eager to share it, because truth be told, at a certain point in the story most would stop listening and pick up their own judgments and then everything else falls on deaf ears. I had to lose myself in order to gain the pearl of great price, but it's worth more than you'll ever know.

I am so thankful that God always has a plan to outwit the enemy. I've learned to thank God for my failures. As my daughter Tausha always says, "I wouldn't choose His methods, but I would choose His outcome every time." All I can say is what others meant for harm, God turned it around for good. I have testimony after testimony of how God has done incredible things for us that I never could have imagined. The truth is failure isn't all bad. Yes, it hurts, but there are things we must each learn from personal failure in order to grow. Failure is only bad when you allow it to keep you down. I thank God for my failures because it's shaped who I am today.

If it hadn't been for failure at that little church long ago, my life wouldn't have gone in a new direction. I wouldn't have gotten married or had my two little children. They are precious and absolutely have a plan and purpose of God to fulfill. They have always been a part of His plan! If I didn't have them, I wouldn't have bad doctor's reports and children that never should have been born, but they were. Praise God for His miracles! If it hadn't been for failure, I wouldn't have moved to Florida and experienced tremendous streams of living water from the Holy Spirit. If it hadn't been for failure, my husband and I would not have experienced the miraculous provision of God time after time after time and have those testimonies to share. If it hadn't been for failure, we wouldn't have experienced the greater workings of God in our life, marriage and family, or have the experience and testimonies how to help other families get free, healed and restored. If it hadn't been for that failure, we wouldn't have met or joined forces with some very power-ful prayer leaders in that part of the nation. If it hadn't been for failure, we wouldn't have taken a very bold step of faith to sow our livelihood and watch amazed as God launched a ministry off of a little tuna casserole. We received a breakthrough so powerful it gave us influence with city leaders and brought many churches together in unity. If it hadn't been for failure, we wouldn't have broken new ground in ministry to the homeless in the city of Pensacola, and witnessed much powerful deliverance. We wouldn't have seen many forgive and go home to their families. We saw the people living in the local crack house get delivered and filled with the Holy Spirit. We have seen many physical healings, too. People delivered from seizures, healed from disease, barren women get pregnant, legs grow out and many more incredible miracles of healing. If it hadn't been for failure, I wouldn't have anything to write about or use to encourage others towards their healing. You see, what the enemy thought would destroy both of us actually got turned around and God used everything for good, just like He promised. Thank God for your enemies and your failures, for He uses them to anoint you!

For those reading this, I hope it has helped encourage your heart. If God can use a woman like me, He can certainly use you. He restored me, and He will restore you. No one has the ability to keep you down except you. God is rooting for you!

His grace is ABUNDANT and He does not condemn you, so please don't live in condemnation. Rise up and take new ground. You cannot afford to keep your testimony silent, no matter how messy it might be. This is how you overcome. This is how you take new ground. This is how you help someone else get back up on their feet and get back into the army of God. Be bold! Be strong! The Lord YOUR GOD is with you!!

Dear Lord Jesus,

I thank You for giving me a fresh start. Your words in Lamentations 3:22-23 tells me Your mercies are new every day. I do not need to fear because You are my Creator and you are able to make all things new. Every day of my life story has been written and recorded in the books of heaven. Let me fulfill what You have written for me this day, and every day hereafter. You saw the end from the beginning and have already written victory, restoration and blessing into my life story. It's filled with resurrection power and my future is bigger than I can imagine! Amen. So be it, Lord. Thank you.

CHAPTER TWELVE

Pulling Out the Root of Bitterness

You may wonder how a person can go through difficult and painful life experiences and come out without bitterness. I was very, very bitter after enduring some of the things I've had to deal with. In my younger days, it was that anger and a fighting spirit that enabled me to be able to endure some of the things I went through. Anger served a purpose in that it made me stubborn and tenacious. I resolved not to be taken down by people that wanted to destroy me. Anger and a lot of determination caused me to persevere. The enemy wanted me to succumb to despair, throw in the towel of defeat and walk away from God. There comes a time though, when God wants us to surrender the anger and all the things that we relied on to survive, and turn to Him. He's after our heart. He wants us to surrender and say, "Ok, Lord. I do not want the benefit of those things any more. I do not need rebellion, anger, or bitterness to survive anymore. I don't want to reproduce those things in the people I love. I'm willing to surrender all of it so that I can truly be free." This is what it means to worship God in Spirit and in truth. He wants us to pursue righteousness in our heart.

My husband says, "We can live focused on the woes of life, or we can live focused on the 'wows' of God. Focusing on our woes invites misery, but focusing on gratitude for the many ways that God wows us invites the presence of God to invade our circumstances. Praising God creates an atmosphere that is inviting to Him, and extends an invitation for God to invade your life and change your woes into wows." Norm is a very positive person. He is full of joy. He always chooses to think the best about others and his motto is life is too short to live with anger, bitterness or regret. Let it go. I thank God for my husband. One lesson he taught me early on is to praise God no matter what, especially in the midst of the storms of life. Worship is a decision of the heart to honor God whether or not we feel like it. Worship transforms us. Worship actually makes us more compliant, willing to change, and gives us a desire to please God.

A heart that refuses to worship God will retain negative emotions, lies in their belief system and unforgiveness towards others. Bitterness is often associated with anger and grudges. We will get to that, but I would like to first address that which is the result of deep unresolved emotional pain. Grief and loss attribute to a root of bitterness just as much as the kinds of wounds that are incurred at the hands of those that treat us with ill will, rejection and injustice. Some disappointments in life are directed towards certain life events that have occurred. Death of a loved one, broken relationships, financial loss or things that cripple a person's ability to bounce back, such as prolonged illness, can all cause deep disappointment and disillusionment. When a person's heart is broken and unhealed on the inside, it can make them hard and unfeeling on the outside. Bitterness always works together with a spirit of self-pity. Self-pity is more interested in feeling victimized, complaining and blaming God and others than it is in taking personal responsibility over those things and cooperating with healing and deliverance. Those spirits are like chameleons that manifest in numerous different ways, which can be hard for a person to identify. Bitterness and self-pity will release destroyer spirits into the life of the one bound by these things. Destroyer spirits, under the strongman of Appolyon, are given authority to hurt, torment, rob and plunder. Grief, despair and disillusionment have turned many people into accusers against Him. They believe He could or should have prevented their pain and disappointment. Blaming God always sets us at odds with Him. He resists the proud. Accusing God of failing us is the same as calling Him a liar. It's saying He is unfaithful and unable to be trusted. **"So God has given both his promise and his oath. These two things are unchangeable because it is impossible for God to lie. Therefore, we who have fled to him for refuge can have great confidence as we hold to the hope that lies before us,"** (Heb. 6:18 NLT). God is not man like us; He is our Creator and is deserving of honor and respect. Retaining bitterness is a choice. It is unbelieving, faithless and irreverent.

There are also life events in which people are offended with others for various reasons and refuse to forgive. The Bible says that unless we forgive those that have sinned against us, we are not forgiven, (Matt. 6:15). If we do not forgive, we are thrown into a spiritual prison and turned over to the tormentors until we have paid every last penny, (Matt. 5:24-26). To the degree that we forgive someone else's sins, our sins are forgiven. If we retain their sins, in like manner, so are ours. **"Whose so ever sins ye remit, they are remitted unto them; and whose so ever sins ye retain, they are retained,"** (John 20:23 KJV). 1 John 4:18 advises us of fear that produces torment. Fear with torment is the consequence for disobedience to God. I believe the fear aspect comes from our subconscious being aware that our heart is guilty before God. There is a part of our mind that may not be completely aware or in tune to the cause of the issue, but is not at peace. The tormenting spirit is there to drive us to God in repentance. It should be like a red flashing light screaming "WARNING!" in our spirit, because fear, anxiety and torment are symptoms that we have open doors to the enemy.

A key indicator that one has retained unforgiveness towards someone else is the evidence that long after the incident occurred; they continue to rehearse old offenses, perceived wrong and injury. Bitterness is a poison that grieves the Holy Spirit. It defiles and reproduces offense in others and causes many kinds of sin and iniquity. The fruit of bitterness is corrupt and will always produce evil. How often we chalk up bad fruit to something we consider human or harmless, when in fact the root is defiled and can only produce more corruption. An evil root will never produce good fruit. According to Romans 3:14-18, the person defiled with bitterness speaks in such a way as to curse themselves and others with poisonous words. Harboring unforgiveness and bitterness can cause a person to act with injustice, and destruction and misery are ingrained in their ways. They are not peacemakers. They have no fear of God.

> "How often we chalk up bad fruit to something we consider human or harmless, when in fact the root is defiled and can only produce more corruption. An evil root will never produce good fruit."

Misery loves company, and bitterness relives and repeats the woes of life. The chorus of complaints is led by a spirit of self-pity. The danger of self-pity is that it is the same as idol worship. Self-pity demands worship. It elicits worship from others in the form of seeking attention, sympathy, and affirmation (a form of praise). "Self" (the person controlled by the spirit of self-pity) becomes god and those that feed this spirit become the person's co-dependent supporters and worshippers. Self-pity cannot survive without feeding its need for worship, but the very essence of this root is bitter. It will only ever produce bad fruit. Narcissism also comes from these spirits, and narcissism is so deeply rooted that a person no longer feels a need to repent or take responsibility for their actions. The danger of one who allows self-pity and bitterness to remain is that it presumes a wrong view of eternal security. The person is deceived into believing that they are in right relationship with God, or that grace will always be available to them, though they walk in stubbornness of heart. It is the presumption of grace that causes a person to harden their heart towards genuine repentance, choosing a lifestyle of sin and compromise over obedience to God. The Spirit desires to do the right thing and forgive. A person's mind, will and emotions can be resistant, but it takes consistent, determined effort to resist the Holy Spirit and His desire to see them healed. That is why this is a sobering topic, for the penalty for retaining bitterness and unforgiveness is severe. It can literally cost a person everything, including their salvation. The ultimate fruit of bitterness is apostasy.

If it were not for the torment in our soul, would we stop to consider the cause? Would we not grow so tired of ourselves and our misery that we would then be willing to change? The enemy uses bitterness to defile a person's heart and defile others. His goal is to slowly but deliberately draw a person into deception so that they act presumptively to grace and make allowances for disobedience. This kind of behavior causes a person's heart to ever so slowly become insensitive towards conviction and the Holy Spirit trying to draw them back towards the Father. They gradually become so desensitized to their need to repent that at some point it becomes impossible for them to feel the desire to repent; and so, they become lost forever, eternally separated from God. Though it pains us to think that God would willingly afflict us with torment, every purpose of God is redemptive. The affliction does not come from God, it comes from the enemy. God *allows* affliction to torment our thoughts and sometimes our physical body to drive us into Him so that we can be healed. He is the Great Physician. How great is His love! How great is His mercy! He wants us to come to Him and inquire what is wrong so that we may be healed and set free from all toxic roots and deadly sins, but we are not set free from the consequences of disobedience until we repent. True repentance is a willingness to forsake that which has us entangled with sin. As long as sin festers, we are in chains, but in the day that we draw near to Him, His immediate response is, "Do not fear!"

The enemy is still the serpent from the garden that whispers in our ear, always about our head, whispering accusation, leading people into temptation and suggesting all manner of justification to do whatever we please. One day I was talking with my kids about the serpent in the story of Adam and Eve. When I told them all he did was hiss and whisper lies, my kids remembered the snake from the old Disney movie, Robin Hood. The snake's name was Sir Hiss. Now we think of the enemy and can laugh and say that's all he does, so we call him Sir Hiss-A-Lot. When one of us is acting badly or saying something that isn't truthful, we help hold each other accountable by issuing a gentle reminder and asking, "Have you been listening to Sir Hiss-A-Lot again?" It's a great way to get us back on track.

Let this be a little nudge to stop listening to that old snake, Sir Hiss-A-Lot. He's nothing but trouble, and if we listen to his suggestions we will always end up separated from God and others. It's when we realize how deeply our Father loves us, and the ultimate sacrifice Jesus paid for our sins, that we again bring ourselves to the foot of the cross, look up and wonder how on earth we are again crucifying our Lord and accusing Him of being unfair, unloving or uninvolved in our lives. It's the revelation that He is nothing BUT love, that it makes us feel sheepish and embarrassed for listening to the serpent and fighting against God that we can finally, with all sincerity, offer up our heart in our hands as an act of mutual love, trust and surrender to the One who gave it all up for us. This is where we are truly in Christ to such a degree that we are actually hidden in Him. The enemy can no longer see us, but he sees only Christ, and the Christ that defeated him before defeats him again and again and again as we remain hidden in the Lord. We are literally cloaked in invisibility but full of all power and authority. This is the enemy's nightmare, because Satan must obey the word of the Lord from His servants. This is how we cut the head of the serpent off and claim our victory; through submission to the Lord. A submitted heart is at peace with themselves, God and others, even if the world is not at peace with them. A submitted heart is not angry or fearful and doesn't take out their frustrations on others. A submitted heart yields to the Holy Spirit and learns how to demonstrate gentleness, kindness and love.

I pray that today is the day of revelation, truth and freedom from all the lies of the enemy. God's only desire in asking for your complete submission and for you to surrender yourself to Him is so that He can give you the exchange of

His power and His presence, and to be so lost in Him that you truly overcome all that has beset you. His desire is to bring you to a place of greater intimacy, to know His heart, His secrets and His strategies. What a great exchange! Our anger, fear, sin and twisted insecurities for His love, power and abundant life. May this be your day for inner transformation and lasting change!

Prayers of repentance and renouncement often take time to work into deeper levels of release. Our mind and will can acknowledge the necessity to move towards obedience to God and forgiveness, but the actual healing comes one layer at a time. Bitterness is demonically empowered and is very resistant to letting go of the individual. Even when a person cooperates with God, it can still take a period of time for the full healing to manifest, because every person is unique. The period of time it takes is strictly between the individual and God.

Genuine forgiveness loosens the root of bitterness and allows it to come out, for the only response more powerful than this toxic spiritual weed is love. When it comes to diagnosing our own heart, sometimes we can be pretty slow and downright inaccurate. We can't always trust our own opinion of ourselves, so we have to look for symptoms to make an accurate diagnosis.

DIAGNOSING THE HEART

A root of bitterness produces feelings like this:

- The desire for the person that wounded or offended you to experience insecurity, embarrassment, shame or hurt.
- A feeling that the person who hurt you is not worthy of blessing.
- The feeling that the person who offended you hasn't done enough to make up for the wrong they have done.
- A desire for them to receive punishment and judgment from God.
- They don't deserve to live.
- Criticisms begin to be directed at others and other situations.
- Bitterness loves to rehearse the past. It also manifests in defensiveness, slandering those that hurt or offended you and involves others in venting toxic thoughts and feelings.
- A bitter heart is an offended heart, and is quickly offended and frustrated with others, quick to lash out in anger. An angry person wounds others with harsh words and they may even catch themselves saying things they wish they would never have said, yet can't seem to stop

doing it. It delights in a superior attitude that infects others with poisonous words.

- Bitterness produces a desire to hurt, belittle, embarrass, shame or put guilt on others. It targets others with undeserved punishment, even though the perpetrator would be quick to deny it to themselves or others.

DIAGNOSING SELF-PITY

- Shifts blame onto others.
- Is easily angered and offended; pouts.
- Sees themselves as a victim. Makes excuses and refuses the redemption of Christ.
- Takes advantage of the compassion of others and manipulates their emotions so that others sympathize with them.
- Would rather complain about their problems than be healed.
- Elevates self-will rather than submission to God.
- Refuses to take responsibility and ownership of their areas of guilt and sin. Unrepentant.
- Prefers spiritual weakness rather than strength from obedience.
- Wears people out with incessant complaining and a need for attention for their issues.
- When confronted with truth, quickly changes topic of conversation. Has a knack of intimidating others and accusing them of not caring.
- Rejects true spiritual authority and embraces counterfeit authority or those that will not challenge them with truth.
- Focuses on self rather than Jesus; denies the power of the cross of Christ.

When bitterness and self-pity throw a party they invite all their friends. It's dangerous company. Those that have these spirits often seek others that will be a partner in a co-dependent relationship, because these spirits demand attention. They cannot survive without being fed! Do you see how they also partnership with rebellion towards God? These spirits are not your friends; they are treacherous enemies that create a deadly highway of corruption straight to the soul. Everyone has their down days and needs comfort and friendship; someone that will understand us and lend a listening ear. But, if it becomes habitual complaining about the many difficulties of life; if you have evidence of hell unleashed to destroy, devour and plunder the things concerning your life, I urge you to consider whether or not you may have allowed a spirit of self-pity a place in your life. It is a dangerous enemy that must be confronted and resisted at any and all costs. Self-pity always has an end goal of slowly dragging its victim into rebellion and apostasy. That is death of one's salvation. It is not worth it! Today can be a fresh start to renounce this wicked enemy of your soul and take back the authority that is yours in Christ.

The only way to know if you have truly forgiven someone is to check your heart: do you have compassion toward them? Do you want to see them blessed, happy and successful? How you answer that may be all you need to diagnose your heart. If there is any hesitancy, or you can't give a 'yes' answer, you may well need to examine your heart and ask the Lord to help you get free.

GETTING FREE

How does one arrive at true forgiveness? How does a person know that it is not just us trying to convince ourselves, but in fact an act of divine intervention that supplies the grace that allows us to genuinely forgive another person?

When wounds are deep and it seems that all our efforts fail to free our heart, what is required is both willingness on our part, and divine intervention from the Lord. He never asks us to do something that He does not enable us to fulfill. Jesus said we must forgive others or God cannot forgive our own sins, but He does not leave us without His help. He provides the grace to pull those stubborn weeds out of wounded, bitter hearts so that His love and grace will flow from vessels of integrity.

Until you see the offender in the light of your own human weakness and can bring yourself to identify with them as a person who has been wounded and made prey of by the enemy, it may be difficult to reach a place of genuine forgiveness. Healing comes when we can accept the fact that the person who hurt or offended us did so out of their own unresolved pain, their own fears or insecurities, and we are just as prone to making the same type of error if we had felt what they experienced. What would have happened if we had heard the enemy's logic as it had been whispered in their ears? How would we have reacted if we had felt the same emotions, listened to the enemy's twisted ideas of truth, and become prey to be used for wrongdoing? Could it be possible that we would have committed the same type of fault? Have you, perhaps in times past, done something similar?

I know that there are some things that are just plain heinous, such as unthinkable things predators have done to willfully harm others. Yet, they too were once just children. They were innocent until something or someone did unimaginable harm to their psyche. The wounded, if they are never healed, go on to become predators themselves, lashing out to hurt and offend others or willfully mistreat them. It doesn't excuse wrong behavior, but it helps us understand it. It is truly only God's grace that can intervene and allow us to see deep hurt and offense in this light. It is the piercing light of His love that allows compassion to arise, enabling us to forgive those that have hurt us. This is the divine gift of God's grace, to forgive with genuine humility of heart. The gift of divine grace enables us to do what we cannot do in our own strength. When your heart has truly released the person that offended you, you will know it because you will feel your heart soften towards them. You will experience the gift of compassion that allows you to be forever free from those old wounds.

> "It is the piercing light of His love that allows compassion to arise, enabling us to forgive those that have hurt us. This is the divine gift of God's grace, to forgive with genuine humility of heart. The gift of divine grace enables us to do what we cannot do in our own strength."

It doesn't necessarily mean that the person we have forgiven is off the hook with God, but it means that we are. If we are to ever recover real joy and peace, we must ask God for His ability to see the perpetrators through His eyes, for in doing so He also grants His ability to forgive. All human beings, no matter how grave their sin and faults are prone to being used by the enemy to inflict unnecessary pain. Undoubtedly, we all have been guilty of injuring others at one time or another.

It was for this cause that God sent His only Son, Jesus Christ, to walk among man and demonstrate Divine Love and Grace. Intellectually we may know this to be true and accept the word of God. But until we model it...live it...demonstrate it...we fall tremendously short of being Christ-like. Challenges with human relationships provide endless opportunities to demonstrate that we truly KNOW Him.

We must work through the issue until the emotional sting is no longer present when you think of that person or event. I pray that truth will set you free and that you will come to a place where you can trust God with whatever injustice, offense, and wounds you've incurred. Real repentance that pleases God is when the heart connects with our prayer and we truly *want* to forgive the one who offended us and get in right relationship with God. We have a genuine change of heart that feels compassion, forgiveness or even pity towards the one the enemy used to offend us, and it's not dependent on anything they do or don't do.

When God showed me the reality of my spiritual condition, I was sad at my own lack of faithfulness towards the Lord. Ultimately, that is what He wants us to feel when we realize our own sin, because godly sorrow leads us to real repentance. I realized that I had placed my faith and trust in a desire for justice, rather than praying blessing upon those that had hurt me. I needed to change my prayer and ask God to show them mercy so that they could be healed. I had not placed my faith and trust in the Lord to be my shield and defense. My confidence was in the wrong things. I had changed God into a god of my own understanding, yet I never realized I had done so.

Witchcraft is energized by negative emotions and anger. That is why we must do everything possible to purify our hearts and get rid of all unforgiveness, anger, offense, malice and bitterness. Christian or not, if a person operates in a spirit of bitterness and allows that to be released through their prayers, it will attract more demonic spirits. That is how the enemy reproduces a curse into a person's life. He creates the situation that allows a door to be opened, and then he has legal entrance. The only way to shut the door on him and get him out is through repentance.

BITTERNESS AND WITCHCRAFT

Proverbs 5 talks about the seduction of an immoral woman, yet the reference is to a seducing spirit that leads people away from loyalty to the ways of God and turns them into adulterers.

"My son, pay attention to my wisdom,

   turn your ear to my words of insight,

   2 that you may maintain discretion

and your lips may preserve knowledge.

³ For the lips of the adulterous woman drip honey,

and her speech is smoother than oil;

⁴ but in the end she is bitter as gall,

sharp as a double-edged sword.

⁵ Her feet go down to death;

her steps lead straight to the grave.

⁶ She gives no thought to the way of life;

her paths wander aimlessly, but she does not know it.

⁷ Now then, my sons, listen to me;

do not turn aside from what I say.

⁸ Keep to a path far from her,

do not go near the door of her house,

⁹ lest you lose your honor to others

and your dignity[a] to one who is cruel,

¹⁰ lest strangers feast on your wealth

and your toil enrich the house of another.

¹¹ At the end of your life you will groan,

when your flesh and body are spent.

¹² You will say, "How I hated discipline!

How my heart spurned correction!

¹³ I would not obey my teachers

or turn my ear to my instructors.

¹⁴ And I was soon in serious trouble

in the assembly of God's people". (Proverbs 5:1-14)

The "immoral or strange woman" described in the Proverbs is a warning against spiritual adultery and unfaithfulness towards the Lord. Dreams often reveal hints and clues of this spiritual condition. The seduction of demonic spirits is through twisting perception of truth and the art of deception. Proverbs warns us to guard our hearts against such perverseness and preserve our ability to discern evil. We must preserve discretion lest we follow the wrong thoughts and attitudes down the steps to death. If thoughts come to tempt you towards rehearsing offense, painful memories and other negative thoughts, recognize that this is the "immoral woman" attempting to seduce you away from being loyal to the Lord. It can also be called a Jezebel spirit because of the witchcraft involved. All witchcraft seduces people away from obedience to God and into idolatry, which God calls adultery. Spiritual adultery allows a curse to enter a person's life that will eventually rob them.

Bitterness works in tandem with a spirit of witchcraft to keep a person bound and deceived. In Acts 8:14, Peter encountered a sorcerer that was known to be quite influential in his city. Simon, who was also called Peter, rebuked the sorcerer for attempting to buy the gift of the Holy Spirit in order to gain access to God's power. But Peter said to him, **"Your money perish with you, because you thought that the gift of God could be purchased with money! You have neither part nor portion in this matter, for your heart is not right in the sight of God. Repent therefore of this wickedness, and pray God if perhaps the thoughts of your heart may be forgiven you. For I see that you are poisoned by bitterness and bound by iniquity,"** (Acts 8:20-23).

The King James Version uses the word "gall" in the above scripture. Gall in this portion of scripture means the essence of bitterness or poison. It has a stupefying effect. It is literally like a drug that intoxicates a person and allows them to be under the influence of another spirit. If we can't seem to recognize the truth of our own spiritual reality, often God communicates this truth through dreams involving drinking, drug use or addictions. Sometimes it will also manifest as a person having cancer or gall bladder problems, whether in a dream or in their actual physical body. When I had bitterness, I began to have severe gall bladder attacks. The pain was unbearable and literally drove me to God in prayer. I would have done anything to be released from that horrific pain! I could hardly eat anything because the pain was so intense. God started showing me the spiritual reality of retaining bitterness and what was produced in the physical body. I wanted the forgiveness to be genuine but I was stuck. I thought I had forgiven many times, but my heart was still in bondage. God wanted my heart to be free! I cried out to the Lord with the most sincere prayer I knew.

Bitterness is a poison that is not limited to emotions. It also begins to destroy the physical body. The message that may be communicated through dreams is one of being under the influence of a spirit similar to being drunk. This spirit of stupor literally desensitizes the person that is under the influence and blinds them of their own need to repent. Lying spirits whisper false realities, creating an illusion of deception in the person's mind and heart, keeping them bound to sin and iniquity. Many people get so used to listening to these wrong voices that they mistake them for the voice of God. A spirit of Python utilizes divination and witchcraft to bind a person's faith, vision, and dreams for the future. It causes the victim to feel hopeless. It literally tries to suffocate the life out of the individual. The spirit of Python (or Pythos, from which it originated) causes overwhelming tiredness, loss of desire to fulfill destiny and loss of vision. It steals God's vision and replaces it with a counterfeit. It becomes like a mirage or false vision placed before the person under the influence of deception. It keeps people looking back at past events rather than on the "new" thing God has for their future. It operates in pride, stubbornness, heaviness, depression and bitterness (Acts 8:23). It will counterfeit real prophecy with divination, which is from a demonic origin and a form of sorcery or witchcraft (Acts 13:6, 16:16). Divination defiles and often ends up causing bitterness and rebellion towards the Lord. False prophetic words often end in disillusionment and discouragement and turn a person's heart away from God. Divination utilizes prophecy for greed and profit, or the prostitution of spiritual gifts for selfish gain, (Acts 16:19; Jude 1:11). It also turns the grace of God into lasciviousness. This spirit is manipulative and deceptive. It uses flattery to gain trust and promote pride, (Acts 16:17). It squeezes the life out of individuals, churches, and those under its influence. The nature of a python is to constrict. Python is attracted to the flesh. The curse upon the serpent in the garden (see Gen. 3:14,15) is to "lick the dust," which speaks of our humanity or fleshly nature. (Man was formed of the dust, Gen. 2:7). The enemy is attracted to our sin nature for that is how he finds entrance and influence into our lives. The more flesh we display, the stronger his grip. Python despises worship and can result in "brass heavens" or an inability to break through in worship. Heart and breathing problems, back problems and other health issues, sometimes even death are the result of individuals that give this spirit a place to operate. Python often brings a spirit of infirmity with it. Python works together with the spirit of witchcraft, or Jezebel, a religious spirit that lusts after power and control. A spirit of lust (a consuming desire for power, sex, money, fame, recognition, etc. often accompanies the python and witchcraft spirit). Python quenches the Holy Spirit in a believer's life and withstands breakthrough, (Acts 13:8). It perverts the straight ways of the Lord though working with the perverse spirit. It brings a spirit of error and influences people to believe what is right is wrong, and what is wrong is acceptable and even approved, (Acts 13:8-10). Python promotes bitterness, rejection and encourages separation from others rather than seeking healthy, like minded spiritual relationships. It projects doom and unbelief on the future, stripping people of faith. Those under its influence often retreat from fellowship and isolate themselves from others in order to preserve themselves from further hurt or relational disappointments. It lies to those under its influence to destroy faith in God, and accuses God to the believer. This spirit does everything in its power to wear out the believer until all their strength is gone. The nature of a constrictor is to slowly suffocate and squeeze the life out of its victim. It hates worship, hates the prophetic gifts (which can see through its deceptive ways and identify this spirit), and it hates apostolic authority. It has no problem with titles, name plates or self-appointed labels, but it is terribly fearful of genuine authority in Christ. It will attempt to destroy, defame and defile God's appointed authority because it knows that the authority of the believer has the power to destroy the ungodly yoke of oppression and shed light on its deceptive ways. The reason it has such power is because it is a principality that influences and controls many other demons under its authority. It is important to understand that a principality is a demonic authority structure, and a government structure cannot be 'cast out.' Lower ranking demons can be cast out of individuals while a principality must be dismantled. The way we do this is through submission, and exercising humility and obedience to God. The prophetic word declared against this ungodly structure also serves to be the voice of godly authority to bring it to an end.

This spirit has entire geographic regions under its control. The only way to be free is through obedience to the Lord that denies the enemy a place to operate in a person's life. The more that people begin to repent and change their ways, the more it pulls down the enemy's authority structure. When people come together in humility and repentance, and really begin to walk in love, the enemy's house comes crashing down and it opens the heavens. Don't you want an open heaven in your home and over your city? Open heavens allow revelation, salvation, strategies, creative ideas and breakthrough to be released!

From a personal point of view, if one is blind to their own need to repent for something, it can seem quite harsh to try and seek answers and be stuck in darkness, but again, it is one of God's methods of communicating. If a person is a Christian and cannot hear from God, but *has in the past*, the silence is there to act as a wakeup call so the person will begin to ask the right questions. Disobedience such as refusing to forgive, withholding love, or denying the authority of Holy Spirit grieves Him and allows evil seeds to grow within us. These evil seeds grow and begin to choke out the life of the Holy Spirit, producing bad fruit. Broken fellowship with God and disobedience causes revelation to be withheld. Darkness and confusion keep a person stuck, confused and discouraged. Demonic oppression, affliction, disorder and crisis torment the life of the person that is bound. Understandably, many become angry at God because they do not see nor understand their own cooperation with the enemy. They may blame God for feelings of abandonment. Hurt, disappointment, anger and offense are not just directed at individuals but at God. A spirit of accusation and pride becomes their stumbling block, preventing them from receiving anything from Him until they repent and come humbly, acknowledging His ways are perfect and the fault is not His. Many people blame God for their lack of understanding and therefore perish for lack of knowledge. This is not God's fault. We have a responsibility to seek Him. He has made truth available through His word and His Spirit.

When the disciples came to Jesus and asked why they couldn't deliver a particular person, Jesus responded with the answer that some spiritually rooted issues could not be resolved *except* by prayer and fasting. Sometimes the truth you need to be set free will only come when you humble your body and allow the spirit man to become the stronger influence. Greater is He that is within you than he that is in the world. Bitterness is a poison. It is also elsewhere in scripture referred to as the "poison of asps" that comes through toxic words laced with death. (Ps. 140:3; Rom. 3:13; James 3:8). It brings a curse, often times brought on with our own words of negativity. That is why the Bible warns us to guard our heart, for out of it spring the issues of life.

"Pursue peace with all people, and holiness, without which no one will see the Lord; looking carefully lest anyone fall short of the grace of God; lest any root of bitterness springing up cause trouble and by this many become defiled; lest there be any fornicator or profane person like Esau, who for one morsel of food sold his birthright." Hebrews 12:14-16.

The reason Esau is mentioned in this portion of scripture is because there is a direct connection between a bitter, unbelieving heart and how it affects a person's attitude towards God. How a person relates to God also has a direct correlation to whether or not they receive their spiritual inheritance and fulfill their calling. Esau was defiled by bitterness. We know this to be true because Esau was so bitter he wanted to kill his brother. That is why Jacob took off to find refuge in the house of his Uncle Laban. Scripture ties the relationship of bitterness in the heart to a loss of inheritance. Esau represents the flippant disrespect of a faithless person that is undeserving of God's blessings. Esau is noted to be a fornicator as well as profane. Through this choice of words we understand that he was marked by contempt and irreverence towards the things that were held sacred. Irreverent also means blasphemous. Those are very strong words, but we gain an understanding of how serious it is to treat God with disdain. Scripture says that God loved Jacob but hated Esau. One must understand that the word 'hate' means indifference or *not to choose*. God did not choose Esau to inherit His promises because Esau did not choose to honor God or value the spiritual inheritance God had intended for him. In the natural, Esau was blessed. He had wealth and he had many descendants. But, he lost the blessing that had originally been intended for him. God allowed Jacob to take it because Jacob valued what Esau despised. The Holy Spirit was witness to Esau denouncing his inheritance for a bowl of porridge, and that became binding in the court of heaven. **"For you know that afterward, when he wanted to inherit the blessing, he was rejected, for he found no place for repentance, though he sought it diligently with tears."** Hebrews 12:17.

Esau is representative of the person that refuses to take God seriously and through casual disregard ends up despising God's good plan for their life. God's decision to not choose Esau is based on Esau's rejection of God. It is not a light thing to despise the goodness of God. Unforgiveness over a prolonged period of time becomes bitterness. Allowing bitterness to take root in our heart is dangerous because it causes a person's heart to be hardened. Our own sin cannot be forgiven under these circumstances, according to scripture. What is even more dangerous is to hold on to bitterness and resist God's gracious offer of healing. When we refuse what God has made available it is to deny the *cross* and disregard the blood that was shed on behalf of our healing and deliverance. It rejects Jesus Christ and tramples on the blood that he shed willingly on our behalf. **"How much more severely do you think someone deserves to be punished who has trampled the Son of God underfoot, who has treated as an unholy thing the blood of the covenant that sanctified them, and who has insulted the Spirit of grace?"** (Heb. 10:29).

It takes faith to trust God with our heart issues. It takes faith to trust God with those that have treated us unjustly. It takes faith to honor God with our responses. God is not looking for us to be perfect; He has provided for Himself the answer to our sinful condition through the atoning blood of His perfect Son, Jesus Christ. What God looks for is a heart that is perfect towards Him. He looks for a heart that is wholly turned towards Him and is quick to repent of wrongdoing.

If we were to count sin, who could stand? For no man comes to God on their own good works or proclaiming their own righteousness; man is allowed to draw near to God because of the propitiation of sins provided by God's own son, (Romans 3:25). Righteousness is imputed to us by the faith we profess in Jesus Christ, that His word is true and His character just. If we say we trust Him, then we must demonstrate that reality by turning over our offenses, hurts, wounds and desire for retribution towards those that have hurt us. Anything else is a lack of faith. It needs to be mentioned that once a person has truly forgiven the enemy will continue to look for ways to ensnare them again. We must be diligent to guard our heart and continue to pray that we don't allow bitterness to creep back in again. Pay attention to your dreams. Sometimes the Lord's warning comes in the form of a dream, especially those that somehow reference something from the past. Always seek Him for answers!

Previously I made the comment that I found myself at a crossroads. I was unable to remove the root of bitterness through simple prayers of renouncement, yet I was willing to be obedient. I earnestly wanted the forgiveness to be genuine. I did not want the ramifications of this bitter root in my life anymore. I told the Lord I was stuck and did not know how to proceed. Holy Spirit gently reminded me of times when I had been guilty of committing the same type of sin that I had judged someone else of doing to me. He reminded me of memories I had long forgotten. Yet, it was my own personal experience that allowed me to understand why I had acted in a similar manner many years ago. I then understood the emotions, thoughts and feelings of the person that perpetuated the hurt towards me. God gave me compassion towards those the enemy had used to inflict hurt. Faced with the truth, I realized I had no right to judge anyone else. All of us were sinners; each person has the same opportunity to be forgiven, healed and set free. If I elevated my judgments rather than mercy, the mercy I wanted God to extend to me could be taken from me.

"Speak and act as those who are going to be judged by the law that gives freedom, because judgment without mercy will be shown to anyone who has not been merciful. Mercy triumphs over judgment," (James 2:12,13). If we want to be the recipient of God's mercy, then we must do something to demonstrate we qualify for His mercy. It's called repentance. The decision was clear and my heart readily agreed. This was an uncollectable debt; it was no longer owed. And, at that moment, my own debt was released. My heart testified that forgiveness was genuine and it was complete. The root of bitterness had been extracted and I was free. Shortly thereafter, the gall bladder attacks went away. The body cannot begin to heal if it is not at peace. Releasing unforgiveness and bitterness and other toxic emotions allows physical healing to begin to take place. When compassion enters your heart towards those that have hurt or offended you in some way, you know you have arrived at a place of deliverance and healing.

Divine grace is a gift. God never commands that we do something that is impossible for us. He provides the means necessary to carry out our obedience. What He did for me, He can do for you, if you simply ask. Tell Him where you are stuck. Ask Him for this gift. Ask Him for the revelation that will move your heart towards compassion. It may be hard, but it's the right thing to do. His grace is sufficient for anything you need.

THE POWER THAT HEALS

So many people struggle with unforgiveness and bitterness. What is bound up inside of us causes restriction, constriction and can literally stop the flow of the Holy Spirit in a person's life. Bitterness will literally shut off the power of God. It is the power of the Holy Spirit that produces strength to overcome any problem. The joy of the Lord is our strength. It is the power of God that needs to be loosed in our life and in the lives of those we encounter that will reverse the curse and set people free so that they too can experience the goodness of God and worship Him.

Families are broken, churches and Christians are powerless and barren, businesses crumble, communities feel the weight of the sin and everyone that is affected suffers the effect of curses that need to be broken. Bitterness can cause poverty, barrenness, unproductivity, illness and death. The prophet Elisha understood the cause of barrenness. In 2 Kings 2, there is a story about some men in a particular city that sought him out and said, **"Please notice, the situation of this city is pleasant, as my lord sees; but the water is bad and the ground barren."** Bitter water is toxic and unable to be consumed. Whether it's in the natural water that we drink or spiritual food that we feed to others, if it's defiled, it will make people sick. Bad religion, anger, unforgiveness, jealousy, competition and other negative emotions will make a person sick and bitter. Elisha understood the solution to the problem, though. It's found in each one of us. **"And he (Elisha) said, "Bring me a new bowl, and put salt in it." So they brought it to him. Then he went to the source of the water and cast in the salt there, and said, "Thus says the Lord: 'I have healed this water; from it there shall be no more death or barrenness."** (2 Kings 2:19-21). Jesus said in Matthew 5:13 that we are the salt of the earth. He also warned us not to lose our 'saltiness,' or we'd be good for nothing. Salt is both a preservative and natural remedy used for healing. Water represents the sea of humanity. God wants our healing to be complete: body, mind, soul and spirit. Too many people are living with things in their emotions that make them sick, whether physically, emotionally or spiritually. The sea of humanity is walking around with unresolved bitterness and has allowed the enemy an open door to steal from them. The effects are found everywhere. God wants to heal what's in each and every one of us, and His plan is to use us to heal one another. This is the kingdom of God. The "new bowl" is the form of Christians moving out of the buildings and into their communities. It is being salt and light, releasing the wonderful 'flavor' of God into our families, workplace and communities through our prayers, testimonies, love, and grace; allowing the gifts of the Holy Spirit to minister to others. The act of 'being salt' is to release the healing power of God through the love of a pure heart, bringing gentleness and comfort to those bound by cords of sin. We can't take our bitterness with us. God wants us healed so that we can heal others. It's time to unload the baggage so that the power of Holy Spirit can flow unhindered.

The significance of water in Christianity is that Jesus described Himself as the living water in the story of the Samaritan woman found in John 4:13. Jesus told the woman, **"Whoever drinks of this water will thirst again, but whoever drinks of the water that I shall give him will never thirst. The water that I shall give him will become in him a fountain of water springing up into everlasting life,"** (John 4:13-14). Jesus also described Himself as the word of God that washes us clean, renews our mind, and makes us holy

(Romans 12:2; Eph. 5:26). Jeremiah 2:13 refers to God as a 'spring of living water.' The scripture in John 7:38 remind us of Jesus' words, that **"He who believes in Me," as the scripture has said, "out of his heart will flow rivers of living water."** Some translations say "belly" or "innermost being". When the Holy Spirit is released, healing and wholeness flow out of the very depths of our being. The LIFE of the Spirit will flow like a river. Ezekiel 47 also mentions a "river" flowing with life, and the leaves are for healing of the nations. Wherever the river flowed, there was life. By the same token, where water is stagnant, it allows for many impurities, parasitic microorganisms and toxic elements to collect. This is why it is so necessary to release the life inside of us. When we do, the river continues to flow, and the anointing is continuously replenished. Many fish (which represents souls) are drawn to the healing waters. The trees planted by the river gave good fruit which was used for food, and the leaves were like medicine for the nations.

God wants to release you from bitterness and the toxic effects of poison and give you a divine exchange. He wants to release rivers of living water inside of you. He wants you to be full of the Holy Spirit and full of joy, peace and strength. Holy Spirit wants to come and fill you with power that will be medicine to others.

Father God,

I want to be free and healed. I do not want bitter memories to prevent me from walking into a blessed future. I surrender my heart to You so that Holy Spirit can give me the power to change. I want no benefit of anger, a desire for vengeance, bitterness or rebellion any more. I surrender every lie, every bit of deception, every hurt and bad memory to You. I renounce all unbelief, irreverence and ask that You forgive me of grieving Your Spirit. I surrender the injustice, self-pity, the bitterness, unforgiveness, offense, resentment and judgments I have had towards You and others. I choose to forgive those that have hurt me (insert names where possible) and I ask that You forgive them, too. Heal their areas of brokenness. I thank You that as I have chosen to forgive others, I can receive Your forgiveness for my sins. I want to please You, so I ask for a gift of divine grace to be poured out into my heart. I ask You to enable me to see those that have hurt or offended me through Your eyes. Help me to see them through eyes of compassion so that I can truly forgive and be healed. I ask that You help me to have a soft answer that promotes peace and not anger. I ask that You heal my heart and help me to change my responses so that my words are kind and promote healing. Help me to recover my joy, Lord, for it is joy that becomes my strength to overcome. Help me to recover peace and experience Your presence in a greater way. Forgive me Lord, for I need Your forgiveness and Your mercy every day.

"Come, Holy Spirit! Spring up, O well! Let your river flow. Let your power flow. Let your river move all the obstacles out of the way. Let it cleanse, heal and restore my vessel. Holy Spirit, forgive me for any way that I have personally grieved you, retained unforgiveness or bitterness and made room for the enemy in my life. I choose to forgive anyone that has hurt or offended me. I realize those debts are uncollectable! Forgive me for quenching Your Spirit and drying up the river within me. Fill me to overflowing with Your love. Let the new wine fill this earthen jar and fill me with joy unspeakable and full of glory! Let my heart be released and may Your power overflow to my neighbors. Let it flow like a river into the streets and into our cities. Let your power be released inside of me to heal the nations and transform lives, everywhere I go, in Jesus name. Amen."

CHAPTER THIRTEEN

Healed From Abortion Regret

There is something that happens to a woman that struggles with identity, fear, and emotional pain. Far too many women are acquainted with the wounds of abuse, the fear of rejection and feeling unloved. When a woman doesn't feel secure in whom she is or understand that God is fully capable of providing for her needs, fear will drive her to make decisions contrary to her beliefs, personal convictions and desires. Women often compromise their own convictions in order to try and make other people happy. Women are life givers, yet in the United States alone there are about 3,700 babies aborted each day or approximately 1,350,500 annually. This is how far removed from our true identity we have gotten in our nation. Women are restorers by nature and physical design. If we have become anything less, we are denying the very person we were created to be! It's not that every woman has to be a mother, but every woman possesses certain qualities that are hers by the gift of God. We are life givers, but many of us have at one time or another succumbed to the fears that led us to make painful choices we later regretted. Millions of women are still dealing with abortion regret. They are among us as the walking wounded, suffering from symptoms of PTSD yet no one knows their pain because abortion regret is not typically something people talk about.

As in cases of PTSD (Post Traumatic Stress Disorder), symptoms may not show up for several months or even years afterwards. It includes flashbacks of reliving the abortion, upsetting dreams, and avoidance. Emotional numbing may include thoughts and behaviors that are designed to help a person avoid the emotional conflict associated with the abortion or the child that the woman was carrying. Symptoms can include anger, depression, and loss of interest in daily activities or things that were once enjoyable, overwhelming guilt or shame, difficulty sleeping, and self-destructive behavior, such as drinking too much. The majority of women who have an abortion end up regretting that decision and suffering with the pain of that choice for a long time afterwards. I was one of those women. Fear drove me to make a choice for which I later hated myself. I lived in the aftermath of self-rejection, guilt, shame and feelings of inferiority. This chapter is devoted to healing women from the deep and long lasting effects of abortion regret.

Women must be healed because they are the heart of the home. Whatever we carry inside of us produces a ripple effect. We can carry pain, bitterness and regret, but we will reproduce that into the lives of those we love. Or, we can carry the love of God and the power of His kingdom and release the kingdom of heaven where ever we go. When a woman gets healed, she can turn the entire destiny of her household. She will be an instrument of healing to her children, husband and other family members. She will release that healing into her community as well. God is raising up women in this hour to be tremendous instruments of His kingdom. God has taken great care to heal my wounds from the past that contributed to bitterness. He will go to any lengths to heal the areas of our lives where we still deal with unresolved grief. Even when we try to move on and have buried them so deep we have forgotten about them, He knows when we have broken places in our soul, and He wants to heal them. He wants us to be an instrument of healing to others. He wants our words to be medicine for the nations. In order to do that, He wants us to trust Him with all of our hurts, offenses, fears, insecurities and regret - and He is willing to go as far back and as deep as necessary in order to make us whole again. It took 28 years for God to heal me from this issue. I don't know why He waited so long, but He has His timing for everything. Maybe it is your time now. I pray that my story can help release healing to you. This is my testimony of how God healed me from abortion regret. I think you'll find it interesting how He chose to communicate His love.

The medical procedure of having an abortion may be over in a matter of a few minutes, but the effects can last a lifetime. My heart bleeds for the many, many women, children and families that are affected as a result of having an abortion. Like many other women, my choice was motivated by fear, not faith. I found myself pregnant at 16 years old. I didn't have the courage to tell my parents, because I did not anticipate a very understanding response had I told them. My boyfriend at that time was not supportive and resented having to take responsibility. I felt alone and had no hope of real help. I had no other adults in my life I felt I could trust, and was not really aware of where to look for help or other options in my small town. I wanted to keep the child and raise it, yet I found myself at a dead end with no apparent solutions. I was terrified and didn't know what to do. An older sister of a friend of mine who had had an abortion told me it was the practical thing to do to insure I had a chance at a decent future. I grasped that little lifeline of hope and believed at the time I was making the right decision. I was so wrong. Had I known then what I know now, I would have absolutely chosen to do something different.

At first, after I had the procedure I felt relief. I thought my problem had gone away. What I didn't count on was the whole host of other problems that kept coming long after it was over. The truth of what I'd done haunted me for years. I was overcome with guilt. For two years I had nightmares of looking for my lost baby and grieving over that loss. Of course, I was defensive of my choice once I had the procedure done, but several months after the fact I started really feeling the aftermath of my decision. I lost friends that did not share my same viewpoint on the subject. Others called me horrible names reminding me of my crime. I even found notes in my school locker calling me a baby killer. I felt like I was made a spectacle of in front of my peers and I was deeply embarrassed. I felt like everyone in my small town knew my sin, and many did. Someone called to anonymously inform my mother what I had done. I had to face my family in shame. It felt like no one offered compassion or understanding, and they had no idea the amount of emotional torment I was going through daily. Even the doctor had left me with a huge guilt trip, telling me about how I was going to 'pay the price.' Doctors today would probably not say such a thing because abortion is accepted and promoted as a woman's right to choice, but this one did. He was so right. I paid a huge price and had no idea the amount of fall out that one decision would bring. People can try to say that an embryo is only a little lump of tissue, but that is not the truth. There is a soul connection to that other life, and once it lives inside of you, your spirit knows it.

What many people refuse to speak about is the fact that the act of abortion is murder, and committing the act of premeditated murder brings a curse into a person's life. Not just those that have them, but those that assist and perform them as well. It is taking innocent life. So many people do not understand that they could potentially have unbroken curses in their lives. It's an open door that the enemy does not want people to think about. It can cause poverty, miscarriage, barrenness, broken relationships, a wandering, discontent vagabond spirit and other things. It also releases the spirits of death and hell into the life of the one that choose to end the life of another human being. This is the curse Cain had to endure as a result of taking Abel's life. (Study Genesis 4:10-12). Innocent blood cries out to God for justice.

Galatians 3:10-12 tells us that Jesus came to break the power of the curse, but the qualifier for that promise is that the just shall live by faith. Abortion is the result of fear and unbelief, not faith; thus it allows a curse to be activated until it is confessed and put under the blood of Jesus. 1 John 1:9 tells us, **"If we confess our sins, He is faithful and just to forgive our sin and cleanse us from all unrighteousness."**

My life prior to the abortion wasn't exactly what I would call healthy or happy as my home life was pretty dysfunctional, but afterward it only got worse. My spirit was left broken and battered. I had no remedy for the emotional issues. I tried counseling and all I got was more labels, a host of prescriptions and no real inner healing. I did not know Christ and would not know Him for many more years to come. A broken spirit will cause a person to do things they would not choose if they didn't suffer from grief and despair. Inwardly I felt like I was falling apart yet because I could not show it openly and I couldn't confess it to anyone, I suppressed it. Silent grieving became this tangled web of pain, depression, anger, and conflict. No one warned me that the emotional pain would snowball into bigger and bigger issues. The painful effect of all that inward turmoil would bring enormous guilt and regret as I looked for love in wrong relationships, tried to numb my emotions with alcohol and drugs, and the never ending string of bad choices that caused my life to spin out of control for quite a number of years. Somewhere in between all this there was a marriage, the birth of my daughter and a divorce, all by the time I was 22. I was a single mother with a two year old, struggling to make ends meet for many years. Life *was* difficult but not once did I ever regret the birth of my daughter, Jessica. She was the best thing in my life. I had never felt a love as intense for anyone as I loved her. I felt badly that she went through all that dysfunction with me, but I loved her more than life itself. I believe it was my daughter's love and prayers that saved my life. There was absolutely an assignment straight out of hell to destroy me, but love is a force more powerful than death. I know she could never see it then, but it was her love for me, and my love for her, that eventually pulled me in a new direction. God used her to save me. You think children can't fulfill great purpose? Sometimes we're the ones to save a child's life, and sometimes they are there to save *ours*.

At thirty-two I accepted Jesus Christ as my Savior but was nowhere close to being emotionally healed on the inside. That became a long process of healing one layer at a time. More years passed and I had long forgotten about the pain of my youth. Many years later I re-married and had a new family. At the time God unexpectedly showed up, I was 43 years old. Our family had just gone through a long period of financial instability, homelessness and had relocated to California from Florida. I tell you all this to let you know that it was just an ordinary day when all of a sudden the Lord showed up and decided to deal with all those years of suppressed emotional pain.

It was Mother's Day, 2009, and I received the surprise of my life. My husband and I were getting ready to go to church and as he was in the shower, he heard the Lord speak to him. We were getting in the car and he told me that the Lord had a word for me. I asked him to share it. My husband began by telling me that he had no particular thoughts about anything as he showered, and that what he heard was certainly not from his own thoughts. He told me he was absolutely clear it was God. I pressed him to tell me, curious what on earth the Lord wanted me to know. Norm said, "The Lord said that your son, who is 28, wanted to wish you a Happy Mother's Day. He wants you to know, 'it's ok,' and he will see you again one day." Well, I really came unglued and I burst into tears. My husband knew that I had had an abortion when I was younger, but I had never gone into much detail about it. I instantly knew there was no way on earth he could have come up with the age of that child. I had to quickly do the math, and sure enough, the child I had aborted when I was 16 would have been 28 that year. I was stunned. I grieved and grieved and finally let out all the pain I had suppressed for so many years. I cried for two days straight. I grieved over the fact that the child I had written off as dead was still very much alive in heaven. How do you explain that to another person? Nothing sounds like a good reason for why you made the choice to end someone else's life if you have to explain it to *them*. I felt such shame for that. Abortion is something that many women can do in private and think they got away with it, but nothing is actually secret when it comes to the reality of heaven as our witness. Do you have any idea how it feels to be confronted with your own selfishness, knowing that your own comfort and convenience were more important than someone else's life? Try explaining *that* to the person that just showed up to let you know they were still alive. Neither the Lord nor my son asked for an explanation, but the thoughts went through my mind just the same. No earthly judge or jury convicted me. They didn't have to. I was very convicted and I felt guilty. Absolutely horrible. I can't even explain how sick I felt about my own actions all those many years before. You see, a person can try to forget, but their spirit knows their guilt. Your spirit wants to know your sin is forgiven. I had brushed it under the rug with everything else when I accepted Christ as my Savior, but I guess God knew better than I did that I needed to deal with old issues in order to be truly healed from it. He will go as far back as necessary so that we can be made whole. I grieved over the fact that I had never had the consideration to give this child a name or allow him the chance to fulfill his destiny. And yet, I knew he was telling me that he forgave me for that selfish act. Not only did he forgive me, but he wanted me to forgive myself. He wanted me to know that he was ok and someday we would be together again. What a comfort! I can only give hope to other women because of the fact that I am 'in Christ.' I know that because Jesus is my Savior my sins are truly forgiven. I can offer hope to other women who struggle with the issue of abortion regret, because even when we have done the wrong thing on purpose, God can forgive that sin and make us whole again if we are willing to confess it to Him. I can offer hope to other women because I know that without a shadow of doubt that even when a baby's life has ended here on earth, I know with all assurance that they are very much alive in heaven. Aborted babies, miscarried babies, children that have left this earth prematurely are certainly in heaven with Jesus. I recently listened to the testimony of a young boy named Colton Burpo, who testified of his trip to heaven during an emergency lifesaving surgery at the age of four. Colton is a little older now and he and his father Todd have written a book called "Heaven is for Real." Recently Colton testified during an interview with Fox News that babies that died in miscarriage or an early death continued to grow up in heaven until they reached the age of young adulthood, and then they stopped aging. My husband was so encouraged by his testimony because it confirmed what he had heard in the shower that day. If we continue to remain 'in Christ' we have the assurance that someday we will be reunited with the children we have lost, but it doesn't mean that we should use that as a comfort to excuse our own responsibility towards preserving life and valuing every life that comes into the womb.

After all the crying, praying and asking God to send a message back to the son I never knew I had, I was finally able to forgive myself. I knew in my heart that was one of the things the Lord wanted me to gain from this encounter, but I believe there is so much more as a witness and a testimony to be shared with others, too. I had been 12 weeks along when I'd had the abortion. No one can tell me that life does not begin at conception. A 12 week old fetus is a human being and has every right to life as much as someone that has already been born. It is still a child, even if it is not yet completely formed and viable outside of the womb. That child has a mind, is forming thoughts and emotions and has the spirit of life within them. I told the Lord I didn't know what He called him, but I wanted to finally give him a name after all those years. I named him *Justice*. I gave him a name that was significant of what I had taken from him. I felt I owed him that. Giving him a name helped me to begin to really heal.

My hope is for women to find places to share their testimonies and help each other heal. We need to share compassion and love. My healing began on Mother's Day 2009. It helped to know that I finally gave my son a name and acknowledged his life. Sometimes our healing is tied to becoming the voice of the advocate and speaking for those that cannot speak for themselves. We cannot afford to suffer in silence. Injustice is the result of good people staying silent when they should speak up. We need to be a voice for those innocent lives that have their voice taken away from them. Babies enduring the pain of abortion cannot be heard. **Justice has a voice.** Imagine my surprise as *Justice* spoke that day on Mother's Day 2009. He used his voice to ask the Lord to give a message to me; a message of forgiveness, healing and hope. And now I offer you, the reader, the same message of forgiveness and mercy from our loving Father. He is very intentional to extend an olive branch of peace and He wants to heal us from our wounds.

I also write this to help other women take a new look at their convictions for being pro-choice. Perhaps it is time to look for a new perspective on an old argument. I believe we are strong enough and resourceful enough to come up with positive solutions. We do not need to destroy our most precious commodity. Children are our future. I don't believe the majority of women who choose abortion do so because they want to; I think they do so out of fear. Fear that they aren't able to care for that child, fear of becoming a parent or fear of a lot of unanswered questions. Instead of focusing on fear, perhaps you could focus on a whole new set of 'what ifs.' Perhaps there is someone reading this right now and you are pondering your options. What if this child has been sent to you because God saw something in you that you can't see in yourself, something this child will greatly benefit from? What if this is an opportunity to have your heart and life changed forever by the unconditional love of a child? What if this child will someday save you? What if this child in your womb is destined for great works someday in their future? What if this child could only become the person they need to become, are destined to become, only by coming through your womb, and the unique life experiences that can only be attributed to your specific family and situations that pertain only to you? Think back about the Bible stories of Tamar, Bathsheba, or Mary, the mother of Jesus. Consider these women's circumstances. One got pregnant as an older woman through the act of prostitution. One got pregnant from an act of adultery while still married to someone else and her 'boyfriend' (King David) had her husband killed. One was a teenage mom who hadn't even had sex yet and was about to be stoned *and* divorced before she could get married. How's that for some messed up, backwards state of affairs? Those were some pretty complicated situations! But without each one of these women we wouldn't have Perez, Solomon or Jesus. If God could get them through the things they faced, don't you think He can get you through whatever you might face? What if God chose you to raise this child and trusts you with a job no one else would do quite the same? When you stop to think about it, why else would He put a child in your womb? He is not daunted by the things that we fear. There are many things to consider.

Understandably, not all women conceive a child in love. Some are not given a choice, if a predator makes prey of them. It is a most difficult dilemma to try to decide what to do if a woman finds herself pregnant by someone that she despises or has been used to hurt her. Yet, even in the worst of situations there is opportunity to look for a different perspective on the issue if a person is willing to yield to God and allow their heart to be changed. Apart from God, yes, many things would seem to be an impossible task. But with God all things become possible. In our weakness God can give us strength to do what we cannot do on our own. Perhaps what is viewed as an unwanted pregnancy is an opportunity to change a destiny, to be a life giver instead of one who destroys life. Perhaps what the enemy meant for harm is an opportunity to allow God to turn something bad into a testimony of His goodness. Sometimes the greatest gift of life and blessing comes out of tragedy, darkness and despair. Perhaps you have that opportunity now. I implore you to please consider everything I have shared through my own testimony. We can all aspire to make a difference in another person's life. Many people would embrace the chance to love and nurture a child and give them opportunity to fulfill their God-given right to life and destiny. God can take any mess and turn it into a miracle if He is just given the chance!

We live in a nation that demands our freedoms and takes many of them for granted. The demand for free choice and women's rights to decide is in the foremost arguments on pro-life or pro-abortion. We have political leaders that will change their convictions on any given moment as long as it helps their political career path and gets them votes for popularity. We live in a society that has given their approval, whether by vote or by silence, that human life is expendable upon our whims as long as it doesn't inconvenience us. But the moment we stop fighting for one another we lose our humanity. Even the unborn have purpose. Though their lives are short lived, the conviction of these tiny lives brings many people to salvation. I cannot pretend that the child I aborted sent me that message in vain. There was purpose to it not just for my personal healing but as a message to be shared with others. Any sin can be forgiven as long as we bring it to Jesus and allow His blood to wash us clean. We can be reunited with children we have aborted, if we will just hold on to Jesus until the day we are called home. But, in the time we have left, someone has to be a voice crying out against injustice. Someone has to speak up on behalf of the children that are being deprived of life and destiny. It is not ours to take. Maybe if we all speak loud enough, together we can change the course of history.

Father,

I thank You that your grace and mercy is bigger than my sin, mistakes and bad decisions. I thank You that even when I've done the wrong thing on purpose, You are still willing to forgive me and You are able to cleanse me from all unrighteousness. I surrender my secret to You, and ask You to help me forgive myself. I choose to forgive myself and ask for healing from this painful event. Please heal my fractured soul and fill the emptiness with Your love and peace. I'm shattered and broken, Lord Jesus. I need You to put me back together again. Release waves of grace and healing and let them pour over me. Holy Spirit, set me free with the truth You reveal. Please let Your love release the healing that I need.

On behalf of those in my family, my ancestors and the forefathers of my city and community, I confess our guilt and ask You to forgive the sin of innocent bloodshed. Father, as a nation of people, we have made room for a spirit of death. Give us judges, leaders and government officials that will help stop the legislation that allows this great tragedy. Lord, I also know that the conviction of it must start with each individual. Let the value for human life be precious to each person. I pray that women would choose life for their unborn babies. I pray for the hearts of the people in our nation, in my family and in my city; that each of us would change, to value life and take the appropriate measures to protect and preserve it. In Jesus name, amen.

CHAPTER FOURTEEN

Breaking Generational Curses

Many people question why bad things happen. The truth is tragedy and difficult times happen to everyone. The Bible tells us that the rain falls on the just and the unjust alike. Troubles are not always an indication that a person is living with an unbroken curse. We live in a nation of people where many have forsaken God and have failed to teach their children the ways of the Lord. Generation after generation has failed to repent for the sins of their ancestors, and so, the judgment for those sins is revisited upon those that continue to sin without repentance.

The subject dealing with generational curses is a challenging topic for many people. There are a   variety of viewpoints on the matter. A person can easily find those who support and those who oppose various points of scripture. It is not my intention to provoke controversy or debate scripture. I can only tell you what I have found to be true by my personal experience and share my testimony. I cannot tell you how others may have arrived at their understanding of generational sin and the effect of unbroken curses. It is one thing to try to arrive at understanding based on what others may or may not teach. It is something altogether different when God gives it by revelation.

Exodus 20:4, 5 says, **"Thou shalt not make unto thee any graven image, or any likeness of anything that is in heaven above, or that is in the earth beneath, or that is in the water under the earth: You shall not bow**

down yourself to them, nor serve them: for I the LORD your God am a jealous God, visiting the iniquity of the fathers on the children to the third and fourth generation of them that hate me;" (KJV). This particular scripture is what seemingly causes a great deal of controversy. That was not really my starting point, however.

Sin is a word that literally means 'to miss the mark,' as in a standard set before us. The word iniquity, however, implies more than sin; it implies a person that is stubborn, unyielding and bent towards rebellion and wrongdoing. It also suggests contempt towards divine law and rejection of the will of God. The visitation of iniquity, as mentioned in the above scripture, meant that God's judgment occurred when parents passed on a lifestyle of sin and bad habits to their children. God's promise of blessing came to those that served Him and obeyed his commands. The difference is between those that love God, and those that hate; those who serve Him and those that do not. It's important to understand that the word 'hate' in this context does not necessarily mean what we commonly interpret from this word. There are various degrees of hatred described in the Bible. It does not always mean the opposite of love but some forms of the word mean 'not to choose,' or to 'love less.' God's choice in this word is telling us that those that hated Him were those that chose to live apart from relationship with Him and to choose none of His ways. Those that rejected Him would not benefit from His promises or blessings, and therefore received judgment upon their sins.

That sounds pretty common sense to me. If a person doesn't want anything to do with God and they won't honor Him or choose His ways, then why should they expect the benefits that He bestows upon His own children? Why do they have the right to accuse Him when things in their life fall apart or tragedy strikes somewhere in the earth? If people live apart from God then they don't automatically have His blessing or protection. The question that seems to plague Christians, however, is whether or not a generational curse can affect a person that is a believer. Let me ask you something. Have you noticed anyone in your family that seems to have repeated the same pattern as a parent or a grandparent? Do you or anyone in your family have a history of things like addictions, alcoholism, anger, rage or abuse? What about adultery, broken relationships, divorce or controlling behavior? Is anyone in your family an atheist, a practicing witch or warlock, or exhibit an unnatural affection for the occult and supernatural realm? What about things such as mental illness, untimely death, poverty and inherited disease? Has a parent or grandparent gotten pregnant out of wedlock only to have the same unfortunate pattern reproduce into the children and grandchildren? Sometimes the children are even the same age as when the sins occurred in the parents. Many of these things repeat from one generation to the next. Who do you think gave you and your family those things? Sickness, disease, poverty, repeated cycles of loss and all those things are a result of unbroken curses. They didn't come from God because those things do not exist in heaven. So where did they come from, and who placed those curses into the family line? Saved or unsaved, people recognize and understand the words "generational curse." The question isn't whether or not they exist in people's lives; the question is why more Christians don't have the victory.

The evidence is all around us. Many Christians live with marginal victory in their life. If sickness doesn't exist in heaven and God didn't give us sickness and disease, then why isn't every Christian healed? His intent is very clear in scripture that it is His will to heal. If every curse is broken then why isn't every Christian walking in victory? Why don't we see every Christian running around casting out demons, healing the sick, working miracles and turning the world upside down? The problem is not with God; it is with our understanding of His word. We can be saved, but people still perish for lack of knowledge. *Salvation is not the same as deliverance.* The effects of unbroken curses are not always a salvation issue. They are a deliverance and sanctification issue. There can still be areas of a person's life - habits and mindsets that are not yet renewed. We have to appropriate that victory Jesus won for us by cooperating with our own deliverance.

Most of my life, both before and after I got saved seemed extremely difficult. It felt like trudging through concrete. I could understand that life before Christ was difficult because I was on a really bad path. After I came into relationship with Christ there were still things that made me feel like life was more difficult than it needed to be, and it brought a great deal of discouragement to my faith. Although I was saved, loving and serving God to the best of my ability, there were definitely some things I knew were old cycles that didn't seem to be broken. Let me interject some background information from my life. Both my brother and my father died right around the anniversary date of one another. My brother died unexpectedly in boot camp at the young age of 17. It occurred the first week of August. My father died the last week of July some years later. I also suffered a miscarriage the last day of July many years after that. The timing of the dates did not seem coincidental as they all took place within about a week's time from one another. July and August were anniversary dates of death and sorrow. For years I had a curiosity about the odd occurrence of the timing of those events. It never occurred to me that it might be attributed to the possibility of a generational curse. Several generations of women suffered from miscarriage and one indirectly caused the untimely death of my maternal grandmother. Alcoholism ran in both sides of my families. Inherited diseases such as cancer and heart malformations were evident. My father had mental illness, I struggled with depression and others in my family were also affected with mental illness. Three generations of women got pregnant out of wedlock. A poverty spirit hung over my family for at least several generations. I also knew without a shadow of a doubt that there were particular spirits attached to my life. There were certain things that had been with me all my life. Fear was one of them. Lust was another. Even as an adult and a person committed to Christ, no matter how much I asked God to help me something was there to hinder my deliverance. In some ways, I felt as if I was a magnet that drew the same type of troubled people into my life. Each time I was left in a worse state. No one had to tell me I had demonic attachments in my life; I was well aware of it. The problem is, I had no one to tell me how to get delivered because the church I was a part of didn't teach on this subject. They taught that every curse was broken once a person came to Christ. While that is true, it's only half of the answer, and I needed the other half! I had no understanding for any of it at the time. In addition, I was doing everything I knew possible to do to live right and honor God. I went to church, I worshipped, prayed, devoured the word of God, tithed, and I did not socialize with others that were not Christians. I was serious about turning over a new leaf in my life but the enemy was equally serious about hindering me any way he could. I went up for practically every altar call and still did not experience victory the way I thought it should be lived out in a believer's life. I was in spiritual and emotional poverty. I was plagued with spirits of fear, lust, anger and other things I could not get free from. If every curse was indeed broken upon my salvation and coming to Christ, then why was I still living with the effects of unbroken curses? A curse does not occur without a cause, according to Prov. 26:2.

Miriam Webster Dictionary defines a curse as: 1) a prayer or invocation for harm or injury so come upon someone; 2) something that is cursed or accursed; 3) evil or misfortune that comes as if in response to imprecation or as retribution; and 4) a cause of great harm or misfortune: also torment.

There are certain things that open a door to the enemy and allow a curse to come into a person's life. Some of them are:

- Idolatry – Exodus 20:3-6; Deut. 27:15: Jonah 2:8; Isaiah 44:9-20; Jer. 1:16: 1 John 5:21; Ps. 16:4; Col. 3:5; Gal. 5:19-21; 1 Cor. 10:14; 1 Cor. 10:20-22; Rom. 1:23; Rev. 9:20-21.
- Cursing your parents or treating them with contempt – Lev. 20:9; Lev. 19:3; Deut. 27:16; Prov. 20:20; Mark 7:10
- Uncovering or exposing the sins of your father. (Can also be applied to either parent or spiritual fathers/mothers) – Gen. 9:22-24
- Stealing or cheating others –Ex. 20:15; Zech. 5:4; Matt. 5:19,20; 1 Cor. 6:9,10;
- Injustice towards others – Ex. 23:1-3; Lev. 19:15; Prov. 17:15; Prov. 29:27; Luke 16:15
- Adultery – Ex. 20:14; Matt. 5:28; Eph. 5:5; Rev. 2:20-22
- Unforgiveness, taking vengeance against others and bearing grudges – Lev. 19:18; Ps. 37:8,9; Matt. 6:14,15; Mark 11:25; Rom. 12:19
- Witchcraft and bitterness – Lev. 19:31; Ex. 22:18; Deut. 18:10; Deut. 18:9-12; 1 Sam. 15:23; 1 Chron. 10:13; Micah 5:12; Gal. 5:19-21; Acts 8:9; Rev. 21:8
- Putting one's trust in man and self-effort – Jer. 17:5,6; Prov. 28:26; Ps. 146:3; Luke 10:27; Matt. 4:1-25
- Those that do not do their Father's will – Matt. 25:31-46; 1 Cor. 6:9; Gal. 5:20,21; Matt. 7:12
- Those that practice deceit – Jer. 48:10: Prov. 6:16-19; Ps. 101:7; Rom. 16:18; Ps. 5:6; Gal. 1:8,9; Acts 5:1-11; 2 Cor. 11:13; Rev. 22:15; Eph. 5:6
- Murder – Gen 9:5; Ex. 20:13; Ex. 21:12; Lev. 24:17; Lev. 20:9; 1 Sam. 15:33; Matt. 26:52; Matt. 5:17-22; John 8:3-11; Matt. 7:1;
- Those that curse others or curse God – Gen. 12:3; Lev. 24:16; Prov. 24:28; Ps. 109:17-20; 1 Pet. 3:10; Prov. 18:21; Mark 3:21; Luke 12:10; Matt. 12:31,32

I can't list every single reference but you can read the scriptures for yourself. The principles of scripture are consistent and applicable in both Old and New Testament. Violating the commands of scripture can not only release a curse, but they can also act as spiritual blocks to healing and answered prayer. All of these sins violate either the law of loving God or loving others. The spiritual law of sowing and reaping is always in effect. If we sow something through disobedience, we may not receive the penalty of death as our sins deserve, but we will reap something. The effects of a curse produce many things. A curse produces loss. The spirits of death and hell advance against the individual to produce defeat, failure, and an inability to prosper. Those unseen forces cause health issues, mental and emotional troubles, hopelessness, fear, loss of finances, employment, broken relationships, divorce and many other troubles. Nothing works right. It's impossible to get ahead. Many scriptures also contrast the blessings of obedience. Blessings cause a person to do well and prosper. It's the complete opposite effect.

I understand all the reasons why people question the validity of this subject. Years ago, I questioned all those things, too. I had a religious answer but I didn't have spiritual insight. I hope that reading the scripture references and principles I noted above helps to clear up any confusion. I didn't have the answers to many questions. I couldn't reconcile the difference between what I thought I understood about scripture and the evidence of Satan's activity in my life. People can tell others what scripture says all day long; but when a person that needs deliverance walks away and doesn't have an answer that heals and delivers them from bondage, it really hasn't helped them at all. Someone is missing the truth somewhere because Jesus assured us "It is finished." The fault lies with people and their understanding of His word. People need answers for their problems. I was left wondering, *"Did Jesus really set us free from the law and the curse?"* If so, why didn't I see more victory in my life? Why didn't I see other Christians living in victory? Everyone I knew was just as messed up as the world. They weren't walking in peace, victory or wholeness either. They had no real power in their life. I knew there had to be something I was missing. It was that conflict between what I read in God's word and what I saw lived out in those around me that made me question everything I had been taught. I wanted to know the God of Moses, Abraham, King David, Joshua and all the heroes that saw the mighty works of God in their everyday lives. I wanted to know the Jesus that the Apostles knew, and do the greater works of Christ. Yet, I was struggling just to survive in my Christianity. Certainly there had to be more to life than what I had experienced. I felt like Gideon in the winepress who cried out to the angel of the Lord, "If God is really with us, then why has all this happened? Where is the God of miracles that we've heard about?"

People can look for reasons to disbelieve, debate the issue and have a *scriptural* answer, but it may not necessarily be a *spiritual* answer. I think perhaps some of the confusion and where people differ is found in the words people focus on rather than on the spiritual principles. The principles of scripture are consistent throughout the Old and New Testament. We are not just looking for the letter of the law, but the spirit of the law that helps us understand the intent of why it exists. Old Testament says, ***"You shall not worship them or serve them; for I, the Lord your God, am a jealous God, visiting the iniquity of*** *the fathers on the children, on the third and the fourth generations of those who hate Me, but showing lovingkindness to thousands, to those who love Me and keep My commandments."* (Exodus 20:5,6) The promise of blessing was conditional upon obedience. The Old Testament was very clear that God was not going to bless disobedience. Jesus Christ is the same yesterday, today and forever. Malachi 3:6 reminds us that God has said, **"For I am the Lord; I do not change..."** Do you think He blesses disobedience today? God is so gracious He doesn't give us what our sins deserve, but we never want to take advantage of that grace. We should honor it. The new covenant of grace was never intended for people to interpret it as though God will put a blessing on sin. The degree to which a person receives healing, deliverance and restoration in any aspect of their life is directly connected with their willingness to cooperate with sanctification. If we say we have no sin, we lie to God and ourselves, according to 1 John 1:8. We all have things for which we need cleansing. This is called sanctification.

Legalism is forcing someone to do another person's will. God gives people free choice to make their own decisions. It is not my intention to cause anyone to feel guilty, condemned or feel as if they constantly have to fear being cursed, but at the same time we each need to take personal responsibility for our choices and the consequences of those choices. The curse came upon people that refused to serve God or stepped outside of covenant through disobedience. When God's people entered into covenant with Him, God demonstrated His love by providing for their needs. His expectation both then and now is that people would love Him in return, and serve Him out of love and loyalty. He made a covenant with them and He was committed to upholding His end of the covenant. He expected them to do the same. A covenant relationship, like a marriage covenant, requires both parties to be willing, loyal and equally committed to one another. Breaking that covenant was considered to be like the actions of a traitor; disingenuous and adulterous in nature. Those that broke covenant were subject to the penalties of the law, which was not the least bit compassionate to human failure. God knew that no one could keep the law meticulously no matter how much they tried and that the law in itself could not make a person righteous. That is why Father sent His Son, Jesus, to pay the price that none of us could pay. He traded His life for ours; and through that act, redeemed all mankind and made a bridge between sinful man and a holy God.

Jeremiah 31:29-30 tells us, **"In those days they shall say no more, "The fathers have eaten a sour grape, and the children's teeth are set on edge.**

But every one shall die for his own iniquity: every man that eateth the sour grape, his teeth shall be set on edge" (KJV). What this means is that God no longer punishes His children for the sins of their forefathers. We don't have to keep living in the same habits, mindsets and sins of our parents and grandparents. We can stop blaming others for the things that have affected our life. We can stop making excuses and saying, "Well, my dad was like this and this is just who I am, or I am just like my mother. I can't change who I am." Yes, you can. Don't use that cop out! God didn't make you like that. We can make different choices and stop those things. We don't have to live with addictions, anger, lust or other things. We don't have to pass down more trouble to our kids and their children. God does not curse His children, but Satan *does*. And, though some things may not necessarily be transferred from our ancestors to us as punishment from God, *we still have to deal with the things that existed prior to our salvation.* Before we came into covenant with God, we were in a covenant relationship with Satan. We might not stop to think about it in those terms, but that is the truth according to John 3:18-21. Before we came to Christ we were under the law of sin and death and Satan was our master. The enemy knows our weaknesses and the areas where we are vulnerable to sin. He is right there waiting to ensnare us and take us back into captivity so that he can resume his place as our master. *It is always a fight for dominion.* If we allow him any opportunity, he will take advantage of us so that he can once again reinstate the curse. He has to have an open door in order to do it. Satan cannot penetrate the power of Jesus' blood, but he will enter any door where our disobedience has permitted him entrance. Our job is to master what once had us!

God gives each person an ultimatum, and it's found in Joshua 24:15. Joshua, who was the commander of the people of Israel, said: **"But if serving the Lord seems undesirable to you, then choose for yourselves this day whom you will serve, whether the gods your ancestors served beyond the Euphrates, or the gods of the Amorites, in whose land you are living. But as for me and my household, we will serve the Lord."** Every person has to make a choice who they will serve. People either serve God, or they serve the world and the ruler of the world. In the New Testament, we are faced with the same choice. **"Salvation is found in no one else, for there is no other name under heaven given to mankind by which we must be saved,"** (Acts 4:12). Thank God that Jesus became the answer we need to redeem us from the power of the curse!

"But that no man is justified by the law in the sight of God, it is evident: for the just shall live by faith." (Gal. 3:11). And, Gal 3:13 tells us:

"Christ hath redeemed us from the curse of the law, being made a curse for us: for it is written, "Cursed is every one that hangeth on a tree," (KJV). He took the punishment and the penalty for our sins upon Himself so that we might live free. 2 Peter 1:3 tells us: **"His divine power has given us everything we need for a godly life through our knowledge of Him who called us by His own glory and goodness."** Jesus made everything available to us through His death and resurrection. The legalities of what He accomplished on our behalf and what he made available to us <u>are</u> finished. Jesus does not need to do anything else. He died for our salvation, healing, wholeness, restoration and victory, *but* if a person never accepts Christ as their Savior then whose fault is that? It isn't God's fault. He made everything available but if you or I never make a choice to choose Jesus as Lord and Savior we would not be entitled to the benefits of salvation or any other promise that comes by faith in the Son of God. In like manner, we know that Jesus won the victory *for* us, but if we do not read our Bible or study His word, then how will we really know everything that is available to us? How will we know what permits Satan legal access to our lives? If we want the benefit of God's promises then there are some things we need to do to insure the promises come to pass. It is all available in seed form. The seed of the promise exists, but we have to cooperate with God. We must make sure we have broken agreement with the enemy and keep the doors closed so that he cannot re-enter. That means we need to take the authority God gave us and cast the devil out of our lives.

In Matthew 18:18-19, Jesus instructs us on the principle of agreement that is at work in the kingdom. Either we are in agreement with faith and obedience, or we are in agreement with a lie and compromise. We speak life or we speak death with our words. We choose life or we choose something that has death attached to it. Every time we make a choice, we choose who we are going to follow. Every promise is ours through faith, but people can be saved and still perish for lack of knowledge. It is our job to understand what the scriptures mean and enforce the victory that Christ made available for us. We don't need to live in fear or feel that we have to make everything about us and our works, but the New Testament is full of reminders that in order to draw closer to Christ, we also need to rid ourselves of the things that separate us from Him. Even the Apostle Paul struggled with sin. He said the things he wanted to do, he found it difficult to do; and the things he didn't want to do, he ended up doing. He wasn't perfect but God was still able to do mighty works through him. There are many people in the Bible that struggled with overcoming sin issues. It is our attitudes towards sin that is the biggest issue. God can handle our sanctification issues as long as we endeavor to keep looking to Him and surrender the things that hinder our transformation. Transformation is not a one-time deal; it's a continuous, life long process. This is what it means to abide in Christ. We abide in truth and obedience to His words and He lives in us to reveal our true identity as sons and daughters of God. Gratitude is the response of one who understands all that grace affords and what has been forgiven them. Gratitude should be the motivation of a person's heart to live a sanctified life. This is not living under legalism; this is the demonstration of our love for all that Jesus has done for us. Living in grace is a tension between two worlds. We don't need to wallow in condemnation if and when we experience a setback, for we all fall short of the glory of God. Yet, we still do our best to live in the truth of what we understand about God and His word. The fear of the Lord is to respect Him and live in right relationship to Him.

The evidence of our faith is living in the best of our ability in right relationship to God and others, and to enforce His word. In John 10:10 Jesus said, **"The thief comes only to steal and kill and destroy, but I have come that you may have life, and life more abundantly."** The enemy is a liar, murderer, a thief and a rule-breaker. Satan is a career criminal. That's his *job*. A career criminal is not going to abide by the rules or obey the law UNLESS someone ENFORCES the law. That is *our* job! If a person thinks that the enemy cannot rob, steal or mess with their life simply because they are under a new covenant of grace, that person is quite mistaken. If we do not exercise the authority that has been made available to us, then we will not experience victory.

Keeping God's commands and His teachings are our responsibility. I am all for the preaching of radical grace as long as it also includes the balanced doctrine of living in right relationship to God. Teaching on this subject is intended to be used as a means of learning from the entirety of God's word, and show the reader how a lack of faith and misunderstanding scripture can cause people to suffer and struggle unnecessarily. We cannot afford to judge ourselves by our own opinions. Jesus Christ paid the price to make it possible for all mankind to live in freedom, health and victory- *in as much as they are willing to appropriate that victory and live inside of covenant with God.* When we step outside of covenant, we are in disobedience and we open doors to the enemy to bring in the penalties for disobedience. I am so grateful for God's grace and mercy as I am sure you are too, but at the same time we cannot afford to have a false sense of security in thinking that it becomes a substitute for obedience. We must endeavor to fulfill our part of this covenant relationship.

Disobedience and idolatry release a curse. Deut. 28 gives an explanation to what released the curse. We find the scripture in the Old Testament, but the principle is still applicable today because **"we shall have no other gods,"** according to Ex. 20:3. We can only serve one god, and we have to choose. Jesus is not going to compete for our affections. Either we give our love to Him willingly or we let other things crowd Him out. When other things are more important than elevating Christ to the number one position in our life, we have idols. That's just the truth. Idols can be anything. They aren't just little statues. Modern day idols can be anything that entices people away from love and loyalty to God or impedes their ability to obedience and service to Him. Idols can be the pursuit of power, prestige, or position. It can be the pursuit of money and material possessions. It can be a home, business, or degrees and titles. Sometimes those idols take the form of extra-curricular activities, pursuits and passions that hinder a person's devotion to the Lord. Sometimes other relationships become the prime focus of a person's life which displaces God to a lesser importance than some other key relationship. While God understands the role we play in the lives of others and the needs that others look to from us, He also expects us to keep a proper perspective on holding Him in high esteem. We should not allow other people to displace Him on the throne of our hearts. Jesus went to the cross and broke every curse, but if we elevate other things to a place of idolatry, then saved or not, we will find ourselves dealing with devils. Idols can be anything that elevates our self-importance, independence and separates our affections from the pursuit of God. Jesus told us in Matthew 7:21-23 it wasn't just those that professed to know Him, but those that did the will of His Father that would inherit the kingdom. **"Not every one that said to me, Lord, Lord, shall enter into the kingdom of heaven; but he that does the will of my Father which is in heaven."** We have to do more than just call Him Lord. There is a need for personal relationship and demonstrating we belong to Him as we fulfill the will of God. When we put our relationship with God first, the rest of our lives and priorities will fall into place.

The question we still need to resolve is what causes generational curses to activate in a person's life? We know that the curse is upon all those that have not accepted Jesus Christ as Lord. What about the believer? We all have parents and grandparents that may have opened doors to the enemy of which we know nothing about. Here is the key factor to why people don't understand this issue: *We still have to deal with whatever was passed down to us through generational iniquity before we got saved.* God revealed to me in a dream that two very powerful demons attached themselves to me at the time of my birth. I didn't find out about that until about a year ago. I could not take authority over them when I first got saved because I didn't know they existed. Many years later I did learn about prayers of renouncement. From time to time I still do them just as spiritual maintenance. When I first got saved I knew my life was a mess but I didn't know how to address demonic attachments. Those things remained with me for years, even after becoming a Christian because I did not know I needed to tell them to go. Demons will only listen to someone with spiritual authority. The reality of generational curses can be understood by the evidence in a person's life. Sometimes those things always seem to be in progress, unraveling every bit of success and blessing in a person's life. At other times, it would seem as if life was generally going ok and then something destructive from the demonic realm was released. What this tells us is that choice matters. There might be something lying dormant in a person's life that is unlocked through the choices they make. Unforgiveness and unresolved sin issues, for instance, allow the enemy to have legal access to a person's life, and may be some of the things that seem to release the effect of a generational curse.

Repetitive Cycles

People tend to repeat patterns and behaviors of their parents. They can inherit spiritual traits just like a child inherits physical traits such as eye or hair color or other physical characteristics through genetics. In a similar manner, families can inherit negative spiritual patterns. Some things can be attributed to children repeating learned behaviors from what they have observed in others in their family. Other things are reproduced spiritually through unbroken patterns and the propensity to have a weakness for certain sins. Though we are saved, there can still be demonic attachments to our lives that need to be severed. Is it God that puts the curse on us? No. The curse comes from the enemy.

People tend to repeat the same familiar patterns and behaviors as their parents or grandparents. Just because the things we do are normal to us doesn't mean those things warrant God's stamp of approval. People may suddenly get a different perspective on the things they do when they read God's word and learn to apply it to themselves. What people consider normal behavior can often be repeating a familiar pattern of things they've grown accustomed to. That is where generational sin originates. The things we think may be harmless enough may not harmless at all. Habits and behaviors that we don't think much of can lead us backwards into things that are tied to generational sin patterns. The things we don't want to let go of can cause us to clothe ourselves in garments that don't reflect the nature of Christ or the new person we have become in Christ. We put back on the old man instead of putting on Jesus Christ. Romans 13:14 advises us, **"Rather, clothe yourselves with the Lord Jesus Christ, and do not think about how to gratify the desires of the flesh."** Learned behavior does have something to do with it, but spiritual bondage is much more than that. A demonic presence is active in a person's life that pulls them back into the same sins.

The Pharisees and those that lived by Old Testament law were concerned about requirements of the law. Jesus told us that we must surpass the righteousness of the Pharisees in that we were to honor God with more than just duty or obedience. The kingdom of God is concerned with heart, motive, our thoughts, and our actions. Although the kingdom is about obedience; it is about what has our heart. When we look at all scripture in the light of God's intended purpose it was not to cast curses upon His people. God is not some evil warlord that likes to punish people unnecessarily. When he established our worlds and enacted spiritual laws, it was to keep God's people inside the boundaries of accepted behavior that would also serve to keep them safe from the repercussions of breaking spiritual laws.

The law as it was given in the Old Testament was never designed as a means of salvation, because no one could be saved by keeping it. In Galatians 3:24 scripture indicates that the law was given as a guardian, a schoolmaster or a tutor to instruct mankind in the spiritual laws of God. The law was never given as a way to achieve righteousness. It acted as a school teacher in the sense that it corrected and instructed God's people to know His ways. It taught people the difference between sin and righteousness. Its purpose was to give mankind a means of defining sin and also protecting God's people. They were graciously taught to follow God's ways for their own protection. Adherence to the law was for their own benefit, so that they did not incur misfortune, disaster or harm, (otherwise referred to as a curse). The law in itself was not considered a curse; it was considered a gift from God to His people. God gave His people an acceptable standard of conduct and boundaries to keep them in right behavior. Those that kept God's testimonies were blessed. Remember that when Jesus appeared, He came as the fulfillment of the law. In Matthew 5:17, 18 Jesus said, **"Do not think that I have come to abolish the Law or the Prophets; I have not come to abolish them but to fulfill them. I tell you the truth, until heaven and earth disappear, not the smallest letter, not the least stroke of a pen, will by any means disappear from the Law until everything is accomplished."** Jesus did not come as an opponent of the law. John 1:1,2 says, **"In the beginning was the Word and the Word was**

with God, and the Word was God. He was in the beginning with God." It's important to realize that Jesus was the Word of God in the Old Testament and He came as the fulfillment of it in the New Testament when he took the form of a human child. When we use the word "law" it simply means God's word, or instruction. Jesus is the living word of God. It was ultimately designed for our greater good so that mankind would learn what it meant to walk in love and treat others the way they would want to be treated. That has never changed. The principles are valid as our teachers. The scripture in 2 Tim. 3:16 tells **us "All Scripture is inspired by God and is useful to teach us what is true and to make us realize what is wrong in our lives."** (NLT) The KJV says, **"All scripture is given by inspiration of God, and is profitable for doctrine, for reproof, for correction, for instruction in righteousness."** The Word corrects us when we are wrong and teaches us to do what is right. The curse that comes as a result of trying to keep the law is because self-effort and pride cause a person to try to manufacture their own sense of righteousness apart from God's grace. It denies the sacrifice Jesus Christ paid for all mankind. Our trust cannot be in ourselves; it must be in what Jesus afforded to us through His death and resurrection. This is what brings us into the New Covenant of grace.

In Matthew 22: 34-40, one of the Pharisees came to test Jesus in His knowledge of the law and he asked Jesus what was the greatest command-ment. In verse 37 Jesus replied: **"'Love the Lord your God with all your heart and with all your soul and with all your mind.'[a] 38 This is the first and greatest commandment. 39 And the second is like it: 'Love your neighbor as yourself.'[b] 40 All the Law and the Prophets hang on these two commandments."** What I hope to impart to you is that we learn to look at all scripture in light of what causes separation from ourselves, God and others, and what impedes our love. If we have unhealed emotional wounds and we can't love ourselves, we are not going to be able to love others very effectively. If we are carrying offense and unforgiveness, we are separated from God and others. If we are full of selfishness, we are not going to love God or others very well, because our selfishness will make us stingy and self-centered. Where ever we deny God's authority in our life, sin becomes the master. Over time the things we refuse to part with will be reproduced by demonic influences and attachments in the lives of our loved ones. This is how similar behaviors, sin and curses repeat from one generation to another. People did not stop to repent and ask God to forgive their sin. I had one person tell me, "You don't need to keep asking for forgiveness if you're under grace." I disagree. If I do something to offend someone I love, I feel a need to acknowledge that wrong and ask them to forgive me. It clears the air, I don't need to carry unresolved guilt, and having a conversation allows the relationship to be restored properly. It is our confession of sin that allows unrighteousness to be cleansed from us, according to 1 John 1:9. I feel better for doing the right thing and talking to the Lord about my error, and I know He forgives me. It is the ultimate response of pride to think that a person can go through life and not have to apologize for wrongdoing or modify their behavior once in a while. How much more should I honor the Lord by asking for His forgiveness if I have done something to insult the Spirit of Grace? True repentance is when an individual turns away from the things God calls wicked and changes their ways. Obedience and repentance interrupt the cycle of generational iniquity. When we cleanse ourselves of sin we break demonic attachments. Every time a person breaks the old cycle, they become a world changer, giving hope to the next generation that follows after them. If we want our children and grandchildren to fulfill the good plans that God has for them, it must start with us. We must be the one to set a new example and break the iniquitous sin patterns that were a part of our lives. God changes the world one life at a time, one person at a time.

Curse or Judgment?

I would like to briefly touch on other instances where a Christian can have a curse working in their life but not necessarily from inherited generational sin. We already addressed the fact that the evidence of curses working in an individual's life comes from disobedience and being outside of God's covenant. For instance, if I attempt to prove my own righteousness apart from the righteousness Christ has provided for me, I am outside of covenant. The New Testament tells us through the Book of Galatians that the law is a curse to those that try to justify their righteousness based on works rather than on the imputed righteousness that comes from the blood of Christ. There is a responsibility of obedience, faith and action required in order to demonstrate faith and reap the benefits of God's promises. The just shall live by *faith*.

The New Testament still demonstrates the spiritual principles at work although it does not use the specific word 'curse.' Let me give you an example. 1 Cor. 11:27-30 advises God's people to be cautious about taking communion in an unworthy manner otherwise it could invite judgment upon the one doing so. An unworthy manner could be retaining unforgiveness towards someone, broken relationships or perhaps failing to repent for things such as speaking curse words against someone else. Retaining unforgiveness, no matter how justified someone may feel, carries a severe penalty. Our own sins are not forgiven; prayers are blocked and so is our entrance to heaven until we are cleansed from our sin. Anger and slander are things that Jesus equates with murder in the heart. Being angry is not sin; it's what a person does with that anger that can invite judgment. These things are scriptural. Let's look at what the scripture in 1 Cor. 11:27-30 says: vs. 27 **"Wherefore whosoever shall eat this bread, and drink this cup of the Lord, unworthily, shall be guilty of the body and blood of the Lord. 28 But let a man examine himself, and so let him eat of that bread, and drink of that cup. 29 For he that eateth and drinketh unworthily, eateth and drinketh damnation to himself, not discerning the Lord's body. 30 For this cause many are weak and sickly among you, and many sleep,"** (KJV). The word clearly says that taking communion in an unworthy manner invites the penalties of spiritual weakness, sickness and premature death. Scripture does not use the specific word 'curse' yet in all practical indications that is exactly what is implied. The reality is that though certain things may look like an active curse, it may be the result of God's judgment because an individual failed to rightly judge himself or herself. How often people prefer the blessing but ignore the truth. We are far too desensitized to sin; so much so that we often completely disregard the warnings of the consequences of it. The body of Christ is weak, sick, and powerless and some have gone on to an early death all because we fail to judge ourselves properly.

Onward to Victory

The fact that we are under a new covenant of grace does not nullify the responsibility to work out our own salvation with fear and trembling before a holy God. It simply means that we have time to work out our issues and get them resolved before the day we are taken home. Jesus has made every promise that we find in God's word available. However, if a person is ignorant of what His word says, or if they live a life of compromise and halfhearted commitment to Christ, that person will not live victoriously simply because they are 'under grace.' We will never have authority or victory over things that we don't understand. A person that is not willing to part with certain vices and sins will never have authority or victory over those areas of their life. This brings us to another important question. If someone cannot see or discern the door the enemy is using to gain access to their life (including the lives of their spouse and children), then how will they be able to shut the door to him? 1 John 1:9 reminds us that God is faithful and just to forgive us of all sin and cleanse us from all unrighteousness, if we confess that sin before Him. Titus 2:11 advises: **"For the grace of God (his unmerited favor and blessing) has come forth (appeared) for the deliverance from sin and the eternal salvation for all mankind. (vs 12) It has trained us to reject and renounce all ungodliness**

(irreligion) and worldly (passionate) desires, to live discreet (temperate, self-controlled) upright, devout, (spiritually whole) lives in this present age..." (Amplified Bible). True freedom comes from the revelation that compels a person to tear down the stronghold where the enemy has circulated his lie, and through it, held a person's redeemed nature in captivity.

A stronghold is where the enemy has reinforced his lies and twisted logic in order to keep people stuck, captive to old mindsets and habits that defeat their spiritual and emotional progress. These things cause blind spots. When blind spots are at work, it robs a person of spiritual sight and a correct perspective. Sometimes people get so accustomed to seeing the problems that they can no longer see the blessings or correctly discern what God has said about them and their future. They actually give the enemy a place to work in their life through unbelief and negative words. When a person stops agreeing with the enemy they can realign their confession of faith to agree with the word of God. A person's behavior changes when faith and agreement come into proper alignment with God.

There are times when a person finds themselves with severe troubles and trials. I do not subscribe to the thought that these things always occur as a result of some curse. I do not automatically believe that people have to have an open door to sin in order to incur loss or tragedy. As I mentioned earlier, Satan is a career criminal and he will always try to get away with something. There are times when God does allow severe trials in a person's life in order to prepare them for a future purpose. Many sincere but mistaken people think that people have to be guilty of something in order for Satan to steal, kill or destroy in another person's life, but this puts unnecessary burdens of guilt and condemnation on those that are suffering. Consider Job's friends. They felt so self-righteous as if they had all the answers to Job's suffering, but in the end God showed them their own need for repentance and humility just as much as He did Job. It should be a lesson to us that none of us, no matter how much wisdom or revelation we may think we have, are qualified to judge another person's life or trials. We may all experience things we cannot explain and have to walk through a dark night of the soul. I don't know if any of us can expect to have all the answers to our questions. Maybe we will only find out once we get to heaven. But we can do our very best to seek God, live in obedience, and serve God out of a grateful heart. This is our reasonable expectation of service to Him.

Now with all that said, I want you to know there is a big difference between the pursuit of purity and living religiously. The pursuit of purity is something we do because we see the value to living a holy life. It allows us to draw closer to God and allow His love and anointing to flow through us unhindered. Religiousness is offensive to everybody, including the Lord. Not because it's an attempt to live righteously, but because it reeks of self-righteousness, arrogance, an attitude of superiority and pride. Religiousness wants to be seen and flaunted before others. God has taken such pains to deliver us from religiousness. He wants to reach the unchurched, the lost, the wounded and untrusting. We will never do it if we don't lose the religiousness and just be real. It's not about evangelizing with our words or needing to wait for a break in the conversation to toss in a few comments about Jesus just so that others can see how righteous we are. It's not about trying to get people to come to church, more programs, evangelistic crusades or getting a building in which to meet. It's about *being* the church. More is said with loving actions than any amount of religious preaching. Jesus didn't preach. He demonstrated the kingdom. He loved. He healed, delivered and restored anyone that was willing to come to him. If He was here today in human flesh we would see him eating his meals with the homeless, chatting with the prostitutes, and comforting those who have just come out of the abortion clinics. He would be telling stories with runaway kids on the streets and speaking kindly to the angry youth who have looked for family and acceptance in gangs. This Jesus is not a religious Jesus. He is a friend that cares and loves the people who might look a bit scary and sometimes act unlovely. This is the Jesus that scares the religious, puts the fear of hell into demons (literally!) and is so gracious that people walk away feeling good about themselves no matter what their situation. Just go be like Him. His love is perfect every time.

Our Journey

There was a period of time in 2007 when God spoke to us about being committed to a new direction and the changes that were to come. It began a very challenging time of stripping, testing and many trials. We lost everything because we said yes to God. I went through some really angry, frustrated times with God and there were many days I did not want to talk to Him. I didn't understand the process or why it had to be so difficult.

During those many months, it seemed like God was giving me some warm up exercises in learning how to deal with witchcraft issues. I could not figure out why! The first one was a neighbor who had previously been a witch. She had been experiencing some marital issues and asked if she could talk about it with me. She told me, "The Lord told me He moved you here for me!" I was a bit amused and wondered what all that meant, but I think we both ended up learning some valuable things from one another. We had some awesome prayer sessions and her marriage got a healing. There was another incident a few months later when a woman who I had not seen or heard from in a couple of years called me out of the blue. We had attended church together in the past but I had not seen her in quite some time. She began to go into detail about some terrible situations concerning her daughter. She explained that her daughter was terribly ill with a form of cancer; her marriage was falling apart and some other issues. A couple of ladies went to her daughter's house to pray but got so ill after they came into the house that they had to leave. Then she told me that as she was desperately praying for someone to help, the Lord told her to call me. "Me?" I sputtered in disbelief. "Why me?" I asked. "I don't know," she said, "but the Lord said you would know what to do." I was astounded. "Jesus!" I whispered, "What am I supposed to do? I feel like I'm in over my head on this one! What are You doing?" This woman had been looking for my phone number for two days when she called! I was absolutely stunned because I did not consider myself to be well versed in witchcraft and deliverance issues. I am so grateful for Holy Spirit. The moment I started praying certain things came to light and she went back to tell her daughter what I had said. She called back within an hour and told me that her daughter identified some things she had in the house and got rid of them. It wasn't a quick fix for all the matters concerned, but things began to improve.

During that time, we also had a ministry on the streets of Pensacola where we fed the homeless in a local park. We were constantly coming in contact with people who were tormented with demons. One day, as two women approached me I saw that one of them was clearly struggling in her health and the closer she got the worst she looked. Her friend, who was another Christian woman, explained that although this woman had recently accepted Christ as her Savior, she had been a practicing witch and was now in a lot of physical pain, emotional torment and financial trouble. Other witches had been sent to harass her where she lived. It was Satan's way of rebuking her and trying to intimidate her to come back into service to him. I heard the devil tell me, "Leave her alone, she's mine!"

I heard him say it again a second time, only this time with a threat that he would come after me, too, if I didn't listen to him. I said, "Shut up, Satan. You come after me anyway so what's the difference?" I proceeded to pray with this woman. I saw her again a few months later and prayed with her again. This time she renounced generational rebellion and got filled with the Holy Spirit. Shortly thereafter, she relocated to another state to live in a Christian ministry and start a new chapter of her life.

For many months we struggled to survive. Satan meant what he said. He was definitely making life difficult. We literally had to go out to the park ministry every Tuesday just to get fed by our ministry team! They would send us home with leftovers that would help us get through the next week. We also ate a lot of leftover bread from the donations we had been given. Someone else had an agreement with Panera bread to pick up their leftover day old bread and they helped donate quite a bit to the ministry we were doing with the homeless. After we passed out the bread, muffins and pastries to those that wanted it, we were able to take home the rest. Some days that's all we had. Breakfast, lunch and dinner we ate leftovers from Panera bread. I truly understood the complaint of the Israelites that were tired of manna! I was so tired of bread but so grateful at the same time. There were days we wouldn't have eaten at all except for that bread. God bless Panera! I bet it never occurred to them that they were really helping keep people alive when they agreed to donate their leftovers, but we did, and we were grateful. God was stretching our faith until I felt like we were going to break. I remember my husband coming out of our prayer closet one time and this grim look was on his face. Alarmed, I asked, "What? Did the Lord say anything?" "Yes," Norm said. "He said YOU said you would pay the price!" I about knocked him over trying to get into the room to go pray. I knew the exact moment he was referring to and what I had said to the Lord, but that had been years prior. I started to wonder what in the world I had agreed to! Have you ever experienced a time when you suddenly realized that saying yes to God caused a big mess in your life?

We had to pray in every meal, every tank of gas, and every little bit of provision. I had a newborn son that was 6 weeks old when it all started. I was so full of fear not knowing where our provision was going to come from. I remember one day when I ran out of diapers. We had no money to go buy more. I was frantic and frustrated! I paced back and forth in my son's room and started declaring every promise I could remember. I said, "Lord, You said in Psalm 23:1 that You are my Shepherd and I will not lack. So according to Your word, I will not lack diapers, in Jesus name!" I started commanding diapers to fill the empty diaper basket. I was very insistent! It wasn't long before my son needed another diaper change. I am not sure what made me walk back in the nursery because I knew the basket was empty, but I went back to look again. Lo and behold, there was one diaper sitting in the basket. One! I thanked the Lord for the diaper and marveled at the power of faith. When you refuse to take no for an answer, faith really does pull what you need out of the kingdom of God! Later that day we received a check in the mail that allowed us to go get a few essentials.

There were many small victories like that but we did end up losing everything and becoming homeless for almost a year. I know a lot of our Christian friends didn't understand what we were going through at the time. We didn't either. We got a lot of religious responses from people that made us feel condemned. That surely didn't help, but it taught us a lot. No one can look at someone else's life as an outsider and have all the answers for what God is doing in the life of others. God's 'educational plan' is tailor made for each individual because that is how He teaches people His ways. Norm and I had always said we wanted to see the miraculous work in our lives. God honored it by giving us miracle needing situations and teaching us to demand more from our faith. When God decides to take you through the wilderness, you learn to look at scripture in a whole new light. He always provided and rations were meager, but thankfully we never went without a place for our family; we just didn't have a home of our own any longer. We bounced around out of suitcases and moved every few weeks or however long we had from one little oasis to another. Many Christians started to hear about our story and strangers started to offer us a place to stay for a short time. The Lord was leading us through the wilderness and we had no choice but to depend on Him. Every connection for work, a place to stay or any of our needs was divinely orchestrated by Him. We never knew where it would come from. That was such a hard time! Through it all we learned to trust Him. It was not a comfortable place to be in, but God demonstrated His faithfulness every single time. We never went hungry. We had a place to sleep and it wasn't on the street. Even in the midst of some very trying situations, and though the answer didn't come until we were stretched to the last moment, the answer *did* arrive. God never left us without help. We have so many testimonies of how God provided in miraculous ways. The enemy was trying to choke the life out of us in every way possible. Phones broke and no calls for work came in for long stretches at a time. Nothing worked no matter how hard we tried to get something going. Our finances were being squeezed to death. Finally I decided there had to be a reason why it was all happening. We did not have any open doors to sin in our lives that either of us were aware of. We had a lot of unanswered questions. How could the enemy withstand us like this? Why were God's promises not working the way we thought we understood from scripture? We needed answers quickly.

God started communicating a lot through my dreams. The dream setting in many of them had to do with my childhood home and things from my youth. I also had some very vivid dreams. Most involved some form of witchcraft or Satanists attacking us. Needless to say, after a number of dreams like that it got my attention. I knew God wanted to communicate something but I really didn't know what. One night my soul was very troubled and I got up to pray. I prayed for about half an hour in the Spirit, asking God to give clarity about the dreams. Suddenly, and quite clearly, I heard Him speak. "Renounce voodoo," He said. I started to argue with Him, thinking that it didn't apply. "Lord," I said, "How is that possible? I have never been involved with voodoo, have I?" It was literally as if I could feel the Lord standing right behind my shoulder, waiting for my obedience. I said, "Ok, Lord, I renounce voodoo. If I have ever done anything to open a door to the enemy - whether I knew it or not, please forgive me. And, if anyone else in my family opened a door to that spirit, forgive us. Let the blood of Jesus cover that doorway and please let me understand what this is all about." Now keep in mind that at that time I really did not have much understanding about generational sin issues. I believe the Holy Spirit directed the words that I prayed to include my ancestors so that I could receive the revelation God wanted to show me.

Immediately the Lord began to speak. He asked me a question. "It's not just about what you think you may or may not be guilty of, Laura," He said. "Do you know what others in your family line have opened a door to?" I said, "Well, no Lord, how could I possibly know that?" "That's my point exactly," He said.

Throughout the next days and months the Lord began to show me more and more. Memories that had been suppressed began to surface, and I remembered things I had forgotten for many, many years. Holy Spirit began to connect the dots in my mind between the strong unnatural curiosity I had as a child towards things in the occult and how the enemy wanted to draw me towards darkness. He showed me things that were working in my family that had reproduced itself into my life at an early age. God showed me that there is a huge difference between our perception of things and how the spirit realm sees things. We process information by a variety of factors. We rationalize our behavior based on our emotions, our intentions, how others treat us, and whether or not we feel we are justified in retaining certain attitudes and behaviors. In other words, we unknowingly create loopholes for our areas of compromise. The spirits of darkness, like their unholy ruler, are legalists. They take advantage of our ignorance. They look for weaknesses, wounding and areas where a person is prone to temptation. They also look for any area of spiritual weakness, pride, a lack of conviction towards sin or areas where a person has resisted and rejected God's authority. For by doing so, the individual can easily come into agreement with the spirit of rebellion and leave the door to the enemy wide open. Every time I have struggled in an area, either with myself, God or the enemy, it was because there was something in my life...a thought, attitude or behavior that was not in proper alignment to God.

1 Sam. 5:23 reminds us, **"For rebellion is as the sin of divination, and presumption is as iniquity and idolatry. Because you have rejected the word of the LORD, he has also rejected you from being king."** Any form of rebellion is empowered by the spirit of Satan. Break down each one of those words and study them.

Rebellion: a show of defiance towards authority;
is the same as or equal to
Divination: the practice of seeking to foretell future events or discover hidden knowledge by occult or supernatural means.

Presumption: Behavior or attitude that is boldly arrogant or offensive; the act of presuming or accepting something to be truthful based on evidence that may or may not be true.
is the same as or equal to
Iniquity: Gross immorality or injustice; wickedness (and)

Idolatry: Blind or excessive devotion to something; the worship of idols.

Pride causes people to resist the knowledge God has made available. The Bible calls this rebellion. Rebellion causes open doors to the enemy so that people actually reject the wisdom and counsel of God in exchange for the lies of the enemy. When a person presumes to know better than God they accept the enemy's version of deception; this equates to making a god of our own imagination, or a false god. Elevating a commitment to self-deception makes an individual the primary god in his or her life. God's desire is for His people to wake up out of their stupor and stop feeding off of fraudulent information. Many of God's people are spiritually impoverished and weak. The answer to our need for strength is to renounce divided loyalties and throw down the lies. Many people read the above scripture in 1 Sam. 5:23 but fail to apply it to themselves. This is where people suffer for lack of knowledge. The spirit realm sees things according to how God's word is written and the enforcement of His spiritual laws.

This is what the Lord says – your redeemer, the Holy One of Israel: **"I am the Lord who teaches you what is best for you, who directs you in the way you should go. If only you had paid attention to my commands, your peace would have been like a river, your righteousness like the waves of the sea."** (Is. 44:17,18). He compels His people, in Isaiah 52:1, to awake and put on the strength of the Lord. We are to clothe ourselves with strength and put on the garments of splendor. God resists the proud but gives grace to the humble. God is so very good to us and His grace so far beyond what we can comprehend. He answers many of our prayers in spite of ourselves, not because we are so good, but because He is. His grace is abundant, but with that said, we also need to realize that God does not want us to be ignorant of Satan's schemes. Sometimes our struggles are to teach us to be wiser than our enemy and gain power over him. God teaches us through adversity in order to convict us of sin and our need to change so that we can truly be overcomers in every sense of the word. He wants us to walk with our heads held high; not in pride, but in confidence that the enemy has nothing in us that he can exploit. If we truly understood all that was waiting for us on the other side of repentance, we would literally be tripping over ourselves to get to God! We would be so eager to submit to Him and repent for holding on to our wrong attitudes and behaviors that it would be a joy to offer ourselves in total surrender.

That is the enemy's worst fear and his nightmare. It's no wonder he spends all his time lying to us. He only has power over us if he can convince us of his lies. Ultimately, Satan's goal is to keep us from completely trusting God and find ways to separate us from intimacy with God. Intimacy is where secrets are shared, strategies are revealed, and the enemy's plans are thwarted. Satan is terribly, terribly frightened by the Christian that understands the value of surrender! The kingdom of darkness shudders at the mere mention of their name. A surrendered person has an intimate relationship with the Lord that allows them to experience strategic gain in order to advance God's kingdom. The enemy has no choice but to shut up and take orders. The Christian that enters into the relationship of total surrender will find that nothing will be impossible for them.

Holy Spirit began to connect the dots in my understanding how things we do leave open doors to the enemy, although we completely go on about our business and forget about them. Scripture tells us in Prov. 26:2 **"As the bird**

by wandering, as the swallow by flying, so the curse causeless shall not come." What this means is, a curse can't just land on you for no reason. A door has to be open in order for Satan to have access, and it's our responsibility to figure out the details of how he got in. But, sometimes we can't. That's the whole point of God asking me if I could tell Him what doors others in my family line may have left open. I had no way of knowing, of course, none of us do, but God wants us to be able to walk in victory. He wants to give us answers so that we take everything back the enemy has stolen. The enemy sees these "open doors" as access points where he has been given an entrance. God taught my husband and me how to cooperate in our own deliverance and healing. Holy Spirit began working with me to write prayers. Some of them are in this book. The Breakthrough Prayer is quite extensive but it is also quite effective at closing many possible open doors to the enemy. It releases inner healing and revelation as well and continues to work long after the prayer has been made.

There are a number of things each person deals with in life and God has a myriad of ways to releasing His healing. God's servants often have "specialty areas." Our experiences with God all have a profound ability to impact not just ourselves but others. Many times these testimonies of our experiences become a key aspect of a person's life message. God doesn't want us to be stuck just trying to survive; He wants us to thrive. He wants our soul to prosper and be in health. The prayers in this book are here so that you can get beyond the barriers of just barely survival mode and break through into true prosperity. I am talking about having peace, joy, and righteousness in your life that also unlocks the blessings and hidden riches of the Lord. The Bible tells us in 1 Cor. 13:9 that when we receive revelation or a prophecy, we know *in part*. God wants to continue to lead us into deeper revelation of truth. We cannot afford to stop seeking! With every generation, we recover more truth that has been lost throughout the generations. That is why it is so important for the body of Christ to come together and share with one another. We should not be so stuck on the part of the revelation we received as to think that someone else doesn't also have something equally true and relevant to contribute. It allows more of the complete picture to be seen and understood. To some, it may be the revelation of the Father's heart of love; for others, it may be the message of grace, deliverance, or holiness. God has many dimensions of His character. God is a God of justice just as much as a God of mercy and grace. He is a loving, protecting Father as much as He is a man of war. He is the good shepherd of the sheep as much as He is the deliverer. Doctrine must be balanced if it is to be effective in healing, deliverance and transforming the individual. Each message has it's time and place in how it applies in an individual's life to release healing and wholeness. This sort of prayer is just *one component* that God may use for your peace, healing, wholeness and blessing. Please understand it is not my wish for anyone to be overly sin conscious and fearful; we should be JESUS conscious and focus on His righteousness working in and through us. It's also not about being religious. It *is* about being *intentional*. With that said, there are prayers of renouncement that are quite effective at getting the ball rolling in the right direction. We have increased authority and anointing over everything that we <u>overcome.</u> It is preparation for moving into a higher level of authority in a person's prayer life. I hope that if you have found this prayer you are at a place in your life where you are not bothered by being thorough. This prayer came as a result of a long journey of stretching, stripping and deep cleansing. We know from personal experience this prayer is effective, and the many testimonies from others that it has helped. I pray and believe that each person that puts this prayer into practice will experience a divine shift out of the old and into the new. May you be blessed with every good thing God has waiting for you!!

Dear Heavenly Father,

Right now I declare that I break every agreement with Satan and the works of darkness. I choose this day to divorce the enemy, to renounce and repent of any covenants that have been made by myself or other family members in my generational line. According to YOUR word in 2 Chronicles 7:14, Father, You said that if I would humble myself, pray and seek Your face...If I would turn and repent from my wicked ways, You said You would forgive my sins and heal my land. Whether I or other family members have partaken of these sins knowingly or unknowingly, I ask Your forgiveness and I renounce:

All spirits of fear, the fear of man that brings a snare, self-pity, inse-curity, and inferiority. Forgive those in my family line for the need to control or manipulate others out of a sense of fear, insecurity or inferi-ority. Forgive us for not trusting in your provision or your timing, and for failing to rest in Your love.

I renounce all spirits of heaviness that bring depression, mental ill-ness, obsessive compulsive disorders, schizophrenia, suicide, and grief. I renounce the spirits of unbelief, double-mindedness, the cares of this world and all things that would give me give me divided loyal-ties in my heart and mind towards God. I renounce every seed that Satan has sown into my heart and mind that would cause divided loy-alties and weaken my convictions towards Jesus Christ. I renounce bi-polar disease and unbelief. I renounce all compulsive behavior and all addictions rooted in fear, rejection, or anxiety. I renounce self-pity and the lie that I cannot or will not be healed. I renounce the tendency to think of myself as a victim or a martyr in these forms of mental illness. Father, You love me and did not give me sickness, disease, torment or problems. Those came from the pit of hell. Jesus died for this truth and I will not reject Your truth. I reject the lies from the enemy and declare that I receive the truth and the healing that is afforded to me as a child of God, for it is written, "By His stripes, I AM healed," in Jesus name.

I renounce and forsake all spirits of discontent, complaining, a vaga-bond spirit, wandering and irresponsibility that have come from iniq-uity and idolatry. I renounce and forsake any sins and demonic spirits associated with gambling, poverty spirits, laziness and sins of poor stewardship. I renounce all addictive behaviors given to excess, greed or stinginess.

I renounce bitterness, jealousy, strife, anger, hatred, profanity, gos-sip, lying, slander and murder. I renounce the bitterness that comes from being hurt or mistreated or injustice that has occurred towards myself or others in my family. I renounce the spirit of Cain, which is a murderous spirit. I repent and forsake the sins of slander, hatred and evil speaking. I renounce the bitterness that comes from being hurt or mistreated, injustice towards me or others in my family. I repent of my judgments against others. Forgive me and those in my family for any sins of hard heartedness, being critical or condemning, or showing lack of compassion towards others in their time of need. Forgive me and those in my family line for turning a blind eye towards those in need and withholding good when it was in our power to help.

I renounce and forsake unforgiveness, including unforgiveness to-wards myself, retaliation, and vengeance. Forgive me, Lord, for any time that I or my family members have sown seeds of discord or caused pain to others through our actions. Forgive us for acts of malicious-ness or things that I or other family members have done with the intent to hurt and cause pain to others. Forgive me and those in my family line for selective obedience or ignoring the prompting of your Holy Spirit when You wanted us to show love, mercy, grace or compassion.

I renounce and forsake the sins of pride, lawlessness, rebellion, selfish ambition, presumption, and testing God. I renounce and forsake athe-ism, mockery, scoffing the things of God and Your Holy Spirit, griev-ing the Holy Spirit and unbelief. Forgive me Lord, for allowing spirits of inferiority or insecurity to drive me to feel as though I have to prove myself to others, myself or to You. Forgive me for believing these lying spirits when they tried to form a false image in me. Your word says I am fearfully and wonderfully made, and I am made in Your image. I am accepted just as I am. Forgive me and my family line for despising godly wisdom and authority or rejecting Your counsel. Forgive us for self-rule and choosing authority figures that did not represent Your government or authority for our lives. I repent from any time that I have cursed God or others. Forgive me Lord, for loving gossip, slander and my judgments more than I loved your law of showing love and kindness. Forgive me for not blessing others more freely, even those I do not like or those that have been an enemy.

I renounce and forsake all soul ties to illegitimate spiritual fathers or spiritual leaders, religious attitudes, and spirits of legalism, disrespect, self-righteousness, prejudice, controlling behaviors, manipulation, imposing my will on others, racism, disobedience, independence, critical spirits, arrogance, vain and judgmental attitudes. I forgive everyone that has knowingly or unknowingly contributed to my hurt.

I renounce and forsake spirits of rejection and abandonment, all lying spirits and command them to leave me at once. I repent for sins of judging or rejecting others, withholding love, acceptance or forgiveness. I renounce and forsake spirits of self-hatred, self-rejection, unloving spirits, guilt, unforgiveness and anger towards myself and others. I renounce the lie that sins done to me by others were my fault. I renounce the shame and condemnation that have come in as a result of deep wounds, embarrassment and sins that were done to me from others. I surrender my pain and anger and I want no benefit from it anymore. I surrender the memories of hurtful events in my life. Take it Lord, I offer it all to you right now. Help me not take it back! I forgive those individuals, Lord. I put them in your hands. Forgive me for not being able to separate the sin of those that have hurt me from them as human beings that have also been hurt and used by the enemy to hurt others. Forgive me for the times when I have not honored nor shown respect to those in authority, parents, spouses or others. Forgive me for not humbling myself or apologizing when I should have done so. Forgive me for broken relationships, broken vows and covenants, and please help me to do whatever I am responsible for to make things right. I ask You to heal the breach in relationship between myself, others and You.

I renounce and forsake all worldly addictions including drugs, alcohol, nicotine, gambling, gluttony, compulsive physical exercise, compulsive spending, sexual sins against myself and others, pornography, and sins of excess that feed the lusts of the flesh. I renounce and forsake the spirits of lust, bondage and drugs.

I renounce and forsake the spirit of pride and Leviathan. I renounce and forsake the perverse spirit and all that is connected to it. I renounce and forsake incubus and succubus spirits, spirits of voyeurism, homosexuality, beastiality and anything connected to demonic sex. I renounce and forsake unfruitful thoughts, fantasies, all unclean and seducing spirits, and the deceiving spirits connected to the perverse spirit. I renounce ungodly soul ties, those of former lovers, false authority figures, and soul ties to anyone that would keep me from moving out of my past and into the good future You have for me. Let those ties to the past be severed now, in Jesus name. I repent of all sexual sins. I renounce and forsake the strongman of Baal and divorce all ungodly spirits of lust, sex and witchcraft. Please heal the fragmentation in my soul and spirit.

I renounce and forsake all false gods and masters and all evil inheritances in my generational line. I renounce all lies and false teaching that blinds me to truth and mocks and resists God. I renounce all ungodly symbols that connect me to false teaching, false gods, ungodly alliances and pagan symbolism. I accept and receive no inheritance from evil sources, only that which my heavenly Father permits and allows. Let all evil inheritances be broken off of me and my family. I put them under the blood of Jesus. I renounce and forsake the spirit of mammon, greed, and selfishness. I renounce and forsake the divided loyalties that come with a love for money, covetousness, idolatry and envy. I renounce bitterness and the lie that I am not blessed by the Lord. I renounce the lie that I will be happier with more material possessions. I renounce the lie that somehow I am rejected or unworthy because I do not have more possessions. I renounce the sin of comparing myself with others.

I renounce and repent for any involvement with secret societies and the ungodly covenants they demand. (If you know which ones are involved in your family history, name them). I renounce and forsake all pledges, oaths and involvement with Freemasonry, lodges, societies or crafts by my ancestors and myself. I renounce all false marriage covenants and mock ceremonies of secret societies. I renounce and forsake blasphemy and taking the Lord's name in vain, as well as blasphemous oaths and pledges to Satan by any other name and alliance. I renounce and forsake all witchcraft spirits. I renounce and forsake the Rosy Cross, the Rosicrucian's and all ungodly alliances, oaths and associations to Grand Knights. I renounce and forsake all false gods of Egypt as well as the lust of power, prestige and position. I renounce and forsake all secret signs and handshakes. I renounce and forsake all false gods, false doctrines, unholy communion and abominations. I renounce and forsake the Luciferian doctrine; I renounce and forsake the oaths spoken to pledge loyalties to man or idol that violated the commands of God and conscience. I renounce all false masters associated with Freemasons, Shriners, Mormonism, Paganism, the Klu Klux Klan and other lodges and secret societies. I renounce and forsake the false god Allah. I renounce and forsake all words and phrases used as secret codes and I break agreement with all curses that were once agreed to be placed upon any and all family members, including myself and future generations. I renounce and forsake the compass point, the cable tow, the hoodwink, the ball and chain, the apron, the noose around the neck, the sword and spear, the blindfold and the mind blinding effect of those things. I renounce and forsake all penalties associated with breaking these ungodly oaths and covenants. I renounce and forsake all play acting and rituals depicting murder and death, and the spirit of fear associated with death as a curse. I revoke and break the power of agreement with these ungodly servants of darkness, Satanic worship, and all associations with those in fellowship of demonic alliances. I command the curse to be cancelled and all ungodly covenants and agreements broken and nullified both in the earthly and spiritual realm, in the name of Jesus Christ. I ask You, Father, Son and Holy Spirit to heal and restore every area of the physical body and ailments that have been suffered as a result of the curse brought on by any involvement by anyone in my family line. Forgive us, I pray, for committing sin and iniquity and blasphemous acts against a Holy God, ourselves and others.

I renounce, forsake and divorce myself from and break any and all agreements, covenants or involvement with: all lying spirits, the occult, demonic spirits, Native American and cultural rituals and traditions involving the use of idols, witchcraft, voodoo, the practice of hoodoo, root workers, witch doctors, conjuring, the practice of juju, pharmacia, black magic, white magic, wicca, and the use of mediums, familiar spirits and seducing spirits. I renounce and forsake all oaths and rituals to false gods, witchcraft covens, sorcerers, Satanists or workers of iniquity. I renounce and forsake any and all sins involving the abuse of trust, authority, and power or using our influence in an ungodly manner. I renounce and forsake sins involving magic, sorcery, practicing charms or incantations, the use of horoscopes, tarot cards, fortune telling, astral projection, psychic energy or astrology. I will burn and destroy all books, spells, incantations, rings, and other objects that connect me to ungodly occult practices, lodges, secret societies or their unholy rituals and practices.

I renounce and forsake all spirits of divination, the spirit of Python/ Pythos, the Serpentine spirit and all that take the form of the demonic serpent. I renounce and ask Your forgiveness, Father, for speaking things in Your name, even prophesying, that has been out of the flesh rather than the unction of the Holy Spirit. I renounce and repent for all broken covenants, unfulfilled vows and promises, betrayal and divorce. I ask You to please disentangle me and release me from ungodly covenants, vows, and peace treaties, and all unrighteous agreements that would bring me into relationships where I am unequally yoked with things of the kingdom of darkness, evil and wrong relationships. Lord, let there be a release of every curse that has come against me or my generational line as a result of these things. I decree a cancellation of every form of witchcraft and curse that has resulted from my involvement or that of my generational line. I ask You, Lord Jesus, to come and deliver me and my family from all demonic spirits that have come as a result of a curse. I ask that You deliver me and my family from every affliction, illness, disease, allergy, or physical condition that has affected us. I ask that You restore all the years that the enemy has stolen. Let finances, health, and relationships be restored. Let peace, joy, mental health and emotional stability be restored. Let the blessings that have been held back, stolen and hidden by the enemy be released into my hands now, in Jesus name. Let all demonic attachments be severed from me and my family line, both in the heavenly places as well as in the earthly realm. I declare that every seed that was sown by Satan in order to perpetuate a curse or cause myself or someone else in my family line to reject my heavenly Father, the Lord Jesus Christ and Holy Spirit must now shrivel and die immediately. Jesus, I give You permission to change what You know needs to change in my life and to convict me if I resist your Holy Spirit.

Your word says in Isaiah 54:17 that "No weapon formed against me shall prosper, and every tongue which rises up against me in judgment shall be condemned," and that this is my inheritance in the Lord. Right now I condemn every negative word that has been spoken over myself, my family and my future in Jesus name. I lift up (___, ____, ____) and I repent for, and I condemn every negative word I have spoken over myself, my family, and our future. I repent for negative words that I have spoken over others and I declare they will not boomerang back into my life or theirs. I break the power of those negative words that hang in the spirit like a curse. I declare that those negative words will no longer ring in my ears or in those that have heard or repeated negative, condemning words. I declare that words that have been used as a weapon will no longer ring in the ears of my loved ones and hinder their faith or their future in Jesus name. From this day forward, I declare their ears shall be deaf to condemning words and only faith shall prosper in their heart, mind and spirit in Jesus name.

Father, I repent for these sins on behalf of me and my family to the tenth generation back. I thank You for Your forgiveness and cleansing of these sins. I declare that when I am tested, the Spirit of God will arise within me and bring me into a place of victory. I give You permission in advance of any situation I may encounter that You and Your Holy Spirit may change my actions, words and responses so that I honor You. Please reign and rule over my emotions. Enemy, according to the scripture in James 4:7, as I am now submitted to God, you must flee from me. I command you to take everything that you have put on me, everything that you have tormented me with, every sickness and GO! I command you to pay restitution at no less than a 7-fold return, according to Proverbs 6:31 in every place that you have brought poverty, defeat, robbery, or death and destruction. Father God, I ask that You cleanse my mind of all unfruitful thoughts, fantasies, and works of the flesh. I thank You for the blood that Jesus Christ has shed on my behalf, and I appropriate the power of His blood and the resurrection power of Your Holy Spirit to every sin, transgression and generational iniquity over myself and my family line. By the power and authority of the blood of Jesus Christ, I declare my victory. Satan, you no longer have authority to torment me or my children with iniquitous sin patterns. Your plan is cut off now in Jesus name. God has promised in Hebrews 8:12 that He will be merciful to our unrighteousness and our sins and lawless deeds He will remember no more.

Jesus, You are the Son of God, and You are seated victoriously at the right hand of the Father. Today I declare that the enemy is defeated where I am concerned. You are my Master, my Lord and my Savior. Please come with Your Holy Spirit and heal my mind, my emotions, my thoughts, my confession and my memories. I forgive those that failed to reach out to me when I was hurting. I forgive those that have intentionally caused hurt and pain to me and my family, and those that have done it unintentionally. I ask You to bless, heal and deliver those that have acted in ways that have hurt me or caused harm to me or my family. I will trust You to judge fairly and mete out any justice in these issues. Bless those that have hurt me, lied about me, or deliberately caused harm to me or my family, and set me free from offense. I release them to you now. Please forgive me Father, Jesus, and Holy Spirit for willingly disregarding Your words and Your Spirit when You have tried to get through to me. Please heal my trust issues with you and others. Please heal the issues related to my past, my present and my future. Heal my hope, my faith and my love. Heal any areas of grief, heaviness, unbelief, and let the renewed mind of Christ be strengthened and formed in me each and every day. Thank You for releasing into me a spirit of Faith, a spirit of Obedience, the spirit of Adoption, the spirit of Revelation and Truth. Now tell me Lord, what I need to do as an act of faith that will release my breakthrough. Confirm it and convict me that I will not neglect to do whatever You tell me to do. Thank You for eternal life, health, and victory, and for restoring my life and my future, in Jesus' precious name, amen.

CHAPTER FIFTEEN

Becoming World Changers

We live in a culture where disdain for God and Christianity are evident all around us. People are disillusioned with church because they don't see the integrity, character, holiness or power that the church should model. The church has been judgmental, lacking in love and grace. We cannot change the world unless we are willing to change ourselves. We have no place trying to tell the world how to live when the church has not fulfilled the law of love even to those in the family of God. Jesus said that the world would know we are His disciples by the love that we demonstrate to one another. If the world cannot see Jesus, why do we blame them for being blind? Whose fault is it if the world does not see love, acceptance, forgiveness and restoration demonstrated by those that profess to know Christ? It is not the world's fault for not being able to see Jesus; it is the church's fault for not living it. We need to move into a greater love that demonstrates the real Jesus to others, because when God wants to change the world, He starts with one man, woman or child. He changes a person then changes their family; he changes a family and changes a community, a city, or a nation. There is absolutely nothing stopping *you* from becoming that person!

The reality I see in many of the unchurched is that people are disillusioned with those claiming to be Christians. They are disillusioned with what they see from the church because what they see is a form of superficial Christianity. There are many people that are hungry for something real. They are thirsty for the presence of God. They're not interested in faking their faith or partaking of dead religious works; they want something authentic and spiritually satisfying. They are looking for Christianity that looks like the real Jesus. People are not impressed with counterfeit Christianity. My desire is for people to witness the reality of the kingdom of God and have people be impressed with Jesus. Some people are so dissatisfied with the form of religion many have left church. They would rather be outside the camp than stuck in the wilderness. God is building His church but it will be built upon the revelation of Jesus Christ. It will be built upon forgiveness, mercy, grace and compassion. Holy Spirit will rebuild and restore the foundations of His church to model everything that Jesus represents: equity, justice, mercy and righteousness. *This is the Jesus the world is waiting to see!*

God's promises to His people include a covenant of peace, safety, rest and freedom from slavery. He promises to make His people a garden of renown. He has His shepherds in the fields, waiting to seek and find the lost, the scattered and the wounded. He will feed His flock with good food that restores their strength and vitality. He will nurture and take care of them so that people do not just survive, but *thrive*. He will lead His people to leaders that represent His heart, and He will lead His people to freedom. He is leading His people into freedom all across the world as He delivers them from the chains that bind their faith.

Could it be that we have seen so little movement from the Holy Spirit because we have not been willing to be cleansed? Many Christians live powerless and frustrated. The reality is no one can separate Jesus Christ from the Holy Spirit or the Kingdom of God. The godhead cannot be separated from itself. No one can separate God from His power, yet so many people live as though they are weak, powerless, and fearful of whatever life throws at them. The gift of the indwelling Holy Spirit was given to us in order to make us effective disciples. The gifts of the Holy Spirit are the evidence of the power of God's Kingdom. Though they might never admit to it, many churches attempt to separate God from the gifts of the Holy Spirit that have been given to the church to flow in supernatural power. God's power is not for show or self-importance. He does not come in like a Las Vegas magic act. The Spirit of the Lord is humble and unpretentious. Kingdom power is demonstrated through answered prayer, and the evidence of the miraculous as well. The greater we walk in love, surrendered to the authority of God in our lives, the greater the power will be evident in our lives. Some people are embarrassed to speak in tongues and resist the gift giver. Holy Spirit is a gentleman. He will not release

Himself into a person that is fearful or embarrassed to receive Him. That is simply pride. He comes to the earnest seeker and those that are jealous for Him! We can no longer afford to be satisfied with a form of godliness but lack the power. This should not be so! When we lose our virtue, we lose our conviction, and where we lose conviction, we make the unconscious exchange to surrender integrity. Once we begin to surrender, we become captive to those that are stronger and determined to rule over us. The Kingdom of God is righteousness, peace and joy in the Holy Spirit, but along with these distinct qualities are evidence of its integrity, power and effectiveness. Every Christian needs to examine them self and ask the question, "What have I traded in exchange for power?" The King cannot be separated from His Kingdom, and if the Kingdom of God is within us, then <u>why</u> are we devoid of power? Do we lack holiness and sanctification? Do we lack teaching or training in the gifts? Have we asked for the fullness of the Holy Spirit and the baptism that fills us with His power? No one has to live a powerless life when they are in Christ!

We have looked into a mirror and seen ourselves dimly, but we can no longer afford to walk away unchanged and unrepentant. God is separating those that are His from those that are not. People assess themselves according to their own perception, their intent, or by reason; God, however, measures us according to His word. We have learned that He measures us by how well we love others and whether or not we have allowed ourselves to be changed into the image and likeness of His Son. This love that He has for us is patient and kind, almost more that a person can bear. He is as close as our next breath! Jesus compels people to repent, for the kingdom of heaven is 'at hand.' All one has to do is step into it by faith. He waits, with a look that conveys He is both pained at our bondage, unhealed wounds and excuses, yet full of longing, compassion and mercy. God's love, like a parent's love, is not conditional upon the other person's ability to reciprocate and show love in return. He simply says, *"I'm here for you..."* and with an outstretched hand He whispers, *"Taste and see that the Lord is good. My love is real."* He is waiting for us to look into the spiritual mirror of His word and confront ourselves with truth. He is waiting for us to open our blind eyes and take a good hard look at ourselves. He is waiting for us to discard all our feeble excuses, the pride, and the lies we like to hide behind, and allow Him

> The greater we walk in love, surrendered to the authority of God in our lives, the greater the power will be evident in our lives.

to shatter our pretentious masks into a thousand pieces. Because, once we surrender our heart, we become candidates for the mercy that heals. Truth exposes the deception of who we are _not_. The presence of His Spirit draws us closer to Christ so that we can experience waves of divine love pouring in healing. He blesses us with the desire and the grace to change.

I can't tell you the number of times I've been shattered and undone, but I'm grateful for them. Hebrews 12:11 says, **"Now no chastisement seems to be joyful for the present, but painful; nevertheless, afterward it yields the peaceable fruit of righteousness to those who have been trained by it."** If we are truly sons and daughters of God, we should expect correction, for scripture tells us that whom He loves, He chastises. The scriptures in Revelation 3:17-19 tells us this: **¹⁷"You say, 'I am rich; I have acquired wealth and do not need a thing.' But you do not realize that you are wretched, pitiful, poor, blind and naked. ¹⁸ I counsel you to buy from me gold refined in the fire, so you can become rich; and white clothes to wear, so you can cover your shameful nakedness; and salve to put on your eyes, so you can see. ¹⁹ Those whom I love I rebuke and discipline. So be earnest and repent. ²⁰ Here I am! I stand at the door and knock. If anyone hears my voice and opens the door, I will come in and eat with that person, and they with me. ²¹ To the one who is victorious, I will give the right to sit with me on my throne, just as I was victorious and sat down with my Father on his throne. ²² Whoever has ears, let them hear what the Spirit says to the churches."**

God's desire for each of us is to be a world changer. He has given us this commission as it is found in Mark 16:15-18, but we cannot reach people if our hearts are insensitive to their pain and suffering. People get so accustomed to wearing the yoke of the enemy that they confuse the enemy's enticements and deception with their will. If our spirits were set free from our body we would see how deeply our spirit longs for holiness and communion with God, but we have grown so accustomed to living in compromise that our hearts have become desensitized and indifferent towards things the Bible calls sin. Don't let that little three letter word get you all defensive and worked up. It doesn't mean you're a bad person or you need to feel bad about yourself. People already feel bad enough about themselves. Neither God nor I want you to live under condemnation. That little three letter word that some people find so bristling and offensive simply means that none of us are perfect. We're never going to be perfect. No matter how hard we try it just ain't going to happen! Can we all face that truth about ourselves? I think so!

Revelation 3:17 challenges us to consider our own pitiful condition. Let's examine what is being communicated. Similar to the Laodicean church, many people have deluded themselves into thinking they are covered by grace and can live in compromise. Christ was very vivid in His explanation of how He rejects the half-hearted efforts of self-satisfied Christians. He said He would vomit them out of His mouth. Half-hearted love and commitment is repulsive to Him! Wealth means nothing if it means that we have become so independent that we no longer feel we need God. One can also feel self-assured that wealth is an indicator of God's approval, yet it can be the farthest thing from the truth when it has been gained at the expense of our relationship with Him. If the compromise is at the expense of our soul, we impoverish ourselves of power, integrity and true spiritual authority. People can be equally deceived by being well clothed in fine garments, when the truth is they may be spiritually naked. Many people in the church today have exchanged popularity for passion and left their first love for the praise of men. This causes them to become blind to the spiritual reality of their own need to change. The body of Christ as a whole has not worn the garments of righteousness, power and strength – *but*, that is beginning to change. People are starting to realize they have been left completely naked to their own shame and they don't like it. They don't like losing loved ones to death and disease. They don't like the enemy getting one over on them and robbing them of their health, family, finances and future. God designed His body to be the answer and use the spiritual gifts He left us with to overcome and defeat all the power of the enemy. Although many churches are in a state of spiritual decline, the eyes of the blind are coming open. The day and age we live in demand the body of Christ to rise up into strength! **"Awake, awake! Put on your garments of strength, O Zion! Put on your beautiful garments, O Jerusalem, the holy city! For the uncircumcised and the unclean shall no longer come to you. Shake yourself from the dust, arise; sit down, O Jerusalem! Loose yourself from the bonds of your neck O captive daughter of Zion!"** (Is. 52:1-3).

Isaiah 52 is a picture of a woman that shakes herself and gets up out of the dust, a queen ascending the throne, taking her rightful place of royal authority. She is to adorn herself in the beautiful garments of a queen mother. The woman represents the church, or the body of Christ. The 'garments' of the church are the gifts of the Holy Spirit as well as the fruits of the Spirit. When we clothe ourselves appropriately, nations will flock to the glory of God. Our purpose as God's vessels is to reflect Him. That requires 'buying gold' which means being purified and tested by fire. It can cost us everything. Until people are willing to die to themselves, learn the way of humility, and partake of the wounds of the

Lord, they will never truly know Him. We must be broken of our own strength before we can experience Jesus Christ in His sufferings, for it is through suffering that we learn to identify with Him in every way. When our natural strength is broken, then we can take on His nature and allow Him to be manifest in and through us. There is no other way than the cross in order to truly know God. Jesus knows what it is like to experience the judgment, the rejection, and the feeling of being expendable. There was no place for Him inside the religious camp. He was excommunicated from the synagogues because He challenged their sacred cows. He confronted their traditions that kept people out of the kingdom of God. Jesus demanded more from their hard insensitive hearts that were bound by religion, pride and self-righteousness. They were offended with His knowledge of the scriptures and the confidence he had in His God-given authority. That scared them. This Rabbi didn't teach like any of them. Jesus wanted to bring people into a relationship of loving community.

Jesus was hated by the religious and those who opposed His Father's kingdom. He was hated by those who were bound by lust for power, control and a desire to maintain the order of the day. People feared what they didn't understand. God's methodology and our opinions often do not coincide. People tend to resist what they don't understand. When Jesus taught and explained that in order to gain the kingdom they would have to be willing to lose it all, it was a foreign idea to them. It's foreign to us today, too. Jesus' words in Matthew 16:24-26 tell us that if we want to follow Him, we have to deny ourselves. He challenges His disciples to take up their cross and follow Him, and warns us that anyone that tries to save their life would lose it, but anyone that is willing to lose their life for His sake will find it. He challenges us to consider what we are willing to trade for our own soul. In Matthew 13: 44,45 Jesus presents another parable. It is the parable of the pearl of great price. The kingdom of heaven is like a rare, exquisite pearl so beautiful that cannot be compared to anything else ever seen. The man that finds such treasure understands it is costly, but is willing to pay the price because the delight of obtaining something so precious is beyond estimation. He must have it at any cost. I will never forget the day when my three year old daughter woke up crying that she had lost the pearl of great price. She has the Holy Spirit within her and has on more than one occasion, had a word from the Lord. I've learned to pay attention to what my kids have to say! You can trust the Holy Spirit to communicate through those who have purity in their heart. I believe God wanted to communicate a spiritual truth through an innocent child. She represented the state of the church. Each person represents 'the church,' and we must be willing to pursue the pearl of great price. It's the kingdom of God in all its glory, power and presence.

The exchange may seem intimidating at first. It requires great trust, and human beings have a great amount of difficulty trusting someone they are unsure about. I know many people who claim to trust God until the bottom falls out of their world and everything comes unglued. That is where the metal is tested, and that is what it means to buy gold refined in the fire. Some people have this false impression of what their relationship with God is all about. Perhaps some think God just wants them to be happy or blessed. God isn't as interested in our happiness as He is in our willingness to be His disciple and trained for kingdom purposes. He knows that Satan is determined and far more committed to our destruction than we are to the pursuit of holiness and fulfilling the will of God. Living a holy life isn't about being stuffy, religious or self-righteous. It's about getting rid of all the junk that hinders us from seeing God for who He really is, and partaking of that incredible relationship between us and God. Do you realize that the Creator of this entire universe wants to have a personal relationship with *you*? This God…the one that oversees all the heavens and hung the stars in the sky wants to hang out with you and I and get to know us. He wants us to get to know *Him*. Spending time with Him allows us to discover our purpose. God has created each one of us to fulfill a certain purpose, and when we fulfill that purpose, it brings expansion to His kingdom. We will never truly feel fulfilled unless we do the will of God and fulfill His plan for our lives. When we are doing His will, there is a sense of happiness and joy that cannot be obtained otherwise.

God's kingdom is an upside down kingdom. Our spiritual inheritance and ultimately our greatest place of authority lies in the trials we overcome. Examine your life. The nature of your trials and battles are a good indicator of your spiritual gifts and where God is developing the anointing for the future. You will never make it to the end successfully without a few upgrades in your levels of discernment, understanding and anointing. Don't despise your trials; they are there to insure you have the strength to run the full race and finish strong! God's methods of training are uniquely designed to the individual and intended to break us of pride, stubbornness, self-righteousness, independence and the things that resist genuine humility. He has to work out our trust issues and He does it by confronting our fears. When we can confront our fears and learn to trust God through what we're going through, that is learning humility. When we learn to stop reacting to every little piece of bait the enemy puts on the hook, we learn humility. When we consider someone else's feelings more than what we want, we learn humility. When the Lord says, "No, you can't do that," even though others do, and you obey God, you learn humility. When you learn to honor others because you've decided to take the high road and deny your flesh, you learn humility. When you learn that real love isn't about you but about others, you learn humility. There are a lot of important lessons in life, but in the kingdom of God, most of them are about the loving nature of Christ being formed in us.

I'll tell you why humility is so important. It's Christ like, and in it lays the key to reaching the hearts of others. It is the secret of smallness. Humility is God's secret weapon! The weapon that has already been proven is the most powerful weapon in God's entire arsenal and the one which the enemy fears most: *the weapon of love.* When a person's belief system is damaged, it affects how they see themselves, others and God. It can actually cause them to see others as adversaries and opponents, when that is simply a lie circulating in their own head. They have walls up that the enemy keeps guarded, and those walls are intended to keep the captives away from those that God wants to use to help bring about their healing and deliverance. Reactions of impatience or pride push people away. Those that are bound by the enemy often do not have the freedom to be able to make different choices. Some are so bound by hard heartedness, insensitivity and rebellion that they don't feel much of anything. Lies have to be unraveled before people can change their behavior. How often we want people to change their behavior to accommodate our feelings and emotions! Again, that is why humility is so important. Humility is patient and kind, and understands that people change when their belief system changes. It has to come by revelation so that the heart is awakened with a desire to change. Humility allows us to appear small in the eyes of the enemy, so that he doesn't consider us a threat. Do you remember how Goliath taunted David and mocked him for being so small? Goliath didn't consider David a threat at all. The giant had incredible armor and a huge javelin. David had no armor and a slingshot, but it was the weapon that had been proven over and over again. God's secret weapon is the secret of smallness. Humility allows us to get close enough to our Goliaths so that the weapon of love can be effective. Only love softens the angry heart. Love allows the root of bitterness to be pulled out. Love opens doors to conversations that never would have happened otherwise. Love is more powerful than evil, and Jesus gave us the example to demonstrate the weapon that always overcomes. *Love never fails.*

◆ ◆ ◆

God is looking for those that want to change the world. Not too long ago, I had a talk with my kids about purpose. My daughter, Talia, is naturally joyful, sweet, caring and compassionate, but she came to me feeling a bit down. I could tell she had lost a bit of her sparkle. She wanted to get her ears pierced, spend money and shop, thinking it would make her feel better. I began to hear the lament of an eight year old that thought fulfillment had to come from the mall. How familiar that felt! I couldn't believe it started so young. I knew I owed it to her to tell her the truth and try to redirect her focus or she could potentially spend years (and thousands of my dollars!) trying to find contentment through superficial means. A conversation that began as a word of encouragement turned into a discussion about relationship with Jesus Christ and fulfilling her purpose. I told her how God had filled her with His greatness and all she had to do was let it out. Her joy started to return as I explained how God had created her with purpose, and filled her with special talents, gifts and abilities. I told her that she should never put limits on what she thought she was capable of because the Bible said that all things were possible to those that believed in God's promises.

That night I couldn't sleep and I felt the Lord nudging me. He said, "It's not enough to just talk about these things with your kids. If you want to raise world changers then you're going to have to lead them into it. Get them up and activated." The next day we had a "world changer" party. We had balloons, cupcakes, and invited the neighborhood kids. We talked about how we could all change our world with random acts of kindness and make the world a better place by showing love to others. Mother Theresa said, "We may not all be able to do great things, but we can all do small things with great love." I even made a little affirmation for my kids to remind them of who they are. I will tell you what I tell my kids.

"You are a world changer. You are wonderfully made. You are loved, valued and respected. Always treat others with honor because someone honorable lives in you. Honor inspires others to live up to their potential. You are kind, honest and considerate. You are full of brilliant and creative ideas. You can do anything you put your mind to because nothing is impossible with God. You have unique talents, gifts and abilities and there is no one else on earth exactly like you. You are special! You are accepted. You have worth. You are created with purpose. You have value, and no one can take that away from you. You are full of greatness. You will change your world!"

Conclusion

If I can leave you with a few final thoughts it is on the subject of faith. Hebrews 10:35-11:1 says: **"Do not, therefore, abandon that confidence of yours; it brings a great reward. For you need endurance, so that when you have done the will of God, you may receive what was promised. For yet 'in a very little while, the one who is coming will come and will not delay; but my righteous one will live by faith. My soul takes no pleasure in anyone who shrinks back.' But we are not among those who shrink back and so are lost, but among those who have faith and so are saved. Now faith is the assurance of things hoped for, the conviction of things not seen."**

This book covers a lot of topics but ultimately it's about a life of faith. My husband and I have gone through a lot of stripping but it's been necessary in order to strip us of religious pretense, emotional and spiritual wounds, wrong attitudes, false concepts of scripture and other things that hinder the growth of our faith. Faith is the only thing that pleases God. We have seen so many miracles. We have prayed for barren women who later gave birth to healthy babies. We've seen legs grow out, backs straighten and be healed, vision restored and people healed from cancer and other health issues. We've prayed for and received a healthy child when it was against all medical odds for me to have another child. We've laid hands on our car when the gas tank was on "E" and watched amazed as the gas gauge needle moved right before our eyes to the ¼ tank mark. We've seen miraculous provision in so many ways! God has given us a variety of situations to increase our faith. But it's not about us; it's about Jesus. It's about what He wants to do for us to increase our faith so that when we pray for others our faith won't be hindered either by what we see or don't see. When we know His heart, we can pray with confidence regardless of what the natural circumstances look like.

When God called Abraham to be His servant and His friend, He gave Abraham what seemed like an impossible task. He wanted Abraham's faith to be enlarged to such a degree that He actually had to use His faith to extract something he couldn't see out of the anointing. He had to believe in the promise God gave him. God was going to make him a father when both he and his wife were past child bearing age. God reversed the aging process and brought life out of a dead womb. As Abraham walked in faith with God his faith was accredited to him as righteousness and he became a father to many nations. One of the scriptures that has always been true with us is Romans 4:17. **"As it is written: I have appointed you to be the father of many nations. So**

Abraham is our father in the eyes of God in whom he had faith, the God who gives life to the dead and calls things that don't exist into existence." It seems that in everything that God has done with us and for us, He has required us to start with nothing. We had to learn to put a demand on the anointing in order to pull something out of the kingdom of God. We have testimony after testimony of how God would have us in impossible situations with literally nothing to work with except our faith. Friend, God wants each one of us to take part in helping to create the miracles we need, but also take part in creating the miracles others need, too.

I remember last year when we driving to Oklahoma on vacation. It was a bright, sunny, beautiful crisp morning but all of a sudden we went into a valley and it became quite foggy. I looked out my window and everywhere I looked there was fog. Suddenly I saw the top of a radio tower with its blinking red lights on top. It seemed somewhat eerie for it to appear as if it was just suspended in midair! The top of the tower was visible but nothing down below could be seen as it was shrouded in fog. I thought how interesting it was that it was such a perfect picture of faith. Corrie Ten Boom said, "Faith is the radar that sees through the fog." I couldn't see the bottom of the metal structure but I knew it was there nonetheless. God used that moment to impress upon me how tangible the kingdom of God is, if a person will simply believe. Everything that exists in the kingdom of God is just as real as our natural realm. We must learn to see with our heart instead of our natural eyesight. We might not be able to see what's there because it's hidden from our natural sight, but just like that radio tower, it's there, waiting for us to press in closer until we see it. Everything we need exists in the kingdom of God. Faith calls those things that 'are not' (seen) as though they were.

The kingdom of God is within you, according to Luke 17:21. Think about that for a moment. The King doesn't go anywhere without His kingdom. How amazing is it that Jesus thought to put it inside of each person that received Him as Savior?

God has said that His word will not return to Him void but it shall surely accomplish what He pleases and it will prosper in the thing for which it is sent, according to Isaiah 55:11. When we "send" the word back to Him through our prayers and declaration of His word, it has such a short distance to travel to get back to Him. We're really just declaring it until we get the revelation that releases the breakthrough. You know you're getting closer and closer to a revelation of breakthrough when you start to feel an increase in joy and the

Spirit starts bubbling up inside of you. Your faith is waiting to break through so that what you've been waiting for can manifest! We don't declare it for God's sake, but for ours. The Word of God is Jesus. (John 1:1) Jesus also said in John 15 that if we would abide in Him and His words abide in us, we could ask whatever we desire and it would be done for us. That is the obedience we talked about in previous chapters. The WORD is in us. The Kingdom of God is *within* us. Do you remember the principle of agreement that we mentioned earlier in the book? Faith + obedience + the Word of God = results! The Kingdom is released through faith and obedience. The more we remain in faith and obedience, the more we demonstrate love and compassion towards others, the Kingdom inside of us grows. LOVE is a huge key to whether or not we release the miraculous Kingdom of God. The Kingdom expands like yeast permeating a lump of dough. It will literally overtake every part of us! Jesus so wanted people to "get" the concept of the Kingdom being inside of us, that is why He told His disciples to go to the lost sheep of the house of Israel, and as they went they were to proclaim 'The kingdom of heaven is at hand.' He told the disciples, "Heal the sick, cleanse the lepers, raise the dead, cast out demons. Freely you have received, freely give." The King and His Kingdom are as close as your hand. What He was saying was, "Check it out guys! The Kingdom is so close you don't have to go anywhere to find it. You're standing right in the middle of it!" "Now, go - give it away!" What a revelation! The Kingdom is actually closer than your hand. It's within you. He demonstrated the Kingdom so that they wouldn't forget what He was teaching them. Now that is truly an amazing thought, once you wrap your mind around it. You just need to learn how to tap into it with your faith.

What exists in heaven? Is there sickness? Is there disease? Is there poverty? Is there death? What?? Heaven isn't full of dead people? No, no, no... they are very much alive! Jesus said God was not the god of the dead but of the living. There is only life in Him. Jesus cannot be anything BUT life! In Ephesians 18-19 the Apostle Paul prayed that we would be able to comprehend the depth of God's love. It surpasses understanding! Paul understood the Kingdom with incredible depth. That is why when he got bit by a poisonous asp (see Acts 28:5), he simply shook it off and suffered no ill effects. When you get the revelation of "the Kingdom of God within you," the fullness is released. The anointing is released because your faith grows through revelation. In Paul's case, anything with death attached to it had to surrender to the power of the anointing. Nothing is greater than the life of God inside of us. The scripture gives us good news. We have the victory! Faith must be exercised in order to grow. One cannot develop faith in the middle of a crisis. That is called hope, and hope and faith are not the same. Faith is a confident assurance towards God. Faith *knows*. The enemy will do everything possible to wear people down and convince them through their circumstances that he is greater. *No,* friend. The KING and His Kingdom are greater. The devil may present you with facts, but facts are not always truth. The truth of God's word supersedes facts. There may be those times when circumstances defy our understanding, but the key to seeing a prophetic word or promise come to birth is to believe and declare what God has said no matter what the circumstances look like in the natural. Faith believes in spite of what the natural evidence tells us! There will be times when we simply don't understand God's plan or His will, but we should never stop believing. Jesus came to give us life and life more abundantly. He came to have us live in the reality of His Kingdom. His love is so great for mankind that He was willing to die so that we would have access to it all!

Whatever your need, all you have to do is envision the Kingdom living within you. Remember the radio tower; whatever you require already exists in the kingdom! Your job is to declare the scriptures in faith until it manifests. What a great plan! Jesus wanted to remain as close as possible to us so that we wouldn't get lost. He wanted to insure we couldn't be without help in the time of our need. He has already given us Himself through death and resurrection. What else would He not be willing to give? Our only failure is to not under- stand His love, His gracious Spirit, His kindness and His mercy. You don't have to feel angry, rejected or forgotten. You don't have to feel unwanted. You don't have to worry about where the answer is going to come from. God wants you to know He understands, and it's going to be ok. If you've had a response of unbelief, just ask Him to forgive you. Receive His love and grace. How marvelous is His love!! You are not waiting for help to arrive, it is here! When my daughter and I review her spelling words I ask her the question, "What is the difference between 'here' and 'there?' One letter. "t." Funny how it takes the shape of the cross. The cross is the bridge between 'here' (where you're at this moment) and 'there' - (where you need to get to, or where the answer is). Just close your eyes and go across the bridge of faith, get your provision out of the Kingdom of God, and come back with it in your hand. Tap into it with your faith. See yourself doing it, then thank God for releasing it!

If Jesus was standing right in front of you, I think he would want you to pray again and ask for your desire. This time, don't doubt. Jesus said, **"Have faith in God. For assuredly I say to you, whoever says to this mountain, 'Be removed and cast into the sea,' and does not doubt in his heart, but be- lieves that those things he says will be done, he will have whatever he says.**

Therefore I say to you, whatever things you ask when you pray, believe that you receive them and you will have them." (Mark 11:22-24). I leave you with the last chapter that is full of prayers for inner transformation, healing family relationships, tearing down strongholds and releasing heaven into the earthly realm. If you can believe for it, God will do it!

My life is an open book. I hope that this book is a help to everyone that reads it and desires real change in their life. These lessons and prayers are what brought me to the place where I am today. It led me out of captivity and released healing and wholeness. The Bible tells us that we are all living epistles read of all men. Each of our lives is a witness and a testimony to others. Ordinary people do not get the opportunity to write their stories and censor all the press releases. Our sorrows and sadness over the times we forfeit a victory are played out for all to see just as much as our moments of triumph as we beat the game and enjoy that beautiful moment of a celebratory win. Our accomplishments and achievements as well as all of our failures and frustrations are laid bare for all to see. The important thing to remember is that our moments of defeat, no matter how many there are, will always pale in the light of the sweeping win God has written into our story. As we follow Christ, He carries the day so that we come out on top. There is no misfortune or injury that can outshine the glory of God. We are containers for His grace and glory, a lighthouse that sends out beacons of hope guiding others to their safe haven so that they can find peace in the midst of the storms of life. *You* are a miracle, waiting to be poured out into someone's life. You are blessed with all that God has, so that you can give it away as a blessing to others. The key to living a life without regret is to love generously. Forgive quickly. Live graciously, and bless abundantly. It is the unselfish act of loving others unconditionally that fulfills the human heart. *Where there is love, there will always be great miracles.*

CHAPTER SIXTEEN

Prayers for Breakthrough, Restoration and Healing

Family Healing

Father God, Lord Jesus and Holy Spirit,

Please forgive me for anything I have done to knowingly or unknowingly give place to the enemy. My family and the children You have given me are a gift from God. I repent for speaking negative things in my frustration and allowing any word curses to be enacted over my loved ones. Right now I break the power of negative words and ask that the power of those words and any lingering memories associated with those words be broken over each of my family members.

I repent and I renounce all unloving spirits, spirits of rejection, fault finding spirits, unclean spirits, spirits of lust, anger, impatience, inferiority, insecurity, fear, witchcraft (control) and spirits of rebellion. I break the assignment of the enemy and I bind these spirits in the name of Jesus Christ. I forbid them from operating against myself or any of my family members. (name them). Pursuant to what You have already done on the cross Lord Jesus, I appropriate that victory and tell these spirits to obey the voice of Your servant. "Satan, be bound, in Jesus name! You and all those under your power and influence are hereby rendered powerless, impotent, paralyzed and silenced, and you are commanded to leave this family at once!"

Holy Spirit, please release Your healing, Your love, and the ministry of reconciliation into my family. Please fill us with the love of God, a desire for purity, and with the fullness of Your Holy Spirit. Heal the hearts, minds, and belief system of each of my family members. Let Your truth replace the lies of the enemy. Give us revelation so that the enemy is defeated completely. I ask that the power of resurrection life be given to me and my family members to bring healing and total restoration. Let the respect, honor, loyalty and love be restored. Heal our emotions, our memories, our self-image, faith and our trust. In every area where there has been a breach, let it be healed and made whole, filled with the love and Spirit of God, in Jesus' name, amen.

Prayer to Break Word Curses

Father,

Your word says in Isaiah 54:17 that "No weapon formed against me shall prosper, and every tongue which rises up against me in judgment shall be condemned," and that this is my inheritance in the Lord. Right now I condemn every negative word that has been spoken over myself, my family and my future in Jesus name. I lift up (____, ____, ___) and I repent for, and I condemn every negative word I have spoken over myself, my family, and our future. I repent for vows made silently or spoken and I ask that You release me and all those affected by those things to be released from any ungodly vows. I repent for speaking any words that are contrary to Your will, O God, and I break the power of them now in the name and authority of Jesus Christ. I also break the power of negative words of others spoken out of their own fear, anger, criticisms, offense, malice, ill will, envy, jealousy, unforgiveness and bitterness. I break the power of false prophetic words. I break the power of prognosticators, physicians, parents, ministers, teachers, peers, and authority figures in our lives that had power to negatively influence us, create fear or harm our self-image, self-esteem or belief system. I call our belief system back into alignment with God and His Word.

I break the power of negative words, including those that have evil spirits associated with them through the use of conjuring, spells, incantations, potions, and all forms of magic and witchcraft. Words and spirit associations that have been assigned to us in order to perpetuate a curse must now be broken and all curses made void. I command in the name of Jesus Christ that all evil spirits associated with these curses leave me, my family, and all that pertains to our lives, and be sent back to hell immediately. I command all open doors to the enemy that originated with these harmful words to be closed now and the blood of Jesus applied to those doorways. I forbid the enemy from crossing through the blood. I declare that those negative words will no longer ring in my ears, or in those that have heard or repeated negative, condemning words. I declare that words that have been used as a weapon will no longer ring in the ears of my loved ones and hinder their faith or their future. From this day forward, I declare their ears shall be deaf to condemning words laced with a spirit of death. All shame, insecurity, inferiority, fear, failure, unworthiness, rejection, loathing, rebellion, lawlessness, idolatry and perversity that originated from these ungodly words and their effects is now broken off of myself and all my family members. I declare only faith, peace, joy, love, and confidence in the Lord Jesus Christ shall prosper in their heart, mind and spirit in Jesus name. Let the love of Your Holy Spirit, of Your mercy and acceptance be shed abroad in our hearts. Let there be revelation, truth and understanding be released into our hearts and minds. Let the counsel of Your Holy Spirit unravel every lie and bring us back to the truth that sets us free. Father God, I thank You and Holy Spirit for releasing blessing into my life and that of my loved ones. Thank You for breaking every ungodly yoke of bondage and oppression that came as a result of condemning words. In Jesus name, I thank you for a fresh start for me and my family. Amen.

Prayer for Healing from Critical Spirits

Dear Heavenly Father,

It is so easy to be able to find words to address other people's problems. How often I understand what the answer is for someone else, yet how difficult it is to implement change in my own life. Every day I fail in areas where I've prayed for change. Every day I fall short of the good things you want for me. So, today Lord, I just pray for myself. I pray that I would be blessed with the grace to modify my behavior and have it be a permanent change. I renounce all spirits of condemnation, unloving spirits, criticism, fault finding and shame. I command them to leave me now in Jesus name. I receive by faith the grace to change, a spirit of faith and love. Today I pray that I would not focus on my criticisms of others, or my insistence that they change to please me. Today I pray for the grace to overlook things that aren't really necessary to criticize. I pray for the grace to know when to keep silent, grace to know how to handle things that do need correction and when to simply acknowledge and bless the positives. Give me new eyes to see what's good and reward those things with praise. This is the prayer from one mother's heart, to be able to break bad habits and replace them with new ones. In Jesus name, amen.

Prayer for Healing From Self-Hatred and Rejection

Dear Heavenly Father,

Today I come to you to acknowledge that I have sinned against myself by believing lies instead of what Your word says about me. I renounce unbelief! I have let the pain of disappointment or feeling like a disappointment to myself and others influence my thoughts and feelings. Your word tells me I am fearfully and wonderfully made. (Ps.139). Your word tells me I am not rejected, but I am accepted in the beloved. (Eph. 1:6). Your word says I am blessed and not cursed. I am the apple of Your eye. I have worth. I have value. I have had a hard time believing that. Today I break any and all agreements with myself and Satan that have allowed spirits of rejection, self-hatred, a spirit of abandonment, fear, insecurity, inferiority, shame, bitterness, self-pity and unforgiveness to manifest. I renounce all of them and I command them to leave me at once. Help me to shut my ears to the enemy's unloving thoughts. They are not my own thoughts but his. Father, I repent for allowing these things a place in my life. I thank You for forgiveness. I thank You, Lord Jesus, for taking my pain, my sin and shame upon Yourself so that I don't have to bear these things. I thank You that Your blood and Your word cleanse my conscience from unprofitable thoughts and renew my mind. Holy Spirit, forgive me for grieving You and not allowing Your Spirit to influence my thought life and actions. Please come heal my mind, my emotions, my spirit and my physical body. Heal my disappointments, my hope and my faith. Heal my ability to love myself and others. Help me see myself through Your eyes and to walk in my true identity. Father, give me Your love for others and help me love myself and to appreciate myself in a healthy way. I come into agreement with God. I declare that I AM fearfully and wonderfully made. I am loved, accepted, and I am blessed by the Lord. I am surrounded with favor and grace. I can do all things through Christ who gives me strength. Blessings are chasing me down to put themselves into my hands. I am a confident person because you have made me whole and complete. I lack nothing because the Lord is my shepherd and I do not lack. Everything that is available to Christ is available to me, because I am a child of God. I have nothing to fear! Fear no longer has permission to bring torment. I embrace the grace You have provided through Your sacrifice, Lord Jesus, and Your love and acceptance for me. Holy Spirit, I thank You for giving me the fruit of self-control in my thought life and I ask You to empower me to live for God. Fill me with Your fullness. I ask You for supernatural assistance to overcome negative self-talk, and I give You authority over my mouth and my actions. Help me overcome the areas of struggle in my life. I thank You for victory. In Jesus name, amen.

Prayer to Be Healed From Emotional Pain and Trauma

So much of what we carry with us on a daily basis is retained in painful memories and the trauma of past events. It literally resides in the very cells of our bodies, creating room for illness, disease, infirmity and a whole host of other physical, emotional and spiritual problems. God wants to heal us so deep it touches the very core of our being and regenerates healing from a cellular level. Do you believe it? Here is a prayer specifically written for us and our family members to be healed so deeply and completely it renews us from the inside out. Be blessed, dear woman of God. God hears your prayers and knows exactly what each one of us need! Each prayer is a step closer to our breakthrough, healing and restoration!

Dear Heavenly Father,

I lift up myself and all my family members to You right now.(Speak their names). I bring us all to Your throne of grace. I ask that You would supernaturally remove the hurtful memories and the trauma of past events out of our minds, emotions, memories and out of our physical bodies. I ask that You would lift all remnants of painful events and the trauma that was created as a result of that pain. Lift it all out of the very cells of our bodies. Let us each only remember the good about those the enemy used to cause pain. Let us only remember good about ourselves and others. Let us be released from guilt, shame, regret, embarrassment, anger, unforgiveness and the trauma of hurtful events in our lives.

Let our ears not remember hurtful words spoken to us, about us, by us, or by others. Let our hearts not retain unforgivness or anger, fear, pain or shame. Help us to speak to ourselves and others as we would speak kindly to a friend. I speak now and declare complete healing and freedom from every painful event in our lives and that those words will not circulate in our minds or emotions any longer. I release myself and I release my family members from the pain of their past. I release them from guilt, shame, regret and bitterness now, in Jesus name.

I speak now to our physical bodies and command all illness, disease, infirmity and weakness to be uprooted and removed now in Jesus name. I command complete release in every cell of our bodies of any and all residual effects of trauma. I lift the remnant of trauma out of our bodies and command the Holy Spirit, which is the Spirit of Life to release healing into every cell of my body as well as those of my family members. I speak to the hormones, organs and systems of our bodies and command them to come into balance and normal function. I command our bodies to be healed at the cellular level. Everything that has been retained that does not exist in the kingdom of heaven, "Be released out of our cells now in Jesus name. Let every weight be released. Let every hindrance be released. Let all that does not originate from the kingdom of heaven be released out of our minds, bodies, emotions, memories and spirit man. Every weakness be filled now with wholeness and perfect soundness through the name, the power and by the blood of Jesus Christ. Holy Spirit, fill us now with your fullness, strength and power in Jesus name. Fill us with joy, peace, and a release of supernatural healing that radiates from the inside out. I thank You for revival, restoration, healing and complete regeneration in Jesus name, amen."

Prayer to Be Healed from Sexual Abuse, Gender Confusion & Alternative Lifestyles

This is a sensitive subject for many women, but one that is so necessary to deal with so that we can truly be set free from things that have affected our faith, our relationships and the way we see ourselves. Many of the same spirits are involved in sexual sins, whether or not they were done against our will or as willing participants. Soul ties can be formed as well as demonic attachments from anything that was active in the lives of others. It is important to cut those ties! As we deal with deep shame, inferiority, insecurity, fear and identity issues that have resulted from sexual molestation, abuse and sins perpetrated by sexual predators, we can be set free, healed and restored to the identity that pleases God. The amount of people that deal with this issue is staggering and many do not feel comfortable asking for prayer on this subject. You can be set free. Bring it to Jesus, and let Him heal you. Today is a day for a fresh start!

Father God,

You know the things that I have gone through. You know my struggle. You long to set me free from the painful memories and experiences from my past. I ask that You release healing from these issues. Help me forgive things that were done to me against my will. Heal me from my past. Help me to forgive and walk me through my struggles in this issue. Holy Spirit, help me to be willing to yield to You so that You can heal me. Right now I forgive _____ (speak the names of those that have sinned against you) so that I can also have my own sins forgiven, and I ask You to empower me to do so. Give me the desire to forgive and have it be genuine. As a matter of my will, I choose to forgive (_____) and ask that You, Father, give me grace and strength to not take this offense back into my heart. I ask that You heal those that have perpetrated sins against me, and set them free from the perversity and sin that has had them bound, including me.

I loose myself from all shame, resentment, fear, insecurity and feelings of inferiority that have come upon me as a result of sexual molestation and other sins against my body - both those that were done without my consent, and those that I may have participated in - willingly or unwillingly. I reject and refuse all lying spirits, familiar spirits, incubus and succubus spirits and command them to go in Jesus name.

I reject, refuse, renounce and divorce all unclean demonic spirits of perversity: pedophilia, voyeurism, domination, brutality, homosexuality, confusion, gender confusion, mischievous and trouble-making spirits, spirits of double-mindedness, unbelief, sodomy, rape, anger, rage, bitterness, unforgiveness, witchcraft, lust, idolatry, hard-heartedness, accusation, familiar and familial spirits, pride, rebellion, and death. I renounce all soul ties to former lovers and those that committed sexual sins against my will. I repent for any ways that I have knowingly or unknowingly come into agreement with these spirits, and I humbly submit myself to the Lord Jesus Christ and the authority of His Holy Spirit.

Lord Jesus, I believe you paid the price for my sin and shame when you went to the cross on my behalf. I do not have to bear the weight of these things any longer. May Your blood would wash over my mind, my body and my spirit and make me clean. Renew in me a pure thought life. Lift the heavy burdens of guilt, anger, insecurity, fear and shame. Holy Spirit, I ask You to pour out the revelation of Jesus Christ as my healer, liberator and restorer like I have not

225

had before. Give me a fresh revelation of my Father's love towards me, and help me see myself the way heaven sees me.

I submit to You, O God, and I resist the enemy, commanding him to flee from me and take everything he has put on me, everything he has brought into my life, and every seed that he has implanted into my belief system. I reject every seed of distrust, fear, anger, rebellion, accusation, bitterness, spiritual adultery, lust, idolatry, and perversity and command them to die immediately, in Jesus name. I reject every false perception of myself and I choose the image You created for me.

I receive by faith the healing for my mind, my emotions, my body and spirit. I receive by faith the mind of Christ, and I choose this day to pull up the root of bitterness and replace it with the love of God. I ask You Lord to plant forgiveness, grace, love and mercy in place of bitterness.

I receive by faith healing for my emotions, belief system, and perspective towards others. I declare: "Because the Great I AM lives within me, I become what YOU are, O God. Because the living word of God dwells within me; You are transforming me, renewing my mind, to become the living word, as Your truth is lived out in me. You are transforming me to live as the anointed of God. I am not a victim, I am victorious. I do not fear; the enemy is fearful of me. I declare that no weapon formed against me shall prosper, and every tongue that rises up against me is refuted according to Your word in Isaiah 54:17. I walk in the fullness of God, in Jesus name.

I thank you, Lord Jesus, for being my healer, restorer, redeemer and protector. I thank you for replacing every lie in my belief system with the truth that will set me free. Unravel the lies I have believed about my true identity. I am Your bride. I am dearly loved, valued and esteemed. I am an overcomer, a conqueror. I am my Father's praise. I am your joy and the delight of Your heart. I am your beloved. I am a woman of strength, dignity, royalty and virtue. I am a woman who is capable, confident, and compassionate. I am a life-giver, a restorer, and a reformer. I am full of peace and joy. I am the fragrance of Christ in this earth. I am anointed to heal with love. Thank You, Jesus. Thank you for settling me and establishing me in faith, love, truth and righteousness.

Help me, Lord Jesus, to identify and break free from any relationships that are unhealthy and undesirable in Your eyes. Help me to honor Your word, Your will and Your wishes. You know my weaknesses; I pray for strength to overcome them. *For those things that You know I cannot or will not be able to overcome in my own strength, I pray that You would take them out of my hand and let it be done according to Your will for my life and for the benefit of Your will carried out in the lives of others, too. Lord, replace those relationships with better ones that will strengthen me in my walk with you, and fill the void for love, relationship and friendship. Father God, I thank You for overcoming victory. Please fill me with Your Holy Spirit and empower me to live for You. Help me to live a life that honors You and brings You glory. In Jesus name, amen.*

Prayer for Financial Release and Restoration

Father God,

I thank You that finances are not a big deal for You, but You use financial matters to encourage us to pray according to Your will. You want us to prosper, but You also want our souls to prosper. You want us to pray on behalf of what others need, too. So I come to You and I ask for wisdom. I ask for Your counsel and understanding so that I do not suffer from a lack of knowledge.

I also repent for any wrong attitudes and actions that demonstrate selfishness, worry, fear, complaining or doubt. I know that those things do not please you and they do not demonstrate faith. I am grateful, Lord, for my home, my family, and all that you have given to bless my life. I am grateful for You, Lord Jesus. I may not always show it, but I want You to know that I do value You, and how much You have already done for me. Thank you for being my Savior. Thank you for your love and acceptance and the forgiveness of my sins. I choose to forgive anyone that has offended or hurt me. I release them. I ask You to forgive the sins of my generational line, too. I don't know everything that others have done, but please let the blood of Jesus cover those sins, and let a blessing come to others in my family, too. I pray they would receive You and receive Your help. For those that need jobs, please help them get hired at a good job. For those that need their health restored, please heal them. For those that need specific things, please meet their needs over and above what they need. Let them be very blessed, and if anyone is holding unforgiveness towards anyone, please help them to forgive so that You can forgive their sins, too.

Father, as a child of God, I now take authority over the spirit of Python which constricts. I bind it up in the name of Jesus and I forbid it from restricting my ability to prosper. I also take authority over poverty and death, and forbid these thieving spirits of death and hell from advancing against me, my family and my livelihood. I tell them all, "Be bound, In Jesus name." According to what Jesus has already done on the cross, I command you to be silent, impotent, and void of any and all power. Leave me now, in Jesus name.

I release the Holy Spirit, the Spirit of Truth, to show me any areas of my life that may be hindering me from receiving increase in blessing and prosperity. If I need to be realigned in some way, show me. If there are relational changes that need to take place, show me. Let Your divine connections come forth now, I pray. I speak a release of Prosperity, Promotion, Favor, Blessing and Increase. Forgive me, Lord, for areas of selfishness and greed. I know that I am blessed to be a blessing. Let the work of my hands be blessed. Let fruitfulness and increase be released in my family.

I command all illegal encroachers, both in the natural and spiritual to be removed from that which concerns me and my family. Please let angelic assistance be released to help remove any spiritual hindrances to breakthrough. I declare all curses are broken. Let blessing and favor be released over each family member, our employment, business contacts and finances. I command the enemy to restore everything he has taken, according to Proverbs 6:31, and with a 7-fold increase. I call for inheritances to come forth, both spiritual and natural, and I speak release over myself and entire family. I speak the word of RELEASE over the people in my city. I command all mountains of resistance to be removed, every gate unlocked, and every door that is connected to Your opportunities to be opened. I speak a release of Your grace, favor, love and restoration to everyone that is in need of Your touch, and Your assistance. In Jesus name, amen.

Prayer for Direction in Employment

Father God,

I thank You that You are trustworthy. I admit that letting You lead is not always comfortable for me, but I choose to live by faith. I do not want to put limits on what I think You can or will do. Please take me by the hand and lead me into the good plans that You have for me. I need a good paying job that will provide for me and my family. You know my skills and abilities better than anyone. Please help me find the right employment that will also be a joy and a blessing. Your word says the blessing of the Lord adds no sorrow to it. *Please give me the blessing of employment that adds no sorrow to it. Father, every time an obstacle appears, I ask You to get me around it. I ask You also to move every mountain out of my path or dig a way through it, but get me connected properly. I ask for You to make divine connections for me and my family, for my friends, and for others in the body of Christ. I pray for the people in my neighborhood and in my city of _____ that they too would have good employment. Holy Spirit, please give me the inspired ideas, creative solutions and the plan of Your design that will help me know what to do next. Let Your thoughts become my thoughts. Those things that are truly of You, let them keep pressing me to take the appropriate action, even if it doesn't make sense in the natural. I choose faith over fear. I thank You for Your sudden interruption in my circumstances to lead me into the blessing you have for me. Tell me what door to knock on, what to ask for, and let Your favor grant my requests. In Jesus name, amen.*

Prayer for Divine Protection

I ask You, Lord, to set up safety and protection for all those that come under the umbrella of my prayer. I pray for myself, my family members (_____ , _____), people in the body of Christ as well as those in my city. Father, You said your wisdom would make us wiser than our enemies, and I ask that You give people wisdom and discernment to understand the motivation of people's hearts. Let people be able to clearly see what is motivating the actions of others. Let those that rise up with a voice of accusation be clothed with shame and their plots come to nothing. You said in Isaiah 54:17 that NO weapon formed against us would prosper, and every tongue that rises up against Your people would be condemned.

Help your people to stand in the day of temptation. Deliver us from evil and the temptations aimed at us in order to lure us into sin. Lead us not into temptation, but deliver us from the evil one as it is written in Matthew 6:13. You are able to make us stand and keep us from falling into sin. You are able to keep us blameless. Send your angels to keep us in all YOUR ways, so that the enemy cannot find anything in us to use against us.

I ask that You arrange the timing of our days and interrupt the plans and schemes of the enemy so that we avoid accidents, premeditated plots, spontaneous trouble and dangerous situations. Let the wicked that try to come against me stumble and fall, according to Your word in Ps. 27:2. You, O God, are the strength of my salvation and You have covered my head in the day of battle. Do not grant, O Lord, the desires of the wicked. Do not further their wicked schemes lest they be exalted, as it is written in Ps. 140:7,8. Do not let a slanderer be established in the earth. Keep us from the snares set by wicked men, and from the traps of workers of iniquity. Let those that would set traps for us get caught in their own nets, while Your people escape safely, according to Your word in Ps. 141:8,9. I ask for angelic protection and divine intervention to interrupt the plans of the enemy. I thank You that the angel of the Lord encamps around those that fear You, and Your angel is with me, my family members and those in the Body of Christ wherever we go. Situations and individuals, demons and darkness do not control the atmosphere; I walk in dominion and therefore I dictate the atmosphere, and what is allowed and what is not. I bind up the spirit of fear, anger, and retaliation and according to what You have accomplished for us on the cross, Lord Jesus, I declare these evil spirits to be rendered powerless, silenced and paralyzed. Let them be frozen by the declarations made by Your people, and carried to the place where You tell them to go. Send Your angels for our help, Lord Jesus.

I declare *the Lord will lead me, my family members and others that are His servants out of all temptations and deliver us from evil, as it is written in Matthew 6:13.*

I declare *the Lord is our help, and if the feet of His servants begin to slip, His mercy will hold them up, as it is written in Ps. 94:18.*

I declare *the Lord will keep His servants from falling and present us blameless without fault before His presence, according to Jude 1:24.*

I declare *the Lord is able to make His people stand, as it is written in Romans 14:4, and I claim this promise for me and my family.*

I declare *the Lord is my defense and the rock of my refuge. Anyone that rises against me or my family, or others in the body of Christ that are the Lord's servants shall have the Lord for their defense. He shall bring the iniquity of troublemakers upon their own heads as it is written in Ps. 94:22,23.*

I declare *our hope shall not be cut off. The plans and purposes of God shall not be cut off. God delivers His people out of the hand of the wicked and light is sown for the righteous, according to Ps. 97:10.*

I declare that anger, fear, rage, a spirit of murder and the spirit of Cain, (including slander with the mouth, which is considered murder of one's reputation), vengeance, and all the works of the enemy must be interrupted and unraveled now in Jesus name.

I declare that that spirit of anger must be bound where ever I step foot, and I take authority over the atmosphere, worshipping You, Lord Jesus, and releasing peace where ever I am. Greater is He that is in me than He that is in this world, and I command fear and anger to bow to the name of Jesus Christ, for it is written, the Lord is Peace.

I declare the Lord's reign and rule, and Your kingdom authority be released into the atmosphere wherever I go. I call all things into divine order and command them to come into alignment with Your will, plans and purposes now, in Jesus name.

Declaration Over The Works of the Enemy: *Fall Like Lightening*

When the heavens are like brass, it's because sin has created strongholds where principalities and powers rule. It is like a blanket of heaviness and apathy, kind of like spiritual smog, but the scriptures call it 'the valley of the shadow of death.' Only the Word of God can defeat the enemy. Only light displaces darkness. When we use the sword of the Spirit, the enemy must bow and submit to the Word of God, for all the works of darkness are under the feet of Jesus. The Word of God commands the ungodly authority structures to be torn down so that principalities can no longer block our prayers. It releases the wind of the Holy Spirit to bring an open heaven.

Lord of Hosts, King of Glory, I ask that You take the sword of Your Spirit, and release angelic assistance to dismantle the ungodly authority structures in the heavenlies as I make these declarations.

I declare: I have pursued my enemies and overtaken them, neither did I turn back again until they were destroyed. I have wounded them so that they could not rise; they have fallen under my feet. (Ps. 18:36,37) And, 'May the God of peace crush Satan under my feet shortly,' according to Rom. 16:20

I declare: "Let the principalities and powers fall like lightning out of their heavenly places," and I shall say, 'I saw Satan fall from heaven like lightning.' as it is written in Luke 10:18. Let Your light strike the mountains of pride, swiftly, Lord Jesus! Let Your light strike the mountains of resistance! Let the light of Your Word strike principalities and powers! Move, mountains, move, in Jesus name! Mountains of sickness, poverty, debt, and bondage come down now in Jesus name! Mountains of division, discord, and doubt, be removed in Jesus name! For it is written, 'Who are you, O great mountain? For before the Lord you shall become a level plain.' I declare multiplied grace to the works of the Lord and of His servants, in Jesus name!

I declare: 'For You are good, O Lord, and Your mercies endure forever!' The heavens do not belong to the enemy, for it is written, 'Indeed, heaven and the highest heavens belong to the Lord our God, also the earth with all that is in it.'

I declare 'For You are good, and Your mercies endure forever!'

I declare: It is written, 'He brought them out of darkness and the shadow of death; and broke their chains in pieces.' (Ps. 107:14) and, it is also written, 'The people who walked in darkness have seen a great light; those who dwelt in the land of the shadow of death, upon them a great light has shined.' (Is. 9:2).

Enemy be dismayed at the strong arm of the Lord! Be vanquished, be removed from your high places, for it is written, 'For behold, I create new heavens and a new earth, and the former shall not be remembered nor come to mind.' Is. 65:17

'The heavens declare the glory of God,' according to Ps. 19:1, and we say, 'His mercies endure forever!'

I declare: "The Lord will open to us His good treasure, the heavens, to give the rain to our land in its season, and to bless all the work of our hands." Deut. 28:12 And I shall say, 'For He is good, and His mercies endure forever!'"

I command all ungodly altars to be silent now, and I declare the enemy shall no longer be worshipped through sin and iniquity. I loose all evil spirits off of ungodly altars, shrines and places where false gods are worshipped and I ask for the Lord of Hosts to rebuke and remove those spirits out of the airwaves and tear down the high places of the enemy. I declare they are displaced by the light of the Lord Jesus Christ, in Jesus name.

Decree an End to the Spirit of Python

I declare an end to the Python spirit today, in Jesus name, over this geographic region, (the city where I live), over the state of _____ and over our nation.

I declare Jesus Christ is the stronghold of our family, our city, the people in this geographic region and over our nation.

I command you, Python, to come out of every person you are working in. I loose you off of them now and command you to go where Jesus tells you to go, in Jesus name. (Acts 16:18)

According to the victory Christ secured by the work of the cross, let the spirit of Python and all its power be rendered null and void in Jesus name. I bind the spirit of Leviathan and pride working in and through others. Let the influence and voice of divination be silenced. Let the power of witchcraft and the spirit of infirmity be broken now, in Jesus name!

Where there has been constriction, I speak enlargement: over my family members, over this geographic region, and this nation, according to Genesis *28:1,* in Jesus name.

Let the wind of the Holy Spirit breathe new life into those that are weary. Let the wind of the Holy Spirit release resurrection power into those that are empty, dry, and without strength. I prophesy to the breath according to Ezekiel 37:9 and say, **'Thus says the Lord God: "Come from the four winds, O breath, and breath on these slain, that they may live."'** I prophesy to the whole house of Israel as I say, **"Thus says the Lord God: "Behold, O My people, I will open your graves and cause you to come up from your graves; and bring you into the land of Israel. Then you shall know that I am the Lord, when I have opened your graves, O My people, and brought you up from your graves. I will put My Spirit in you and you shall live, and I will place you in your own land. Then you shall know that I am the Lord, have spoken it, and performed it," says the Lord.** (Ezek. 37:12-14.)

Thus says the Lord to His anointed (insert your name) : "I will go before you to make the crooked places straight. I will break in pieces the gates of bronze and cut the bars of iron. I will give you the treasures of darkness and hidden riches of secret places, that you may know that I, the Lord, who call you by your name, am the God of Israel and (insert your name)." (Is. 45:2,3) Lord we agree, that what you did for your anointed servant Cyrus to subdue nations and go before him to loose the armor of kings; to open before him the double doors so that the gates would not be shut, you have done for us. We thank You for breaking through the barriers and leading us beyond the outer gates and through the doors you have for us. In Jesus name, amen.

Prayer and Declaration over the Spirit of Leviathan

Father God,

I want to be free and healed. I do not want bitter memories to prevent me from walking into a blessed future. I surrender every lie, every bit of deception, every hurt and bad memory to You. I surrender the shame, rejection, self-hatred, self-pity, the feelings of condemnation, guilt and blame that I have turned inwardly onto myself, as well as those thoughts and feelings of judgment that I have placed upon others. I choose to forgive those that have hurt me (insert names where possible) and I ask that You forgive them too. Heal their areas of brokenness. I receive by faith that You sent Your Son to die for my sins and that Jesus paid the price for my victory. I thank You that as I have chosen to forgive others, I can receive Your forgiveness for my sins. I ask Your forgiveness for others in my family line that failed to acknowledge Your Lordship and receive the offer of salvation for their own life. Lord, please cut off every generational sin. Please pull down every stronghold in my thinking that is based upon a false belief system, controlled by fear, insecurity or inferiority and held in place by the lies of the enemy. I renounce every lie and every agreement that I have made with the enemy. I renounce all lying, deceiving spirits, all spirits of anger, unforgiveness, bitterness, jealousy, resentment and vengeance. I renounce all spirits of double mindedness and unbelief. I repent for entertaining the wrong ideas, assumptions and belief system. I renounce the seed of every lie that I have taken into my spirit, Holy Spirit, please visit me with your salvation and healing to my mind and emotions. Lead me into the truth that will unravel the lies and set me free. Fill me with the fullness of Your Spirit, which is wholeness, healing, life, light and purity. Fill me with pure love that will wash away the pain and hurt. Please transform my thoughts and belief system to form new, healthy thoughts that are void of pain, mistrust, anger, unforgiveness, insecurity and inferiority. May my responses demonstrate self-control, love, peace and joy. Thank you for the victory and for realigning my future to walk into the newness of what You have for me this day. Therefore,

According to what You have already done, Lord Jesus, I bind the spirit of Leviathan and pride, and all the works of the enemy. "Satan, be bound," in Jesus name. I render the works of the enemy silent, impotent and paralyzed in Jesus name. I send the unclean demonic spirits back to the pit of hell. I ask for You to release your Holy Spirit, full of truth and revelation, and send out Your arrows of truth. Make Your people free, Lord Jesus. I ask for the Spirit of Grace and Repentance to be released all over the land. Let the Spirit of Liberty and the Spirit of Adoption be released now, in Jesus name.

Father, You said, "For they shall not be ashamed who wait for Me." You asked, "Shall the prey be taken from the mighty, or the captives of the righteous be delivered?" We say, "YES, LORD!" Today we release the decree against the spirit of pride and Leviathan, and all the works of the enemy.

According to Your word in Isaiah 49:25, **"Thus says the Lord:"**

"Even the captives of the mighty shall be taken away, and the prey of the terrible be delivered; for I will contend with him who contends with you, and I will save your children." I will feed those who oppress you with their own flesh, and they shall be drunk with their own blood as with sweet wine. All flesh shall know that I, the Lord, am your Savior and your Redeemer, the Mighty One of Jacob."

I declare this is the day the Lord with His severe sword, great and strong, has punished Leviathan the fleeing serpent, Leviathan that twisted serpent, and He has slain the reptile that is in the sea, according to Isaiah 27:1.

I declare this is the day the heads of Leviathan is broken in pieces, according to Ps. 74:14.

I declare Your arrows have pierced the armor of pride and Your hand presses Leviathan down.

I declare the arrogance of the proud has been halted and the haughtiness of the terrible has been brought low, according to Isaiah 13:11.

I declare that those who walk in pride You are able to put down, according to Daniel 4:37.

I declare the pride of man brings him low but the humble in spirit retain honor, according to Prov. 29:23.

I declare the pride of the haughty is brought down according to 2 Sam.22:28.

I declare that those that are hardened in pride are deposed from their kingly thrones and their glory is taken from them, according to Daniel 5:20.

I declare the crown of pride has been removed. The humble are exalted and the exalted are humbled, according to Ezekiel 21:25.

I declare the arrow of the Lord's deliverance is released, 2 Kings 13:1.

I declare that You shall save Your flock, according to Ezekiel 34:22, and that they shall no longer be a prey.

I declare blessings to the Lord, for He has not given us or our children to be as prey to the enemy; we have escaped as a bird escapes from the fowler's nest; the snare is broken and we have all escaped. I declare help is in the name of the Lord Jesus Christ, the name of the Lord, according to Ps. 124:6-8.

I declare the Lord's voice has thundered from heaven, that You have sent out Your arrows and Your lightning bolt to vanquish the enemy. I declare the Lord's rebuke according to 2 Sam. 22:14-16.

I declare the Lord's deliverance according to 2 Sam. 22: 18-20.

I declare the enemy has been destroyed according to 2 Sam. 22:38-41. You have given us the necks of our enemies.

I declare a release of the Spirit of Truth, and that truth is the arrow that will find it's mark in Jesus name.

The answer we have is the prophetic word that releases the voice of God into the earth. He sends out His voice, a mighty voice; the God of Israel is He who gives strength and power to His people. Psalm 68:11 reminds us that when the Lord gives the word, great is the company (an army of people) who proclaim it!! The prophetic voice, released by a company of people will declare God's will into the earth. "Leviathan, today you are defeated," in Jesus name! Today we declare the prophetic word against the spirit of Leviathan. "Leviathan, your pride has brought you low!"

Prayer to Heal the Brain, Mental and Emotional Illness & Addictive Behaviors

Father God,

I thank You for Your Holy Spirit that gives us wisdom to know what to ask for in prayer. I lift up myself and my family members, (be specific if you have people that you know are struggling in some of these areas) and I lift up my friends, those in my community, in this geographic region and my city of _____. Please send the answer to this prayer for every person under the umbrella of my prayer!

I thank You Jesus for your forgiveness and restoration. I believe You are the Son of God and You can heal me. You took my sin and disease upon yourself so that I could live victoriously. Please help me live freely. Let faith rise up in me and Your Holy Spirit fill me with wholeness, power and the fullness of God.

I renounce fear, depression, anxiety, and addictive behaviors. I renounce and repent for any ways I have come into agreement with the enemy. I ask that You would heal the cerebral cortex in my brain and those I have lifted up to you as well. I ask that You would fill any areas of deficiency in our brain chemicals with the fullness of Your Holy Spirit. Let the amounts of seratonin, noradrenalin, norepinephrine, epinephrine, dopamine and all chemicals produced by the brain be correctly balanced. Let every deficiency be filled and every over secretion be reduced to just the right levels for each individual. Let there be no over production of cortisol. Let every amino acid neurotransmitter function with perfect wholeness and soundness as it is in Jesus Christ.

Let every gene that carried defective or mutated DNA that would perpetuate weakness, compromised health, mental instability or that which carries the result of a curse be healed at the cellular level. Infuse every cell, every gene, every strand of DNA with the DNA and healing of Jesus Christ. Let every curse be broken and sent back to the source, for You O God did not give us any DNA that would carry a curse. It came from the evil one, and as we submit to Your authority, we resist the devil and command him to take back everything that he has brought into our family.

I pray that any damage to the brain itself, the neurotransmitters, and the centers for impulse control in the cerebral cortex be healed now in Jesus name. Let there be light in every darkened area of the brain, emotions and in their spirit man. I declare the amino acid and peptide neurotransmitters be rewired to function in perfect health and send the proper amounts of chemicals to regulate impulse control, stress management, peace, pleasure and pain management in perfect balance. Let the acytlcholine functions be healed and restored to perfect health. Let the chemical agents and the communication messengers between brain cells function in perfect harmony, balance and soundness in every cell. Let all things in the molecular structure that affect mood, anxiety, appetite, sleep, temperature, heart rate, self-control, discernment, impulse control, aggression, fear, stress management and other physical and psychological appetites, desires and occurrences be healed and restored to the perfect wholeness that exists in Jesus Christ.

Holy Spirit, let Your fullness fill our lack, for it is written the Lord is our Shepherd and we shall have no lack, according to Ps. 23:1. Let all areas that have been damaged, those areas that are genetically unsound, weak, impaired or afflicted be healed, for it is written, "Surely He has borne our grief and carried our sorrows; yet we esteemed Him stricken, smitten by God and afflicted. But He was wounded for our transgressions, He was bruised for our iniquities, the chastisement for our peace was upon Him, and by His stripes we are healed," in Is. 53:4, 5. Lord Jesus, You told us, Your disciples, to lay hands on the sick and they would recover, (Mark 16:18). You said in John 14:7 and again in John 14:16 that if we abide in You, we could ask whatever we desire in Your name and Your Father would do it, because it would bring glory to Your name. So I ask that those I have prayed for would be healed in the cellular, molecular level of their genes, in their DNA, and that anything that resides there that is not of Your placement, nor Your will for that person would be supernaturally removed, replaced with Your fullness and restored to perfect health right now, in Jesus name.

Holy Spirit, please give me (as well as others I pray for) a revelation of my heavenly Father's love and acceptance so that perfect love will cast out all fear. Reveal my Father's heart towards me, and them. Show me my truest identity as it is in Christ. Lead me to the salvation that is through Jesus Christ. I thank You and give You glory for the healing that is taking place now in Jesus name. Amen.

Prayer for a Healthy Pregnancy

Father God,

I thank you that children are a blessing from the Lord. I stand before You today and declare You are faithful. I will enjoy the blessing of children for you have given me your promises.

Your word declares in Psalm 127:3 that the fruit of the womb is a reward and Psalm 128:3 also promises that I will have children that flourish like young olive plants in my home.

I declare the blessing of Prov. 31 over myself and my womb, that the day will come when my husband and my children will rise up and call me blessed.

I declare according to Your promise in Exodus 23:26 that because I love you and serve You and worship You, O God, You will bless my provision; you will take sickness away from me and I will NOT suffer miscarriage or be barren. I will fulfill the number of my days, in Jesus name.

Father, I remind You of Your promise in Malachi chapter 3. I tithe and am a giver, Lord, and because of that, You have promised to rebuke the devourer for my sake. You promised that the devourer would not destroy the fruit of my ground and You said my vine would not fail to bear fruit in the field (vs. 11) so I thank You for fruitfulness to come forth from my womb and that the devourer is rebuked in Jesus name.

Lord, You also said in Job 22:28 that I would declare a thing and it would be established for me so that light would shine on my ways. I make this declaration now and ask You to establish this for me.

I declare the decree that I will not miscarry according to Your promise in Exodus 23:26.

I declare that my body is now and will continue to produce abundant levels of all hormones necessary to maintain a normal, healthy birth. I declare my progesterone levels are increasing exponentially daily and will continue to do so throughout my pregnancy.

I declare that I will bring forth a healthy child out of my womb. I call for my children to come forth out of heaven and into my womb. I speak life into my uterus. I break the power of every negative word over my body, my family, my future, and children yet to come. I will not experience placenta previa, leaking of amniotic fluid, premature miscarriage, pre-eclampsia, abnormal bleeding or any other complications. I declare that you have an appointed time for childbirth and I will not give birth before that appointed time. I speak life to the placenta; it will adhere normally and be of correct size and in the right position to support a healthy pregnancy. The fetus will implant in the right place and be securely attached to the uterine wall. All cells will divide normally and each cell will produce healing and perfect soundness as it forms new life inside of me. I will not experience ectopic pregnancy, congenital defects, inherited disease or other abnormalities. If it is not allowed in heaven, I do not receive it. There is no disease in heaven, Father. I resist those things and declare all possible inherited generational curses broken now in Jesus name.

Father, please forgive anyone in our family line that may have neglected to ask Your forgiveness for their sins. Forgive, I pray, sins of broken covenants, broken trust, idolatry, shedding innocent blood, rebellion and any ungodly covenants that may have been made. Let them be broken now in Jesus name. Please forgive any inherited generational iniquitous sin and let the blood of Jesus be applied to those sins. I declare that I am a new creation in Christ and there is life in the blood. I thank You, Lord Jesus, that Your DNA flows through me to make me whole and complete in every way. I thank You for your Holy Spirit that is full of life, strength and power. Let the perfect soundness and wholeness that is in Your Spirit flow through me and release healing throughout my body. I declare no curse will pass through the blood of Christ. I submit to Your Lordship in my life and I resist the power of evil. I refuse it and declare it will not come near me. Father, I ask for a double portion of restoration. I thank You Father for continuing to show me how to pray specifically as I believe for a healthy pregnancy. In Jesus name, amen.

Prayer for Healing from Cancer

Testimony: Some years ago we went to pray for a man that had cancer. He was in very bad shape and the tumors had spread from his pancreas all throughout his body, including his lungs. As I prayed and asked God to show me where the root of the issue came in, suddenly I heard the Lord say, "Breach of trust." I had never heard that phrase before and I sought the Lord for more information. As I continued to pray, the woman of the house we were staying at came and put a book in my hand. It was the book *A More Excellent Way to Be In Health* by Henry Wright. I was not familiar with the book or its content, but I turned to see if it had anything regarding the spiritual roots of cancer. It did. One of the first things it mentioned was broken trust issues and the fruit of bitterness. We sat down together to share what the Lord had shared with us, and we all renounced bitterness, anger, slander, vengeance, unforgiveness, jealousy and broken trust. We took communion together and declared life, healing, blessing and wholeness. Shortly thereafter a new x-ray confirmed the tumors in the lungs were gone. This man continued to gain strength and vitality over the course of the next year and regained weight as well. This testimony demonstrates the reality of spiritually rooted disease as a result of an unbroken curse in a Christian's life. God's truth does not lie. He showed the root of it so that we could draw the connection between where the curse was and what would release the healing.

Dear Lord Jesus,

I know that cancer does not come from You. It comes from the pit of hell, but You overcame all the power of hell when You rose from the cross. The Bible says that YOU took the keys of death and Hades away from the enemy! You took the sin of all mankind and every evil thing upon Yourself. You were beaten - for us. Your word in Isaiah 53:5 declares this truth and that by Your stripes, we are healed. You would not have written it in Your word unless You meant what You said. So today, Lord, I say a prayer for _____, asking that you heal their body. Please fill them with the fullness of Your Holy Spirit and let the wholeness, the power and the peace that is in You manifest within them.

You have given Your children Your authority, and as Your child I command cancer to be placed upon the stripes You took on behalf of: (insert the name of the person you are praying for). I bind the spirits of infirmity, death and hell and forbid them from advancing against them in Jesus name. Spirit of death, flee _____ now! Spirit of Life, infuse _____ with resurrection life, strength, and perfect soundness. Jesus, You are the resurrection and the life! I command the root of this cancer and these tumors to wither and die immediately. Let salvation come to _____ now. Give them room to breathe, room for their organs to work properly, and room for life to flow unhindered in their body. I command the blood supply that feeds these tumors to cease. I command the cancer cells that reproduce uncontrollably to be supernaturally restrained and healed. Let all the healthy cells refuse to let cancer attach to them. Let the DNA of Jesus' perfect blood heal any areas that are predisposed to cancer. Let the broken spirit be healed, and the bones filled with fatness. We ask that the bone marrow be healed and filled with new, healthy red blood cells that continue to multiply exponentially. Let joy and laughter come back to _____ as their strength, for Your word says it is medicine to the body. We command all cancerous cells to leave _____ body now in Jesus name.

Father, I thank You for hearing these prayers and releasing Your answer into this earthly realm. I thank You that You are faithful to watch over Your word in order to bring Your promises to pass. Thank you for releasing healing. In Jesus name, amen.

Note: As mentioned above, we have personally noticed the connection between physical disease such as cancer and unresolved unforgiveness and bitterness. The body often manifests the physical symptoms of a spiritual reality. That is one factor why some people do not get healed or perhaps they do get healed only to have it return. If the root of the spiritual issue has not been dealt with the problem can return. I am not saying this is true in every case, but there is much evidence between unbroken curses, spiritual issues and physical disease. Please ask the Lord if there is something that you need to specifically address in prayer to insure that your victory is 100%!

Prayer for Healing from MS and other Auto-Immune Disorders

Father God,

I bring myself to You and place myself at the throne of Grace. I thank you that my sins are forgiven and You are always available to help me. I ask You for Your healing touch on my mind, emotions, memories, and my physical body. Lord, I do not know the cause of all the physical symptoms I have experienced, but You do. I believe You can help me Lord Jesus. I thank You that You know everything about me and can guide me through my healing. I ask for wisdom from your Holy Spirit to help me correctly diagnose the root of these issues. Lead me to the answers that will release my healing.

Lord, I bring my heart issues to you first, and I ask to be healed from any and all emotional wounds that would keep my heart blocked from giving and receiving love. I ask you to dissolve any root of bitterness that came as a result of parental abandonment, hurt, offense, grief, rejection and disappointment. I choose to accept myself. I reject all lies from the enemy. Forgive me for believing lies and rejecting Your truth, Father. Guide me through my emotional healing and help me to be aware of the love that you have already placed in my life. Help me to trust that love and release any walls of self-preservation I have enacted to protect myself. Let sensitivity return, and let me not see it as a sign of weakness or something to be feared. Let me see it as a part of experiencing life. Help me to love myself and see myself as You see me. I open the door of my heart to You.

I ask for revelation of You as my Father, and that Your great love would dispel all spirits of fear, anxiety, hopelessness, disillusionment, self-pity, cold love and rebellion. I loose myself now from all of these including unloving and critical spirits. I loose myself from spirits of fear, accusation, anger and rejection. I submit to you Jesus and resist these spirits. In the name of Jesus and by the power of Your blood I bind every evil spirit and forbid them from operating against me. I command every unclean, evil spirit to go from me now and never return. I command every assignment of the enemy to be cancelled and unraveled and the assignment from the Lord to be released into my life. By faith, I receive healing from Your Holy Spirit to my mind, emotions, and memories. I thank You for the love that heals and restores every part of me. I thank You that I have great peace and my composure is undisturbed because I put my trust in You.

I speak now to my physical body. I command all swelling and abnormal pressure on nerves on my spine, in my arms, legs, hands and feet to be released. I speak healing into every nerve that may have suffered injury from accidents, compression, drugs, alcohol, lead, radiation, seafood toxins, insect and spider bites. I speak to my arteries, and wherever there is constriction, let there be normal blood flow. Let all pressure on peripheral nerves from enlarged blood vessels, scar tissue or infection be released now in Jesus name. Let all chemical balances of potassium, calcium, sodium, vitamins and other body chemistry be in proper and normal balances. Let any abnormal accumulation of chemical or medication toxins be supernaturally removed from my body now, in Jesus name. Send Your healing to every ulcer, lesion and scar tissue, both on the myelin sheath of my spinal cord and throughout my entire body. I speak to the cells that have been separated from the other cells and isolated into inactivity. "Come back into placement and alignment with other healthy cells." Father, I speak a creative miracle to come forth. Let the body begin to tell itself to secret the proper chemicals to attract the migrating cells and guide them along the right pathways. Cause these cells to recognize and join the other cells of the appropriate type to assemble to form new tissue growth. I command the cells to begin to actively work together, to create life together, to recreate what is missing, and to bond together to form new healthy cells and tissue, forming the myelin sheath, nerves, tissue and all that supports healthy blood flow to the damaged areas of my body. Let this process be actively maintained and stabilized. Where there is lack, let Your wholeness and healing restore and recreate what is diseased, dying or absent. I command resurrection life to begin to flow into every cell in Jesus name! Let every area where the white corpuscles have attacked my body begin to heal and be restored, and let those abnormal signals from the body cease now in Jesus name. Let all nerves be completely healed and restored. Let every scar on my brain be removed and the tissue renewed. I thank You, Lord Jesus, that by Your stripes I am healed. I thank You for your promises in Psalm 103 that tells me You forgave all my sin and healed my disease. I believe in You O God and in Your word! You said in Psalm 91 that no plague would come near me. I thank You that I do not have to fear. I place myself under the shelter of Your wings. You are my refuge and I thank You that no harm shall come to me. Let all viruses and gene defects be healed now, in Jesus name. I command any and all symptoms of MS and other diseases to be eradicated from my body. I command my body's immune system to be strengthened and the immune cells to stop attacking my nervous system, including my brain, optic nerves and spinal cord in Jesus name. Thank You, Father for Your love. Thank You, Jesus for delivering me from the things that want to destroy my health. Thank You, Holy Spirit for releasing healing. In Jesus name, amen

Note: Many auto-immune disorders and diseases have their roots in parental abandonment, self-hatred, rejection, guilt and unloving spirits. When a person rejects himself or herself, the body comes into agreement with a spirit of infirmity, which turns the immune system against the body. The body then begins to be at war with itself. Instead of the immune system protecting the body from foreign things that could be a potential health threat, the immune system begins attacking the body, literally destroying it from the inside out.

Scripture Verses for Healing

Do you have a bad doctor's report? Struggling to believe God in the midst of a difficult health crisis? Here are some Scripture verses for healing, revival, new life, and restoration. Stand with confidence upon the Word of God, Jesus Himself, as He has given you His reassurance of His will. These are promises that will refute every lie of the enemy, every double minded thought that wants to wash out your faith. God said it, so you can believe it!

When the doctors give you the facts, you tell them the truth – the WORD of GOD! Insert the name of the person you are praying for and make the scriptures personal. It will lift your faith as you declare these over the situation!

First of all, know that GOD IS FOR YOU, NOT AGAINST YOU! It is not God's will that we suffer with illness because Jesus Christ paid the price for us. Romans 8:31,32 says, **"If God is for us, who can be against us? He who did not spare His own Son, but delivered Him up for us all, how shall He (God) not with Him (Christ) also freely give us all things?"** God's desire is to freely give us all things – and that includes healing. Don't let the enemy lie to you and tell you anything different!

In the face of illness or bad reports, the enemy wants to gloat prematurely. This is what the enemy says to you. **"All who hate me (spirits of infirmity and sickness) whisper together against me; against me they devise my hurt. "An evil disease," they say, "Clings to him." And now that he lies down, he will rise up no more."** (Ps. 41:7,8) The voice of the enemy speaking through our own mind, from doctors, or from others speaks negative words to strip us of our faith. But the enemy is the Father of Lies! He never speaks truth! He is just a big gossip spreading rumors and lies that aren't true. FEAR is False Evidence Appearing Real. Remember, symptoms are not truth. It may be a fact that you feel lousy or get a bad doctor's report, but the WORD of GOD is TRUTH. The facts must submit to the truth as we declare it. Why? **"God is not a man that He should lie."** (Numbers 23:19)

God is Holy and is bound by His covenant with us. Understand the power of covenant. He cannot deny the nature of who He is: Jehovah Raphe, our Healer. He is so much to us…our salvation, our deliverer, healer, provider, Lord…the names of God are many! But there is help in the name of the Lord. Psalm 124:8 says, **"Our help is in the name of the LORD, who made heaven and earth."**

God's word must also overcome the facts of the situation because Isaiah 55:11 tells us, **"So shall My word be that goes forth from My mouth, it shall not return to Me void, but it shall accomplish what I please and it shall prosper in the thing for which I sent it."** God's word cannot return to Him void, or empty, of accomplishing the very thing that He meant that word to do. It is anointed with supernatural power to produce exactly what God has purposed. BUT! They key here is that we must declare the word and RETURN it to Him by reminding Him what He said. That is how we activate our faith and send the word forth to accomplish what we tell it to do!

Isaiah 53:5 tells us that **"By His stripes we ARE healed."** We ARE ALREADY HEALED because Jesus accomplished that victory for us when He died on the cross and overcame for us all.

Jesus said in Revelation 1:18, **"I AM He who lives, and was dead, and behold, I Am alive forevermore. Amen. And I HAVE THE KEYS OF HADES AND DEATH."**

Satan no longer holds the keys of death, and it is not his right to take your life. Do you realize that the Bible says that every day of your life has been written ahead of time? God has an appointed time for each person to die, and He has a purpose for each one to fulfill before they are taken home. You just tell the devil, "GOD isn't done with me yet and I'm not going anywhere until HE takes me home! Devil, you don't have a right to my life, so go and take your sickness with you in Jesus name!" As a believer in Jesus Christ, Jesus holds the keys of your life. Jesus died to set you free, and He will not turn the keys of death over to the enemy. Let that give you confidence in knowing that JESUS is in control – not your illness, and not the enemy!

"By this I know that You are well pleased with me, because my enemy DOES NOT triumph over me." (Ps. 41:11)

Ask God to reveal if there is a strongman that needs to be bound. Bind the strongman of infirmity, cancer, fear, death, etc. Jesus defeated the enemy with "IT IS WRITTEN…" Bind the spirit of infirmity and death over the person and loose the healing power of the Holy Spirit.

"I shall not die, but live, and declare the works of the Lord….He has not given me over to death." Ps. 118:17,18(b) You must fulfill your purpose here on earth before it is time for you to go home. It is not God's will that your life is shortened prematurely. Jesus paid the price for our healing on the cross. The debt was paid to redeem us. By His stripes we have been healed and we are healed! Therefore, you must stand in faith knowing that Satan has no legal right to your life. This is a legal matter, not just a health issue. The thief has taken what does not belong to him – your health! If God has not given you over to death, then Satan cannot take your life from you. It is not his to take. He must be ordered to relinquish his grip on your health!

"My soul clings to the dust; revive me according to Your word," (Ps. 119:25). To REVIVE means to "cause to live." Lord, you have spoken and it is finished. Healing has been accomplished through the work of the cross, and by His stripes, we are healed!

"But God will redeem my soul from the power of the grave, for He shall receive me." (Ps. 49:15)

"As for me, I will call upon God, and the Lord shall save me." (Ps. 55:16) It is absolutely His will to save you from this illness.

"Our God is the God of salvation; and to God the Lord belong escapes from death." (Ps. 68:20) He has provided a way of escape for you. Stand still and see the salvation of the Lord! Battles were won through praise and worship. (2 Chronicles 20:20)

"Also, Your righteousness, O God, is very high, You who have done great things; O God, who is like You? You, who have shown me great and severe troubles, shall revive me again, and bring me up again from the depths of the earth. You shall increase my greatness, and comfort me on every side." (Ps. 71:19-21) God's promise to revive you, bring health and restoration so that in the end, your testimony of His power in your life brings great glory to the Lord. He increases the greatness of your testimony and the anointing in your life to see others healed and restored!

"Establish Your word to Your servant, who is devoted to fearing You." (Ps. 119:38)

Read and declare Psalm 103.

Exodus 15:26 tells us that GOD does not put disease on people if we follow Him and live to honor Him.

ALL OF PSALM 91!

"He brought them out of darkness and the shadow of death, and broke their chains in pieces." (Ps. 107:14)

When Jesus conquered death through the resurrection power of the Holy Spirit, because He was fully human, he defeated death for us all. He has brought you out from under the shadow of death and He HAS ALREADY BROKE YOUR CHAINS IN PIECES! Receive it by faith…the chains of death can no longer hold you. Ask Him for a fresh anointing to give you resurrection power over death!

"Then they cried out to the Lord in their trouble, and He SAVED them out of their distresses. He SENT HIS WORD AND HEALED THEM, and delivered them from their destructions." (Ps. 107:19,20)

Remember the word to Your servant, upon which You have caused me to hope. This is my comfort in my affliction, for Your WORD HAS GIVEN ME LIFE." (Ps. 119:49,50)

"Let Your tender mercies come to me, that I may live…" (Ps. 119:77)

"O Lord, revive me according to Your justice." (Ps. 119:149) Judge my case in the court of heaven, Father! Take the thief, the enemy, the oppressor, my adversary, to the court of heaven and plead my cause against this ungodly foe, Lord Jesus. Cause me to live – revive me! For You, Father, are a just judge. Thank you for making the thief, the destroyer, repay and restore my health. I belong to You, Father. It is not the enemy's rightful place to take my life. My life is hidden in You. Thank you for restoring me, even greater than before. And Father, thank You for a greater anointing so that I may see others set free and healed, also.

"Forever, O Lord, Your word is settled in heaven." (Ps. 119:89) Your word cannot return to You without accomplishing the very purpose for which You have written it and said it. (Isaiah 55:11)Your word tells me that death is under Your feet, so death is under my feet as well. Your word tells me that "by His stripes we are healed," so I thank you for Your healing power to flow through my body, releasing total and complete healing.

When the devil wants to present me with facts, I will tell him the truth. I am healed, in Jesus name! My body must align itself with truth, for the word of God is truth. I declare that I will live and not die, in Jesus' name! The things that are impossible with men are possible with God. He alone is my strength, my shield. My God is for me, not against me. He has saved me, redeemed me, and He gives life to my mortal body. I am not defeated because Jesus is not defeated, and His word tells me that He always causes me to triumph! As I have declared this healing in my body, it has been established for me, so that light will shine on my ways. What God has promised, He is fully able to perform. It was accomplished at the cross and by His stripes I have been healed - this is God's promise to me. I was healed, I am healed, and my body is in the process of manifesting my healing. As it exists in the kingdom of God, I now call it into the natural realm and say, "Healing, come forth and produce health in my body now, in Jesus name!" I have called those things that do not exist and they have manifested by my declarations of faith. I receive my healing in Jesus' name, for all things are possible to those who believe!

More prayers and articles available at: *Beyond the Barriers*. Visit: xpectamiracle.blogspot.com.

Made in the USA
Columbia, SC
03 November 2018